Classic Hunting Tales

Classic Hunting Tales

Edited by
VIN T. SPARANO

Beaufort Books
Publishers
New York

Library of Congress Cataloging-in-Publication Data

Classic hunting tales.

  1. Hunting. I. Sparano, Vin T.
SK33.C562 1986   799.2   86-32094
ISBN 0-8253-0345-1

Published in the United States by Beaufort Books Publishers, New York.

Designed by Irving Perkins Associates

Printed in the U.S.A.   First Edition

10 9 8 7 6 5 4 3 2 1

To My Grandson Nicholas,
May He Grow to Love the Woods
And Waters as Much as I

Contents

Introduction

IN the early 1980s I collected a whole crateful of the very best hunting stories I could dredge from my memory and research. When I thought I had the very best, I hauled them over to Beaufort Books, and the collection was published in 1983 as *The Greatest Hunting Stories Ever Told.* There is no doubt that this first anthology of hunting classics was a success. The book is loaded with hunting tales that will be read and reread by generations and generations.

There was just one problem with that initial collection. The box I carried over to Beaufort held fifty to sixty stories. My publisher gave me a quick lesson in economics and sent me home with orders to cut the number of stories in half. It was not easy picking Jack O'Connor over Robert Ruark, Gordon MacQuarrie instead of Townsend Whelen, and so on. But I did it, and I went back to Beaufort with twenty-eight stories. If you were one of the lucky ones who read the book, you know all the tales were hunting classics.

I knew that someday I'd put together another collection. I stashed the remaining manuscripts and continued to look for even more memorable stories and adventures that would jar readers into another world, if only for a short time. My criterion was simple: Choose tales that leave readers with a better insight into the outdoors and maybe themselves.

A few years passed, and Susan Suffes, Beaufort's editor-in-chief, and I got together a few times over lunch. It was easy to agree on our next project together. You're holding it in your hands.

Is this better than the first volume published four years ago? Don't ask me to answer that question. I can't. All the stories here are as close to me as those in my first collection. Naturally, I have my favorites.

Two stories very special to me are Corey Ford's "The Road to Tinkhamtown" and "Nat's Dog" by Joan Tyler Fairbanks. The stories are tied together with the same thread—the passing of body and spirit and the strength, comfort, and sometimes pain we get from our memories. Both stories involve hunting dogs, those reassuring symbols of loyalty we take into the woods with us. Even if you're the toughest bear hunter in the mountains, I defy you to read these stories without getting unhinged and glassy-eyed.

Another favorite is "Nervous Breakdown" by Gordon MacQuarrie. This isn't a hunting story, you say? I know it isn't, but it's my book and I can make and break the rules. MacQuarrie's Bill Jones is us— me and you. He sees a hole in the line and he goes for it. Bill is a hero and we should cheer him on.

And it is fun to read about Saxton Pope and Arthur Young, the namesakes of the Pope & Young Club (recordkeepers of bowhunting trophies), hunting grizzlies for the first time with a bow in 1919. It's a hunting feat that has been done many times since then, but let's not forget that Dr. Pope and Mr. Young, sixty-seven years ago, did not have compound bows, graphite arrows, modern broadheads, and other gadgets of technology. They used wood longbows and arrows.

Of course, there's a dose of Africa here. Though most of us will never go on a safari, we still want to read about it. Sometimes old Africa, when there was still a Belgian Congo, is even more exciting. And naturally, Robert Ruark is still scared of buffaloes.

And why did I insist on a bear attack story in both books? Because, many years ago when I saw my first bear in the woods, I got weak in the knees and I ran out of spit. Any animal that can do that to a man deserves a special place in this book. In this case, however, two Alaska brown bears ganged up on a moose hunter and mauled him terribly. The ordeal will keep you looking over your shoulder in bear country for a while.

I could go on and tell a bit about each story, but that's not the way to do it. You pick the stories, in any order, and read and savor them. And read them again and again, whenever you want. There's not a bummer in the lot. They will all stick in your head, but some will find a way into your heart and stay there forever.

Once again, I want to thank *Outdoor Life* for granting me permission to reprint some of these stories. As Executive Editor of *Outdoor Life*, I even bought a few of them.

Finally, as I did in the first book, I want to thank the authors. To those who are still with us, I am grateful for giving me the opportunity to preserve and pass along your work in these pages. To those who are no longer with us, I thank you wherever you are for the precious gifts you have given to me and others who live to love the woods and waters and wildlife of our world.

Vin T. Sparano
New York
March 25, 1986

"The Road to Tinkhamtown" is my all-time favorite. As the tale goes, when Corey Ford wrote this story many years ago, he left instructions with his editor that it was to be published upon his death. I do not know if this is true, and I will not be the one to prove that Ford's request was a product of some publicity agent's mind. True or not, it's a great precedent to a great story. When my time comes, I hope I can meet up with Frank and Shad.

The Road to Tinkhamtown

by COREY FORD

IT was a long way, but he knew where he was going. He would follow the road through the woods and over the crest of a hill and down the hill to the stream, and cross the sagging timbers of the bridge, and on the other side would be the place called Tinkhamtown. He was going back to Tinkhamtown.

He walked slowly at first, his legs dragging with each step. He had not walked for almost a year, and his flanks had shriveled and wasted away from lying in bed so long; he could fit his fingers around his thigh. Doc Towle had said he would never walk again, but that was Doc for you, always on the pessimistic side. Why, now he was walking quite easily, once he had started. The strength was coming back into his legs, and he did not have to stop for breath so often. He tried jogging a few steps, just to show he could, but he slowed again because he had a long way to go.

It was hard to make out the old road, choked with alders and covered by matted leaves, and he shut his eyes so he could see it better. He could always see it when he shut his eyes. Yes, here was the beaver dam on the right, just as he remembered it, and the flooded stretch where he had picked his way from hummock to hummock while the dog splashed unconcernedly in front of him. The water had been

I

over his boot tops in one place, and sure enough, as he waded it now his left boot filled with water again, the same warm squdgy feeling. Everything was the way it had been that afternoon, nothing had changed in ten years. Here was the blowdown across the road that he had clambered over, and here on a knoll was the clump of thorn apples where a grouse had flushed as they passed. Shad had wanted to look for it, but he had whistled him back. They were looking for Tinkhamtown.

He had come across the name on a map in the town library. He used to study the old maps and survey charts of the state; sometimes they showed where a farming community had flourished, a century ago, and around the abandoned pastures and in the orchards grown up to pine the birds would be feeding undisturbed. Some of his best grouse covers had been located that way. The map had been rolled up in a cardboard cylinder; it crackled with age as he spread it out. The date was 1857. It was the sector between Cardigan and Kearsarge mountains, a wasteland of slash and second-growth timber without habitation today, but evidently it had supported a number of families before the Civil War. A road was marked on the map, dotted with Xs for homesteads, and the names of the owners were lettered beside them: Nason, J. Tinkham, Allard, R. Tinkham. Half the names were Tinkham. In the center of the map—the paper was so yellow that he could barely make it out—was the word "Tinkhamtown."

He had drawn a rough sketch on the back of an envelope, noting where the road left the highway and ran north to a fork and then turned east and crossed a stream that was not even named; and the next morning he and Shad had set out together to find the place. They could not drive very far in the jeep, because washouts had gutted the roadbed and laid bare the ledges and boulders. He had stuffed the sketch in his hunting-coat pocket, and hung his shotgun over his forearm and started walking, the setter trotting ahead with the bell on his collar tinkling. It was an old-fashioned sleighbell, and it had a thin silvery note that echoed through the woods like peepers in the spring. He could follow the sound in the thickest cover, and when it stopped he would go to where he heard it last and Shad would be on point. After Shad's death, he had put the bell away. He'd never had another dog.

It was silent in the woods without the bell, and the way was longer than he remembered. He should have come to the big hill by now. Maybe he'd taken the wrong turn back at the fork. He thrust a hand into his hunting coat; the envelope with the sketch was still in the pocket. He sat down on a flat rock to get his bearings, and then he realized, with a surge of excitement, that he had stopped on this very rock for lunch ten years ago. Here was the waxed paper from his sandwich, tucked in a crevice, and here was the hollow in the leaves where Shad had stretched out beside him, the dog's soft muzzle flattened on his thigh. He looked up, and through the trees he could see the hill.

He rose and started walking again, carrying his shotgun. He had left the gun standing in its rack in the kitchen when he had been taken to the state hospital, but now it was hooked over his arm by the trigger guard; he could feel the solid heft of it. The woods grew more dense as he climbed, but here and there a shaft of sunlight slanted through the trees. "And there were forests ancient as the hills," he thought, "enfolding sunny spots of greenery." Funny that should come back to him now; he hadn't read it since he was a boy. Other things were coming back to him, the smell of dank leaves and sweet fern and frosted apples, the sharp contrast of sun and cool shade, the November stillness before snow. He walked faster, feeling the excitement swell within him.

He paused on the crest of the hill, straining his ears for the faint mutter of the stream below him, but he could not hear it because of the voices. He wished they would stop talking, so he could hear the stream. Someone was saying his name over and over, "Frank, Frank," and he opened his eyes reluctantly and looked up at his sister. Her face was worried, and there was nothing to worry about. He tried to tell her where he was going, but when he moved his lips the words would not form. "What did you say, Frank?" she asked, bending her head lower. "I don't understand." He couldn't make the words any clearer, and she straightened and said to Doc Towle: "It sounded like Tinkhamtown."

"Tinkhamtown?" Doc shook his head. "Never heard him mention any place by that name."

He smiled to himself. Of course he'd never mentioned it to Doc. Things like a secret grouse cover you didn't mention to anyone, not even to as close a friend as Doc was. No, he and Shad were the only ones who knew. They had found it together, that long ago afternoon, and it was their secret.

They had come to the stream—he shut his eyes so he could see it again—and Shad had trotted across the bridge. He had followed more cautiously, avoiding the loose planks and walking along a beam with his shotgun held out to balance himself. On the other side of the stream the road mounted steeply to a clearing in the woods, and he halted before the split-stone foundations of a house, the first of the series of farms shown on the map. It must have been a long time since the building had fallen in; the cottonwoods growing in the cellar hole were twenty, maybe thirty years old. His boot overturned a rusted ax blade and the handle of a china cup in the grass; that was all. Beside the doorstep was a lilac bush, almost as tall as the cottonwoods. He thought of the wife who had set it out, a little shrub then, and the husband who had chided her for wasting time on such frivolous things with all the farm work to be done. But the work had come to nothing, and still the lilac bloomed each spring, the one thing that had survived.

Shad's bell was moving along the stone wall at the edge of the clearing, and he strolled after him, not hunting, wondering about the people who had gone away and left their walls to crumble and their buildings to collapse under the winter snows. Had they ever come back to Tinkhamtown? Were they here now, watching him unseen? His toe stubbed against a block of hewn granite hidden by briers, part of the sill of the old barn. Once it had been a tight barn, warm with cattle steaming in their stalls, rich with the blend of hay and manure and harness leather. He liked to think of it the way it was; it was more real than this bare rectangle of blocks and the emptiness inside. He'd always felt that way about the past. Doc used to argue that what's over is over, but he would insist Doc was wrong. Everything is the way it was, he'd tell Doc. The past never changes. You leave it and go on to the present, but it is still there, waiting for you to come back to it.

He had been so wrapped in his thoughts that he had not realized Shad's bell had stopped. He hurried across the clearing, holding his gun ready. In a corner of the stone wall an ancient apple tree had littered the ground with fallen fruit, and beneath it Shad was standing motionless. The white fan of his tail was lifted a little and his backline was level, the neck craned forward, one foreleg cocked. His flanks were trembling with the nearness of grouse, and a thin skein of drool hung from his jowls. The dog did not move as he approached, but the brown eyes rolled back until their whites showed, looking for him. "Steady, boy," he called. His throat was tight, the way it always got when Shad was on point, and he had to swallow hard. "Steady, I'm coming."

"I think his lips moved just now," his sister's voice said. He did not open his eyes, because he was waiting for the grouse to get up in front of Shad, but he knew Doc Towle was looking at him. "He's sleeping," Doc said after a moment. "Maybe you better get some sleep yourself, Mrs. Duncombe." He heard Doc's heavy footsteps cross the room. "Call me if there's any change," Doc said, and closed the door, and in the silence he could hear his sister's chair creaking beside him, her silk dress rustling regularly as she breathed.

What was she doing here, he wondered. Why had she come all the way from California to see him? It was the first time they had seen each other since she had married and moved out West. She was his only relative, but they had never been very close; they had nothing in common, really. He heard from her now and then, but it was always the same letter: why didn't he sell the old place, it was too big for him now that the folks had passed on, why didn't he take a small apartment in town where he wouldn't be alone? But he liked the big house, and he wasn't alone, not with Shad. He had closed off all the other rooms and moved into the kitchen so everything would be handy. His sister didn't approve of his bachelor ways, but it was very comfortable with his cot by the stove and Shad curled on the floor near him at night, whinnying and scratching the linoleum with his claws as he chased a bird in a dream. He wasn't alone when he heard that.

He had never married. He had looked after the folks as long as they lived; maybe that was why. Shad was his family. They were always together—Shad was short for Shadow—and there was a closeness between them that he did not feel for anyone else, not his sister or Doc even. He and Shad used to talk without words, each knowing what the other was thinking, and they could always find one another in the woods. He still remembered the little things about him: the possessive thrust of his paw, the way he false-yawned when he was vexed, the setter stubbornness sometimes, the clownish grin when they were going hunting, the kind eyes. That was it; Shad was the kindest person he had ever known.

They had not hunted again after Tinkhamtown. The old dog had stumbled several times, walking back to the jeep, and he had to carry him in his arms the last hundred yards. It was hard to realize he was gone. He liked to think of him the way he was; it was like the barn, it was more real than the emptiness. Sometimes at night, lying awake with the pain in his legs, he would hear the scratch of claws on the linoleum, and he would turn on the light and the hospital room would be empty. But when he turned the light off he would hear the scratching again, and he would be content and drop off to sleep, or what passed for sleep in these days and nights that ran together without dusk or dawn.

Once he asked Doc point-blank if he would ever get well. Doc was giving him something for the pain, and he hesitated a moment and finished what he was doing and cleaned the needle and then looked at him and said: "I'm afraid not, Frank." They had grown up in town together, and Doc knew him too well to lie. "I'm afraid there's nothing to do." Nothing to do but lie here and wait till it was over. "Tell me, Doc," he whispered, for his voice wasn't very strong, "what happens when it's over?" And Doc fumbled with the catch of his black bag and closed it and said, well, he supposed you went on to someplace else called the Hereafter. But he shook his head; he always argued with Doc. "No, it isn't someplace else," he told him, "it's someplace you've been where you want to be again." Doc didn't understand, and he couldn't explain it any better. He knew what he meant, but the shot was taking effect and he was tired.

He was tired now, and his legs ached a little as he started down the hill, trying to find the stream. It was too dark under the trees to see the sketch he had drawn, and he could not tell direction by the moss on the north side of the trunks. The moss grew all around them, swelling them out of size, and huge blowdowns blocked his way. Their upended roots were black and misshapen, and now instead of excitement he felt a surge of panic. He floundered through a pile of slash, his legs throbbing with pain as the sharp points stabbed him, but he did not have the strength to get to the other side and he had to back out again and circle. He did not know where he was going. It was getting late, and he had lost the way.

There was no sound in the woods, nothing to guide him, nothing but his sister's chair creaking and her breath catching now and then in a dry sob. She wanted him to turn back, and Doc wanted him to, they all wanted him to turn back. He thought of the big house; if he left it alone it would fall in with the winter snows and cottonwoods would grow in the cellar hole. And there were all the other doubts, but most of all there was the fear. He was afraid of the darkness, and being alone, and not knowing where he was going. It would be better to turn around and go back. He knew the way back.

And then he heard it, echoing through the woods like peepers in the spring, the thin silvery tinkle of a sleighbell. He started running toward it, following the sound down the hill. His legs were strong again, and he hurdled the blowdowns, he leapt over fallen logs, he put one fingertip on a pile of slash and sailed over it like a grouse skimming. He was getting nearer and the sound filled his ears, louder than a thousand churchbells ringing, louder than all the choirs in the sky, as loud as the pounding of his heart. The fear was gone; he was not lost. He had the bell to guide him now.

He came to the stream, and paused for a moment at the bridge. He wanted to tell them he was happy, if they only knew how happy he was, but when he opened his eyes he could not see them anymore. Everything else was bright, but the room was dark.

The bell had stopped, and he looked across the stream. The other side was bathed in sunshine, and he could see the road mounting steeply, and the clearing in the woods, and the apple tree in a corner of the stone wall. Shad was standing motionless beneath it, the white fan of his tail lifted, his neck craned forward and one foreleg cocked. The whites of his eyes showed as he looked back, waiting for him.   "Steady," he called, "steady, boy." He started across the bridge. "I'm coming."

Reprinted by permission of Harold Ober Associates Incorporated, Copyright 1970 by Holt, Rinehart & Winston, Inc.

Jack O'Connor needs no introduction to anyone who reads hunting tales. I knew Jack back in the early 1960s. I will always remember him as being irascible, hard of hearing from years of shooting, and loud. I will also remember him as one of the finest storytellers of all times. Jack, who was shooting editor of Outdoor Life *from 1941 to 1972, hunted in Africa and India many times and has written numerous stories about his experiences, but "A Tiger Has Killed" stands out as his very best.*

A Tiger Has Killed

by JACK O'CONNOR

ANYONE who has ever been in the Salt River Valley of Arizona has a pretty good notion what the tiger country near Kashipur, in northern India, looks like. Actually a man who has grown up in any of the irrigated valleys of the West could go to the land around Kashipur and imagine he was home. When I first saw it I was struck by its resemblance to the country around Phoenix when I was a kid, or to the flat, irrigated valleys of Utah and southern Idaho.

Near Kashipur there are big feathery trees, most of which are figs but which at a distance look like the great cottonwoods of the irrigated Southwest. And there are fields of sugarcane and golden wheat stubble and green row crops, and narrow dusty country lanes and little mud-and-wattle villages that look not unlike the adobe and ocotillo huts of Mexico. And there are little wandering creeks and shallow rivers, big patches of reeds along the banks, and occasional patches of jungle, the way there used to be a few acres of mesquite forest along the riverbanks in southern Arizona years ago.

The jungles may be small, but spotted axis deer live in them, and so do monkeys and peacocks and jungle fowl and beautiful little long-tailed parakeets, as green as jade is green, and little birds so incredibly blue they seem fragments of some distant magic sky. And beyond the yellow of the reeds and the pale straw of the stubble fields and the green of trees and hedgerows, blue serrated foothills rise; and beyond them, remote and delicate, often sensed rather than seen, are the great Himalayas.

It is a thickly populated country, a land of many villages. Often one little group of huts is so close to the next that a man with a strong voice can make himself heard from one village to the next. It is a land of many noises, great and small—the lowing of the creamy, hump-backed sacred cattle of India, the barking of dogs, the cackling of hens, the bleating of goats, the shrill babble of children, the singing of women at work. Children drive herds of water buffaloes and cattle to graze in the grass and in the jungles. Peasant farmers harvest their grain with sickles not much more efficient than pocketknives.

But when I first saw this country, I was bitter with disappointment. Tigers here? Preposterous! A man might as well look for a tiger among the flower beds of some American suburban home. Tigers among all these people, tigers in the midst of these farms and right next door to the villages? Don't make me laugh!

In northern India, tigers may be hunted in the national forests only the last two weeks of each month. When we landed at Kashipur we had just completed fourteen days of hunting in the foothills of the Himalayas. My companion, Lee Sproul, had shot a tiger. I had seen the eyes of another by spotlight and one night, shooting from a tree by flashlight at a tiger behind a bush, I had scratched its cheek with a .375 Magnum bullet. Lee and I had sat through dreary nights in machans. We had driven with men and with elephants. We had prowled the high-grass country at night on elephantback with spot-lights. Still I had no tiger.

Two weeks in supposedly fine tiger country, and I was as without a trophy as if I had done my tiger hunting in New York's Central Park. My amigo Herb Klein had hunted a couple of weeks near Nag-pur, India, and had shot five tigers. Another friend, Prince Abdorreza Pahlavi of Iran, in still another part of India, had taken eight in the same length of time. I had come more than halfway around the world for a tiger and I might as well have stayed home to shoot woodchucks.

So now the three of us—Lee Sproul, our outfitter A. D. Mukerji, and I—were driving through this alleged tiger country in our asthmatic jeep after a night in a government resthouse in Kashipur. Bullock carts loaded with wheat straw or sugarcane turned creaking off the industry roads to let us by. Village dogs yapped at us. Scrubby chickens fled cackling from our path.

We were going to meet the three faithful elephants that had made the long trek down the foothills, where we had used them for driving. If by some remote chance there happened to be a tiger in this improbable place, it was absolutely necessary that elephants be used. The cover was too thick for humans.

But fat chance! I had about as much faith in finding a tiger there as I had of seeing my Aunt Gertrude go riding by on a white horse playing Lady Godiva and wearing nothing but pink tights and a blond wig.

Then suddenly, in the dust, beside the road, I saw great round tracks—or pugmarks, to use the correct Anglo-Indian term.

"Stop," I yelled. "Tiger tracks!"

The jeep wheezed and clattered to a stop. While we were inspecting the tracks an excited native came running up and began to chatter Hindustani to Mukerji.

"What does he say?" I asked.

"He says if we're hunting tigers to come and shoot one out of his cane field. He says a big one (possibly the one that made this track) killed a bullock last night and dragged it into the cane. Now when anyone goes near it, it growls and the men are afraid."

"What did I tell you?" said Mukerji. "*Lots* of tigers."

And there were, as improbable as it may sound. Down from the foothills, along with the elephants and their pilots or mahouts (pronounced ma-hoots), had come our crew of shikaris (native scouts and hunters), as well as other mysterious characters who scratched the elephants' tummies and performed other obscure chores. When we joined them they were all jumping with excitement.

"Tell the Old Sahib (prounounce s.o.b.) that he's sure to get his tiger," they chorused. "There are tigers everywhere. We're up to our hips in tigers!"

When we boiled it down, we found that after their arrival the afternoon before, they had discovered tracks in the dusty little roads of a tigress and two cubs and of a middle-sized male tiger, all of whom lived in a big cane patch. There was another male, they said, that made his headquarters not far from the riverbank. Down in the reeds and the high grass of the riverbank lurked the largest tiger of them all. To judge from the signs they made with their hands, his pugmarks were only slightly smaller than those of a bull elephant. And then upstream a couple of miles there lived an ornery old lady tiger who had somehow lost her cubs.

All told, about nine tigers lived along the river bottom there right among the farms. It was a chummy arrangement and for the tigers a very convenient one. During the day they'd bed down in the reeds beside the stream, and when night fell they'd go hunting. Now and then they killed an axis deer in a patch of jungle, and occasionally they'd devour a hog deer out in the shortgrass flats.

But mostly they simply ate cattle, so many that the native Indians felt they were in the chips if they could bring more than half their calves to maturity. Tigers were to be endured—like flies, drought, typhoid, children, mosquitoes, and other catastrophes. Old Shere the Tiger was to them as natural as rain and stars and sunsets, as much to be expected as the hot dry winds of April and May and the torrential monsoon rains of late June and July.

Now and then a farmer would come face to face with a tiger when he went early to his field, or some children after birds' nests would report that they had blundered into Old Stripes in his bed and had been growled at. Always the villagers would see tiger tracks in the roads and in the fields and practically every day some tiger would take a cow or a buffalo.

For the most part such an arrangement is almost friendly. The people leave the tigers alone and the tigers leave the people alone. Of course the tigers take their toll of cattle but that's only to be expected, as the way of a tiger with a cow, like the way of a man with a maid, has been going on since the world began.

But now and then a sport from town or some local skikari takes a poke at a tiger, usually with buckshot fired from some rusty old Spanish single-barreled shotgun. Sometimes he actually kills the tiger, but more often he wounds it. Many times the magnificent creature slinks away to die of infection and to be found only when the vultures drop to the carcass, but very often the tigers are crippled or slowed down by the wounds, so they are not powerful enought to kill cattle or fleet enough to catch a deer. Then they turn man-eater. When we were hunting in the Kashipur area three man-eaters were said to be within a radius of thirty miles.

We were really in tiger country now! In order to get our quarry located, we bought a supply of buffalo calves and staked them out in spots where tigers were likely to pass. Almost every morning a skikari would come peddling up to our resthouse on a bicycle and announce dramatically, "A tiger has killed!"

But we were to discover that even in this odd and excellent tiger country there is many a slip between tiger and rug. Take the lady tiger and her two cubs in the cane patch, for example:

The very first night, she walked out of the field, spied one of our calves, killed it, and dragged it back into the cane to fee her half-grown young. The circling vultures told us where the kill lay, and that she was still on it, or so near that the birds were afraid to come down. We built two machans by a lane through the cane, perched upon them, sent the elephants in to drive. Did we see any of the three tigers we knew were there? We did not! If we'd had a dozen elephants we might have pushed some out. As it was, the wise old gal and her cubs simply sneaked around our elephants. The next night she killed another one of our calves.

And there was the case of the big male tiger in the patch of jungle.

It looked as if getting him would be a cinch. All the villagers could tell us where he lived, when he had killed last, which path he usually took to his night's hunting. Our shikaris tied a calf out. The tiger killed it. The fact that the vultures were perched hungrily in trees in the middle of that little patch of jungle showed us where the tiger was.

It all looked very easy. Tigers are used to the noise of the natives, and when they bed down for the day they stay put. Our men went about preparing for the drive as nonchalantly as if they were building extra bleachers for the world series. They tied two native beds called charpoys upside down in trees to serve as machans. They put sheets of newspaper on bushes so that they would flutter and frighten the tiger to keep him on the desired line of retreat. The men who were to serve as lookouts or "stops" climbed their trees with shouts of glee. It was like boy scout day at the country fair.

Finally, when all was set, Mukerji and I climbed into one machan (the one where the tiger was most likely to pass, since I still had not shot a tiger), while Lee and and Anglo-Indian named Joe Hardy, who'd joined our party as a guide, climbed into another.

Then the drive began, and the little jungle became suddenly hushed and quiet. This was it. This was drama! The three elephants formed a line and worked the place over, patch by patch. Every time they'd come to a particularly thick bit the line would halt and one of the elephants would go into it, knock down shrubs, shake trees. All was quiet except for the crash of underbrush, the occasional crack of a limb.

Nearer and nearer came the slow, relentless crash of the elephants.

Then one of the stops high in a tree yelled, "The tiger is coming. I see him ahead of the elephants!" Then another cried, "The tiger tried to sneak out, but saw a paper and turned back."

I had a fairly good field of view of thirty-five or forty yards. The elephants were about seventy-five yards away now and my heart was in my throat. Old Stripes was on his way and he was—at long last—my meat.

Then all at once, to my right where Lee's machan was located, I heard the sharp blast of his .35 Whelen and looked up to see a tiger sprawl on the ground for an instant and then get up and take off.

In a zoo a tiger looks orange-yellow. See one in the shade and he likewise looks quite orange. But see a big wild tiger in the sunlight and he's bright red. And so it was with this tiger. He had tumbled at the shot, but in an instant he was up and galloping through the brush and tall grass like a scarlet streak.

Lee took another crack at him and so did Joe. From our machan Mukerji let fly with both barrels of a shotgun loaded with 12 gauge ball. By the time I could duck around him, the tiger's front end was disappearing into another patch of jungle, but I swung the cross hairs in the scope on the .375 Magnum ahead of the fleeting cat and blasted off with the same results.

Poor Lee! He felt as low as a man caught pilfering funds for the orphan's home. His machan, where the tiger was not supposed to pass, had been too close to the brush. The elephants were almost upon him, so he had decided that the tiger had slipped out or it was my time to get the shot. Then all at once the big cat had burst out of the brush within twenty feet of him, traveling like a turpentined tom. Lee had only time to throw his scope-sighted .35 Whelen down between his legs and shoot when it seemed to be pointed in the right direction.

We scrambled down out of the trees and ran to the spot where the tiger had disappeared. A few drops of blood that looked as if they'd come from a muscle wound glittered red on the yellow grass, and I discovered where my .375 bullet had plowed through the brush.

The elephants were lumbering up when suddenly Lee wheeled and yelled, "There it is!" Apparently the tiger had gone into the first dense patch it could find and lain down, because later the sign told us that Lee had indeed seen the tiger and that it was probably only scratched, possibly along the flank.

But nevertheless we mounted our elephants, and while we covered the ground in front our shikaris tracked . . . and tracked . . . and tracked. All that afternoon we stayed on the looping trail of the tiger. Sometimes we could see a little blood, and occasionally we found where he had laid down to rest. Then there might be a puddle of blood the size of a dollar. The feeling grew that his wound was superficial. But we didn't want to give up as long as there was any chance we might come upon him.

As the day wore on it became hotter and hotter and Lee and I got thirstier and thirstier. The animal's trail wound back and forth across a clean, cool-looking little stream that was shaded by lovely jungle trees, by tall grass and reeds. Now and then the boys would pile off the elephants and fill up with water. They had never heard of germs and waterborne diseases. Mukerji had, as he is an educated man, but he is an Indian and to a great extent immune to the frightful ailments that seem to lie in wait for the unwary American or European in any unboiled water in India.

Lee and I drooled at sight of the voluptuous water but we knew that dysentery would get us if we drank it. So we simply suffered.

Once a shikari reported a cobra. Another time we flushed out a wild sow and a litter of young, and once we flushed a leopard (which in India is always called a panther). But we didn't want to shoot the sow and couldn't have shot the leopard. Finally the tiger's wound stopped bleeding. We gave up and went back to the jeep, where some boiled water awaited us.

Almost every day tigers killed our baits, and almost every day we drove. But nothing happened. We scared the daylights out of generations of monkeys, moved a good many axis deer, wild boar, and peafowl. But tigers? Not a one.

The big tiger that lived down by the river was a particularly irritating character. Our shikaris staked out so many buffalo calves that he couldn't stir from his reed patch without running into one. But he'd just pass them by.

One morning a shikari came to gather the calves that had been quaking all night with the acrid smell of tiger in their noses. He heard the tiger's heavy tread in the reeds to his left. Presently he heard the great beast taking a bath in the little creek, grunting and splashing like a fat old man. Finally he heard the tiger go off about fifty yards and lie down.

The shikari was so certain he knew where the tiger had bedded that we tried a drive. I was perched in a tree overlooking a road the cat would have to cross, but I saw no tiger. A magnificent wild boar, the largest I saw in India, came trotting by, and later a couple of little hog deer sneaked past, heads down and almost crawling.

Time passed. The elephants belonged to some bush-league maharaja. He wanted them back, as he was throwing a shoot for some butter-and-egg men from New Delhi. We stalled the maharaja, crossed the palms of the elephant men. Came the time when we had but two more days to hunt, as the maharaja had threatened something very drastic and oriental unless he got his elephants back soon. If someone had offered me a few rupees that morning for my chance at a tiger, I probably would have sold out.

For breakfast Lee and I had watery oatmeal flavored with gray Indian sugar and diluted with pale blue boiled milk from a starving humpbacked cow. We drank a cup of ersatz powdered coffee and then tried to kill the taste with the wonderful Indian oranges which were both food and drink to us.

Then we heard excited yells outside the rest house. Mukerji burst in. "The big tiger has killed!" he said, beaming. "The one by the reed bed!"

To me it seemed like an omen. Surely the fates couldn't dangle another tiger in front of my face and then jerk it away. . . .

We really prepared for this drive, and I was delighted to find that the terrain looked like the best for us and the worst for the tiger of any we'd tried in India. The grass the tiger would come out of was tall—just about as high as a tiger's back—but there was a good tree for a machan, and I could shoot down. The belt of high reeds by the creek where the vultures told us the tiger lay was narrow enough so that it could be beaten nicely by three elephants.

So this was it.

To make sure there'd be no slip-up, Mukerji had loaded the three elephants with all manner of odd local characters. He had armed some with shotguns they were to shoot off to add to the noise and thus help move the tiger.

Tensely I waited for the elephants to do their job, but the beat came all the way to the machan without moving anything except a few pea-fowl and a couple of hog deer. I was sick with disappointment.

Then Mukerji and the mahouts had a big argument. Mukerji wanted them to drive again, closer to the creek. The mahouts said it was un-necessary—that if a tiger had been there it would have moved. Not knowing anything about it, I was nevertheless inclined to agree with them.

Finally Mukerji got them to try again. Once more the three lum-bering elephants came through the reeds, but this time farther to the left. Again the whooping and the hollering. Again the shotguns, fired off to move the tiger. Again the swish of elephants.

All at once I saw something big and red round above the grass in front of the elephants. It couldn't be the great massive head of a big he-tiger, but it was. And then the great beast was loping through the grass, quartering but coming gradually closer. At times he was just about out of sight, but at the top of his bounds I could see him well, a massive male tiger shining red in the sun—red as a new copper penny, red as an Irish setter, red as blood.

My first two shots went right over the top of his back because I shot at him on the top of his bound, but on the third shot I made myself shoot a bit ahead and low into the grass. I heard the bullet go *thunk* and I knew I'd hit him hard and solid, probably in the rib cage. He staggered for a moment then and slowed, but didn't go down. He was dead on his feet, though I didn't know it. Careless of the elephants, he turned and staggered back toward the reeds that so long had shel-tered him. He went into the reeds and down into the nullah where ran the cool little stream where he had drunk so often after killing.

But his lungs were full of blood, and he couldn't make it up the far bank. Suddenly I heard the death cry of the mighty tiger. I had never heard it but I knew what it was. It made my breath catch and tears come. It was part roar, part shriek, part lament. Then he col-lapsed and fell over backward, dead.

I scrambled down off the machan and ran to the spot where my great trophy had fallen. Already the elephants had come up, and some of the beaters had gathered around it. He lay there striped and beautiful, orange-red and black. He was as large as a small horse, and between the ears he was wider than the shoulders of a big man. As I stood there looking at the great gorgeous cat crumpled in death, I was a little sad and half-embarrassed. I'd have his hide tanned and his head mounted. I'd spend the rest of my life with him, yet I hardly knew him.

We measured him later—properly, since tiger measurements don't tell much unless the job's done right. A man might say he killed a ten-foot tiger, meaning that's what the tape read after the animal was skinned and the hide stretched. Actually, his ten feet would shrink to less than eight according to the "official" method of measuring big cats.

That is to lay the beast on his side, drive a peg in at the nose and one in at the end of the last tail bone, then roll the carcass away and measure the distance *between* the two pegs—not from center to center—with a steel tape. (Some people measure from peg to peg with the animal still in place, but obviously to lay the tape "over the curves" as it's called, adds maybe eight inches to the reading.)

Correctly measured, my Indian tiger went nine feet nine and was distinctly larger and heavier than my African lion, which my outfitter Don Ker said was the longest he'd ever measured (nine feet seven).

In his book *The Tigers of Trengganu,* Lt. Col. Arthur Locke says he thinks the standard for Indian tigers can best be set by the "Bachelor of Powalgarh," which figures in the late Jim Corbett's classic *Man-Eaters of Kumaon.* Locke calls the Bachelor, hunted season after season by sportsmen because of its great size, "truly a king among tigers" but adds that when measured by Corbett and his sister it went, not twelve feet, but ten feet seven inches *over curves.*

"This animal," Locke concludes, "would probably have been about ten feet if measured between pegs. I doubt very much whether so experienced a sportsman as Corbett would have regarded this tiger as an exceptional specimen had it not been unusually big even for India."

Getting back to my old he-tiger of Kashipur, he was one big tiger. I think he's the biggest tiger I've even seen a picture of.

It didn't take me long to find the bullet hole. It was a bit high, a trifle too far back, but a good solid lung shot nevertheless. With a hit like that from a 270-grain, soft-point bullet from a .375 Magnum he should have gone down in a hurry. He didn't.

Tigers are tough, and if I ever shoot another I'll use the lion medicine of Syd Downey, the African white hunter—a .416 or a .470 soft-point.

Now that the tiger was dead we were all a little drunk with excitement. The mahouts and shikaris whooped and yelled. One of the shikaris who'd been fasting to bring me luck, and whom I called Dopey the Dwarf because of his resemblance to the Disney character, became hysterical and wept. He said that if he died now he'd die happy because his poor old gentleman (me) had shot that wonderful tiger, the largest, fattest, finest tiger ever to live in northern India.

And so we put him on an elephant and we all rode in triumph through the villages to the jeep. The people cheered, the dogs barked, and the bullocks hitched to a cart in a wedding party smelled the tiger 5d ran away. The scared little brown bride got thrown out on the ground, and for a moment it looked as if an international incident was in the making. But when Lee and I passed around five-rupee banknotes, the people bowed and said the American sahibs weren't so bad after all.

And that night we had two more drinks than usual before dinner. Even the curry tasted good!

OUTDOOR LIFE
NOVEMBER 1955

My hunting buddy Jim Zumbo, editor at large for Outdoor Life, *put me on to this story. The adventure of the Chadwick ram appeared in* Outdoor Life *back in February of 1937 under the title "Record on a Meat Hunt." This was long before I joined* Outdoor Life, *and I didn't really know the significance of the Chadwick ram. L. S. Chadwick killed his world-record Stone sheep in August of 1936 in British Columbia. The horns measured fifty-two and one-eight inches along the outside curve. Today, fifty years later, the record still stands. The Chadwick ram is recognized worldwide as a standard by which all other sheep hunts are measured. Oddly enough, Chadwick never really started out to break any record. This ranks as the strangest "meat" hunt of all time.*

The Chadwick Ram

by L. S. CHADWICK

GOING out after food, and coming back with a Stone sheep whose horns measure fifty-two and an eighth inches along the outside curve may be something new in hunting, but that's the way I bagged the head that apparently sets a new world's record for size.

The hunt really began eighteen days before I shot the ram. It was August 1936, and I had decided to look for sheep in a wild section of the Rocky Mountains in British Columbia because, on a previous trip, one of my guides had told me that there were some excellent specimens in a small region apparently never hunted by a white man.

My party consisted of myself and three guides, Roy Hargreaves, of Mount Robson, Walter "Curly" Cochrane, of Rolla, and Frank Golata, of Dawson Creek. Cochrane had operated a trap line near the headwaters of the Muskwa River five years before, and had seen many fine heads. All of these men are good guides, excellent hunters and trappers, and experienced outfitters. It was due entirely to their abilities that I located, and got, the record head.

We went into the sheep country from Pouce Coupé, a place I selected because it had a good hotel where I could stay while getting my outfit adjusted for the trail. From there, we went to Dawson Creek, seven miles farther up, and continued by automobile for eighty-five or ninety miles. We crossed the Peace River at Taylor Flats and followed the river most of the time, going by way of Fort Saint John, to Bear Flats. There we picked up our pack train and struck out into rough country. Going was often slow because, after leaving the regular beaten trails, we had to blaze our own. Some days we made only six or eight miles. We pitched sixteen camps in eighteen days, having twice to remain an extra day in camp because of heavy rains. We left Bear Flats August 9 and worked our way northwest, up Halfway River, over the two Nelson Summits, past Redfern Lake, and then turned north. We fought mosquitoes and gnats all the way.

When we pitched camp on August 27, Curly, who at the time was acting as cook, demanded that some of us go out and get a supply of fresh meat. "We've been living on bacon long enough," he complained. And the rest of us agreed. When you eat bacon day after day for more than two weeks, you develop a craving for something fresher.

We had arrived at about two-thirty in the afternoon, so there was plenty of daylight left. Roy, Frank, and I took the glasses and rifles and started out to scout. We decided that, although we were looking primarily for fresh meat, we would not shoot any sheep unless they had fairly good horns. Thus the scouting expedition had the double goal of food and trophies, but we never suspected that it would turn out the way it did.

Soon after leaving camp, we split up. Roy climbed to the highest point on a nearby mountain that faced our camp and set the 20X telescope on its tripod. Through the 'scope, he searched the neighboring ranges for sheep. He saw about ten or a dozen rams, but none that seemed to have horns larger than thirty-five or thirty-six inches. Then, six or seven miles away, he located three sheep on the skyline of a high mountain range. "One of them looks as if it might be worth going after," he declared. Pursuit, though, was impossible in what remained of that day.

Early next morning, however, we started after the three rams, hoping that they had not strayed very far from the place where Roy had spotted them. We were optimistic, so we took horses to bring back the meat. About one o'clock we stopped to eat lunch high up under a cliff, out of the wind. Not far away there was a high saddle of ground, near the top of the range. Lunch over, we climbed to the saddle and surveyed the country with our glasses. We saw three sheep on top of a neighboring mountain, maybe a mile and a half away. One of the rams seemed to be carrying a wonderful pair of horns. We promptly decided to attempt a stalk.

The sheep apparently saw us. So Roy and I left the horses with Frank, who kept them out in the open where the sheep could watch them, and started after our game. We went down to the valley between the two ranges, along the edge of a glacier that partly filled a steep ravine, then crossed the valley, and scaled the other side. Of course, when we got to our goal the sheep were gone, but we soon sighted them in the next valley.

From this point, the biggest ram didn't look so promising. Roy and I debated whether to keep after him or try to locate something better. We decided finally to keep on, now that we had gone this far, and get some pictures of him at least. Besides, we needed meat.

Aside from being a hunter who uses a gun, I also like to shoot wild game with a motion picture camera, particularly game I am going to try to bag with a rifle. So we crept within two hundred yards or so of the sheep, and I exposed some color film on him.

Finally, I decided to try a shot. I fired from a sitting position, and, as he was directly below me, and almost straight down, I aimed a bit low. I was using a telescope sight for the first time on game of any size. The bullet struck the ram low in the body without hitting any bones, and the ram left in a hurry. Roy and I took after him. All the sheep ran swiftly down the valley for a short distance and then started to climb our side of the mountain. The wounded one soon began to lag behind, and while he was running down the valley, I took four more shots at him before he disappeared. One of the bullets struck him lightly in the hip. I shouted to Roy, who was able to make much faster time than I, to give him a finishing shot. I felt that the sheep was so badly wounded that he eventually would die, perhaps suffering for hours or days before he did.

Roy was fast outdistancing me in the chase. When a man gets to be sixty-two, he has to move a little more leisurely than when he was young. I probably won't do much more hunting in a country where I have to climb mountain ranges ten thousand feet high.

The wounded ram was unable to keep up with the others on the upward climb, allowing Roy to get near enough to get in the finishing shot. The bullet passed through the sheep's body, back of the shoulder and above my first one. The animal dropped down into a deep ravine. When we got to him, he was dead.

Even then we were not too enthusiastic about our prize, a Stone ram *(Ovis stonei)*. His body was small, at least for such a pair of horns. The big surprise came when we put the tape on him. The left horn measured fifty-two and one eight inches along the outside curve, and thirty-one and a quarter between the tips. The circumference of the horns at the bases was a little more than fifteen inches. We were so excited that we failed to notice then that a small portion of the point, perhaps two and a half inches, was broken from the right-hand horn. Except for this, I am sure the right-hand horn would have been at least a half inch longer than the left, as it was larger at the base and throughout its length.

I remembered that the largest previous bighorn head on record had horns measuring about forty-nine and a half inches on the outside curve, so I obviously had the biggest wild sheep head ever taken. Later checking showed that the finest sheep head of any species listed in *Records of North American Big Game* is that of the bighorn credited to James Simpson, who shot it in British Columbia in 1920. The horns had an outside curve of forty-nine and a half inches and a spread of twenty-three and seven eighths inches. The largest Stone sheep head, a trophy taken by C. R. Fahr on the Peace River in 1930, had a curve of forty-four and three quarters inches.

By the time Roy and I reached the dead sheep, Frank had become tired of waiting, and had started with the horses to follow us. Just as we were planning to go back and look for him, he appeared in the valley, scarcely four hundred yards below. As he was able to lead the horses within one hundred yards, we did not have to carry our meat very far.

We estimated, from rings on our ram's horns, that he was about fourteen years old. He had excellent teeth, and otherwise was in good condition. All three of the men with me checked the horn measurements.

To my knowledge, Stone sheep are found only north of the Peace River. There are no sheep of the common bighorn variety in that region. Stone sheep are smaller in body than regular bighorns and have very different markings. Whereas the bighorn has a white "doughnut" on its rump, the Stone sheep has a white patch that extends all the way down to the ankles, like a pair of white pants. Its bluish-gray coat hasn't so much brown as the bighorn. The backs of the legs are white, the underbody white or gray, and the fronts of the legs brown. Some specimens have white faces and necks.

Curly Cochrane told me there seemed to be only about one-fifth as many sheep in the territory near the headwaters of the Muskwa River as there had been five years before. Wolves, he said, were responsible. If something isn't done to clean out the wolves, it won't be many years until the sheep are extinct in that region. The wolves get them when snow drives them down into the valleys.

At a sulphur spring near where we camped, I shot a big male wolf, the leader of a pack of five. In every direction from that spring I found sheep horns, some of them very good. Such slaughter cannot help but thin out the sheep.

Chances of getting heads bigger than the one I took probably are none too good, for big heads are becoming scarce wherever hunters

are active, because of the practice of shooting rams with horns no
larger than thirty-five or thirty-six inches around the curves. Too many
hunters shoot rams with small horns, and then wonder why no big
trophies are left. The only reason I was able to get the big fellow in
the Muskwa River country was that no other hunters had been through
there to get him when he was smaller. He happened, too, to be lucky
enough to escape the wolves. As we did not cover this entire section,
on account of heavy snow, there is a chance that some lucky hunter
will some time find this old boy's daddy with a still larger head.

Most persons ask me what kind of rifle I use. My favorite for all
types of big game hunting is a .404 Magnum, made by the late Frank
Hoffman, of Cleveland. It shoots a 300-grain bullet at a muzzle velocity
of 2,709 feet a second, and has about twice the power of a Springfield.
With a heavier load, it is suitable for African game. There is no game
in North America that it cannot kill with a 300-grain bullet. The gun
weighs about ten pounds.

My guide always carries my Model 54 .30/06 Winchester. In case
anything happens to the big gun, the Winchester will then be on hand,
ready for business.

I realize the Magnum is a bit heavy for Rocky Mountain sheep, but
I like its range, power, and accuracy. It has a remarkably flat trajectory.
As for the range, a little experience I had with the second sheep I
shot on my trip may illustrate that. I got within about 350 yards of
him, and succeeded in taking some motion pictures through a tele-
photo lens. Roy suggested that, if I wanted that ram, I had better use
the gun instead of the camera, because the sheep was moving away.

So I started shooting. I fired six shots, using iron sights, but missed
because the animal was far away and moving fast. Then I decided to
try one shot with the 'scope sight, as I could no longer see him with
the naked eye. We judged the animal to be a good half mile away,
but the bullet struck him in the hip, and did plenty of damage. It was
pure luck that I hit him, but the shot does illustrate the power of the
Magnum 300-grain bullet at such ranges. In the Stone sheep country,
it is difficult to get closer than two hundred yards to one of the animals,
because they have been made shy by constant attack from wolves. So
a gun with considerable hitting power and flat trajectory is necessary.

This second sheep, by the way, had horns measuring forty-two
inches around the curves and thirty inches between the tips. It really
was a much more beautiful specimen than the record one, and its
horns were superior in color and general appearance.

I found plenty of other game north of Peace River, but used my
movie camera more than my guns. In a basin on the south fork of
the Muskwa River, we came upon a grizzly bear. I took movies of him
while he was stripping leaves from weeds and bushes and eating them.

Then I decided to try the rifle. I left the camera standing and moved about seventy-five feet upstream, to be closer for the shot.

The first bullet struck the bear, and he came plunging down the little valley toward me. One of the guides decided to try his luck as a cameraman, so he aimed the motion picture camera and pressed the release. As the bear got fairly close to us, the camera developed a decided tendency to wobble. On the film, which we saw later, the image of the bear jumps wildly all over the scene. And the closer the bear gets to the guide, the more it jumps.

I finished the bear with a shot at close range, but the guide didn't know until afterwards that my gun had jammed because the follower plate had flipped over as I was loading by hand, and that the bolt of the rifle, which the other guide was getting ready to fire, had slipped out of the gun. If he had known, I don't suppose the bear would have stayed in the picture at all. Fortunately, I had shot grizzly before, and was able to keep my feet on the ground while I got my rifle loaded.

I had planned to go about one hundred miles farther north, but snow prevented that. However, I felt more than satisfied with the results of the trip. A number of other hunting expeditions into Alaska, Alberta, British Columbia, and Ontario had taught me that it is almost a rule that the prize trophy is taken on the very last day. The sensible thing to do, now that I had my trophy, was to quit, even if I had bagged it the first day with the first shot. The next time I hunt, it might not be a bad idea to go looking for meat instead of trophies.

OUTDOOR LIFE
FEBRUARY 1937

Everyone loves a dog story, especially a story about an old hunting dog. I'm not going to say much more about "Lingering Greatness," except to say that after you read it, you'll probably want to give your dog a big hug—even if he busts birds in the field, hunts by himself, can't find cripples, and generally embarrasses you in front of your hunting buddies. He's still "your hunting dog."

Lingering Greatness

by FLOYD A. BAKER

THE last half of December had been much colder than usual, and early January wasn't much better. After finally forcing myself to go outside and do the usual farm chores one cold morning, I decided that it would be at least 1 or 2 P.M. before a person would have any business trying to find a few quail.

I owned a pointer bitch that was about five years old and that I believed to be among the better dogs. I had also just started a Brittany pup of about six months that had enough natural ability to make most men brag a little about their dog training, even if unjustified. Dog men and fishermen seem to possess bragging ability now and then.

I had seen many quail seasons come and go, and several good dogs, long gone, linger in my memory—dogs that never loafed on the job. They were always willing partners, no matter how hard the conditions.

I wonder, sometimes, if the dogs we remember as less than great just never understood what we really wanted because our training could have been better. It is always easier to lay the fault on the dog, I guess.

On dark, cold, and dreary days, thoughts such as these seem to find their way into our minds—or maybe they come to mind because we're getting a little older and we reminisce more.

I looked out the window one more time around noon and saw that the sun had finally come out. It looked warmer, anyway. I had a quick bite to eat and stepped out to check the weather again. The wind was still blowing from the north, ten or fifteen miles an hour—not the best day for hunting I had ever seen. But after being unable to hunt for several days, I decided to try it for a little while.

I tried to think of someplace where there was still a covey or two that wouldn't be harmed if I took three or four birds. I remembered an old field that bordered on quite a bit of timber. A pretty good creek ran through the north end of the area. There had been a couple of coveys there earlier in the season, but they had given me the slip after I had taken only four or five birds with twice as many shots.

There was plenty of cover in the field and maybe the birds would hold. That's what that pup needs, I thought, after the wild birds we had hunted last. I would take him by himself. It would do him good. He hadn't hunted alone before.

I put more clothes on than I thought a man could shoot in, and after I loaded the pup in the truck, I decided that an extra pocketful of shells wasn't a bad idea. No one would be there to see how many shells I used.

I drove the four or five miles in about ten minutes. When I parked the truck by an old gate, a feeling of excitement began to make me forget about the cold. I opened the door of the dog box and that bundle of energy leaped out. The pup seemed a little confused and ran in circles, coming back to see where the old dog I had left at home was. The pup was, I guess, uncertain as to whether he could handle the job alone. But after we had walked more than half of the thirty acre field, he was hunting very well. We searched every acre pretty thoroughly, but failed to find one single bird. The cold spell had caused them to change their range, I thought. The pup had hunted everywhere in the old field.

Heading toward the truck, I noticed clouds covering the sun—the kind of clouds that seem to make the cold seep in through your boots and around the collar of your jacket. I looked south, across the country road where I had parked, toward some rolling hills. There was probably a half mile of bare pasture land between me and the hillside farther to the south. I hated to go home without giving the little dog a chance to see what he could do by himself.

Crossing the road, I headed him south. The walk would do us both good, I thought to myself. Besides, two or three weeks earlier, a hunting friend and I had set a good covey near a pond at the base of those ridges and there should be several birds still in that bunch. Maybe we could find them before it got too late.

We walked along an old fenceline on our way there, hoping maybe to find a stray bunch that I didn't know about. The little bit of ice and snow that had thawed down in the valley near the hills was now beginning to freeze again and we hadn't found anything yet. Looking back toward the truck, I wondered if it was wise to go farther, but only about another quarter of a mile lay between us and the pond where my friend and I had found some birds.

The little dog had gone ahead and was out of sight over a little rise. I moved another hundred yards, and when I saw him, he still hadn't found any birds.

While I was standing on the higher ground, I looked up at the hillside where there were a few scattered bushes and grass. Water seeped out of these ridges most of the time, but now everything was frozen because of the bitter north wind. Then something about four hundred yards away caught my eye. It was near the pond. In the darkening light from the overcast skies, I was unable to make out what it was. I assumed it must be a cow's head sticking up out of a little bunch of tall grass growing near the pond.

I moved a little farther south and a little in the direction of the pond, stopping occasionally to watch the pup work. The little valley seemed so quiet; I hadn't heard another hunter shoot the whole evening. I figured that the other gunners had had better sense than to be out on such a cold day. Once more, I moved another hundred yards in the general direction of the pond, until I was again standing on a little rise. Once more, the odd object caught my eye. This time, because I was closer, I could see that it was a dog and that it seemed to be standing still and looking at something on the ground.

I looked around for other hunters but saw no one. As I moved closer, the old dog still stood in the same place. I could see that he was a setter. He seemed very tired, but he continued to look straight ahead. His head seemed to be too big for his frail body. When I got closer, I saw that ice had formed on his undercoat and that his ribs stood out clearly. The long, shaggy tail swept back and forth like a pendulum. Its movement never ceased while I stood there, twenty yards away. It dawned on me that he was very old; far past his prime. The once-bright eyes were sunken and clouded, and I guessed that he had gone deaf from old age and too many shotgun blasts over his head. He didn't even know I was there. Once more I searched the landscape for someone who might be with him, but again there was no one.

I had already decided that the old dog was on birds—if not, he sure thought that he was. I had forgotten about my pup while I'd been studying the old dog. When I looked up, I could see him standing twenty yards behind the old dog. He was honoring that old-timer's point with everything he could stretch out.

The old dog was locked up and sensed nothing but the birds. Yet when I moved to within five steps of him, those dim eyes caught sight of me for the first time and he seemed startled. He looked up at my face just for an instant and I caught a message that only a hunter and an old dog can possibly understand. Immediately, the nose shot forward and the tail that had been moving straightened. No dog ever looked more beautiful and, as I moved forward a few feet to the place where the dog was looking, I felt sorry for him.

When ten or twelve quail lifted into the air, I knew I had to shoot one or two for the old setter. I got a straightaway and folded one that went to my right.

The old dog picked up the first bird and started toward me, but when he got within ten yards, he slowly put the bird down, his eyes seeming to say that he didn't know how much he could trust people anymore.

The pup had picked up the second bird and was nudging me with it. I took it and he fetched the one that the old dog had put down. Then he came to get his pat on the head. Dogs seem to greatly appreciate just a pat on the head.

As I stood and reloaded my gun, I looked around to see where the old dog was. I had no idea where the other birds had gone. I stood there in that late evening cold and wondered if all this had really happened. I felt inside my game pocket and there were two birds there, still warm, to tell me that it was all real.

I moved farther up the hill and looked in every direction. Finally, I saw the old dog crossing the slope above me. He moved as though his back legs were hobbled. He pulled them along behind him and I could tell that every step was extremely difficult, but he never gave in to his misery. The last I saw of him, he was headed south. I called to him but he kept going. Of course he couldn't hear me, but it seemed that I had to do something. I tried to catch up with him, but it was as if he sensed my actions somehow and maybe remembered some past betrayal by a man.

I started back toward the truck and realized that I felt obligated to find someone who knew about the old dog. There were only two or three houses within about two miles of where we were, and as far as I knew, none of those people kept bird dogs.

While I hurriedly loaded my pup in the dog box, I decided to drive the roads in that area and look for someone who had lost the old dog. Maybe he would be parked somewhere waiting for the dog to come back. But I found no one on the roads, and I couldn't find any signs of a place where anyone had parked and let a dog out. Then I thought of the only other place where anyone stayed. It was a pipeline shop about one mile east of where I had last seen the old dog.

I parked in front of the shop and went in just as they were about to leave for home. I asked them if they had ever seen an old setter bird dog around the place. To my surprise, they said yes. An old dog stayed around the shop sometimes. They said that some fellow had brought him out there, knowing that they liked to hunt some and maybe would take the dog. The dog had gotten too old and wasn't much use anymore; he just wandered the countryside and came back to the shop for a little feed when he needed it.

The old dog's plight kept me awake that night. I could still see the greatness come alive in him again when I walked up to his side. He may have been old and crippled, eyesight nearly gone and completely deaf, but no dog that ever breathed showed more greatness than that old setter did on that cold winter evening. I'm not sure I will ever be the same after seeing him.

When I told the men at the shop about the old dog that I had found on point, they asked if he had been onto anything. I took the birds from my coat and put them on the floor before them.

"Here's a present from the old dog," I said.

I suspect that they were the last birds ever taken over him.

OUTDOOR LIFE

JANUARY 1985

When you read about this classic hunting trip in British Columbia by Colonel Townsend Whelen, bear in mind that this happened back in 1906, before the time of nylon and freeze-dried foods. When Colonel Whelen talks about his tent, he means heavy canvas. And he probably didn't have a fancy reloading press when he hand-loaded his .40/72 cartridges with black powder and lead bullets. As you read this story, try to imagine how you would make such a trip without modern equipment. Colonel Whelen, who was only a lieutenant when he wrote this story, was the shooting editor of Outdoor Life *back in the 1930's. He also designed the Whelen sling that many of us now use on our rifles. Colonel Whelen may well have set the stage for most of today's big-game hunters.*

Red-Letter Days in British Columbia

by LIEUTENANT TOWNSEND WHELEN

IN the month of July 1901, my partner, Bill Andrews, and I were at a small Hudson Bay post in the northern part of British Columbia, outfitting for a long hunting and exploring trip in the wild country to the North. The official map showed this country as "unexplored," with one or two rivers shown by dotted lines. This map was the drawing card which had brought us thousands of miles by rail, stage, and pack train to this out-of-the-way spot. By the big stove in the living room of the factor's house we listened to weird tales of this north country, of its enormous mountains and glaciers, its rivers and lakes, and of the quantities of game and fish. The factor told us of three men who had tried to get through there in the Klondike rush several years before and had not been heard from yet. The trappers and Siwashes could tell us of trails which ran up either side of the Scumscum, the river on which the post stood, but no one knew what lay between that and the Yukon to the north.

We spent two days here outfitting and on the morning of the third said goodbye to the assembled population and started with our pack train up the east bank of the Scumscum. We were starting out to live and travel in an unknown wilderness for over six months, and our outfit may perhaps interest my readers: We had two saddle horses, four packhorses, and a dog. A small tent formed one pack cover. We had ten heavy army blankets, which we used for saddle blankets while traveling, they being kept clean by using canvas sweat pads under them. We were able to pack 150 pounds of grub on each horse, divided up as nearly as I can remember as follows: 150 flour, 50 pounds sugar, 30 pounds beans, 10 pounds rice, 10 pounds dried apples, 20 pounds prunes, 30 pounds corn meal, 20 pounds oatmeal, 30 pounds potatoes, 10 pounds onions, 50 pounds bacon, 25 pounds salt, 1 pound pepper, 6 cans baking powder, 10 pounds soap, 10 pounds tobacco, 10 pounds tea, and a few little incidentals weighing probably 10 pounds. We took two extra sets of shoes for each horse, with tools for shoeing, 2 axes, 25 boxes of wax matches, a large can of gun oil, canton flannel for gun rags, 2 cleaning rods, a change of underclothes, 6 pairs of socks, and 6 moccasins each, with buckskin for resoling, toilet articles, 100 yards of fishing line, 2 dozen fish hooks, an oil stove, awl, file, screwdriver, needles and thread, etc.

For cooking utensils we had 2 frying pans, 3 kettles to nest, 2 tin cups, 3 tin plates, and a gold pan. We took 300 cartridges for each of our rifles. Bill carried a .38-55 Winchester, model '94, and I had my old .40-72 Winchester, model '95, which had proved too reliable to relinquish for a high-power small bore. Both rifles were equipped with Lyman sights and carefully sighted. As a precaution we each took along extra front sights, firing pins, and mainsprings, but did not have a chance to use them. I loaded the ammunition for both rifles myself, with black powder, smokeless priming, and lead bullets. Both rifles proved equal to every emergency.

Where the post stood the mountains were low and covered for the most part with sagebrush, with here and there a grove of pines or quaking aspen. As our pack train wound its way up the narrow trail above the river bank we saw many Siwashes spearing salmon, a very familiar sight in that country. These gradually became fewer and fewer, then we passed a miner's cabin and a Siwash village with its little log huts and its hay fields, from which grass is cut for the winter consumption of the horses. Gradually all signs of civilization disappeared, the mountains rose higher and higher, the valley became a canyon, and the roar of the river increased, until finally the narrowing trail wound around an outrageous corner with the river a thousand feet below, and looming up in front of us appeared a range of snowcapped mountains, and thus at last we were in the haven where we would be.

That night we camped on one of the little pine-covered benches above the canyon. My, but it was good to get the smell of that everlasting sage out of our nostrils, and to take long whiffs of the balsam-laden air! Sunset comes very late at this latitude in July, and it was an easy matter to wander up a little draw at nine in the evening and shoot the heads of three grouse. After supper it was mighty good to lie and smoke and listen to the tinkle of the horse bells as the animals fed on the luscious mountain grass. We were old campmates, Bill and I, and it took us back to many trips we had had before, which were, however, to be surpassed many times by this one. I can well remember how as a boy, when I first took to woods loafing, I used to brood over a little work which we all know so well, entitled "Woodcraft," by that grand old man, "nessmuk," and particularly that part where he relates about his eight-day tramp through the then virgin wilderness of Michigan. But here we were, starting out on a trip which was to take over half a year, during which time we were destined to cover over fifteen hundred miles of unexplored mountains, without the sight of a human face or an ax mark other than our own.

The next day, after about an hour's travel, we passed the winter cabin of an old trapper, now deserted, but with the frames for stretching bear skins and boards for marten pelts lying around—betokening the owner's occupation. The dirt roof was entirely covered with the horns of deer and mountain sheep, and we longed to close our jaws on some good red venison. Here the man-made trails came to an end, and henceforth we used the game trails entirely. These intersect the country in every direction, being made by the deer, sheep, and caribou in their migrations between the high and low altitudes. In some places they were hardly discernible, while in others we followed them for days, when they were as plainly marked as the bridle paths in a city park. A little farther on we saw a whole family of goats sunning themselves on a high bluff across the river, and that night we dined on the ribs of a fat little spike buck that I shot in the park where we pitched our tent.

To chronicle all the events that occurred on that glorious trip would, I fear, tire my readers, so I will choose from the rich store certain ones that have made red-letter days in our lives. I can recollect but four days when we were unable to kill enough game or catch enough fish to keep the table well supplied, and as luck would have it, those four days came together, and we nearly starved. We had been camped for about a week in a broad wooded valley, having a glorious loaf after a hard struggle across a mountain pass, and were living on trout from a little stream alongside camp, and grouse which were in the pine woods by the thousands. Tiring of this diet we decided to take a little side trip and get a deer or two, taking only our three fattest horses and leaving the others behind to fatten up on the long grass in the valley, for they had become very poor owing to a week's work high up above timber line. The big game here was all high up in the mountains to escape the heat of the valley. So we started one morning, taking only a little tea, rice, three bannocks, our bedding and rifles, thinking that we would enjoy living on meat straight for a couple of days. We had along with us a black mongrel hound named Lion, belonging to Bill. He was a fine dog on grouse but prone to chase a deer once in a while.

About eight miles up the valley could be seen a high mountain of green serpentine rock, and for many days we had been speculating on the many fine bucks that certainly lay in the little ravines around the base, so we chose this for our goal. We made the top of the mountain about three in the afternoon, and gazing down on the opposite side we saw a little lake with good horsefeed around it and determined to camp there. About halfway down we jumped a doe and as it stood on a little hummock Bill blazed away at it and undershot. This was too much for Lion, the hound, and he broke after the deer, making the mountainside ring with his baying for half an hour. Well, we hunted all the next day, and the next, and never saw a hair. That dog had chased the deer all out of the country with his barking.

By this time our little grubstake of rice, bannocks, and tea was exhausted, and, to make things worse, on the third night we had a terrific hail storm, the stones covering the ground three inches deep. Breakfast the next morning consisted of tea alone, and we felt pretty glum as we started out, determining that if we did not find game that day we would pull up stakes for our big camp in the valley. About one o'clock I struck a fresh deer trail and had not followed it long before three or four others joined it, all traveling on a game trail which led up a valley. This valley headed up about six miles from our camp in three little ravines, each about four miles long. When I got to the junction of these ravines it was getting dark and I had to make for camp. Bill was there before me and had the fire going and some tea brewing but nothing else. He had traveled about twenty miles that day and had not seen a thing. I can still see the disgusted look on his face when he found I had killed nothing. We drank our tea in silence, drew our belts tighter, and went to bed.

The next morning we saddled up our horses and pulled out. We had not tasted food for about sixty hours and were feeling very faint and weak. I can remember what an effort it was to get into the saddle and how sick and weak I felt when old Baldy, my saddle horse, broke into a trot. Our way back led near the spot where I had left the deer trail the night before, and we determined to ride that way, hoping that perhaps we might get a shot at them. Bill came first, then Loco, the packhorse, and I brought up the rear. As we were crossing one of the little raviat the head of the main valley Loco bolted and Bill took after him to drive him back into the trail. I sat on my horse idly watching the race, when suddenly I saw a mouse-colored flash and then another and heard the thump, thump of cloven feet. Almost instantly the whole ravine seemed to be alive with deer. They were running in every direction. I leaped from my horse and cut loose at the nearest, which happened to be a doe. She fell over a log, and I could see her tail waving in little circles and knew I had her. Then I turned on a big buck on the other side of the ravine and at the second shot he stumbled and rolled into the little stream. I heard Bill shooting off to the left and yelled to him that we had enough, and he soon joined me, saying he had a spike buck down. It was the work of but a few minutes to dress the deer and soon we had a little fire going and the three livers hanging in little strips around it. Right here we three, that is, Bill, the dog, and myself, disposed of a liver apiece, and my! how easily and quickly it went—the first meat in over a week. Late that night we made our horse camp in the lower valley, having to walk all the way as our horses packed the meat. The next day was consumed entirely with jerking meat, cooking, and eating. We consumed half the spike buck that day. When men do work such as we were doing their appetites are enormous, even without a fast of four days to sharpen them up.

One night I well remember, after a particularly hard day with the pack train through a succession of windfalls. We killed a porcupine just before camping and made it into a stew with rice, dough balls, onions, and thick gravy, seasoned with curry. It filled the kettle to within an inch of the top and we ate the whole without stopping, whereat Bill remarked that it was enough for a whole boardinghouse. According to the catalogue of Abercrombie and Fitch that kettle held eight quarts.

We made it the rule, while our horses were in condition, to travel four days in the week, hunt two, and rest one. Let me chronicle a day of traveling; it may interest some of you who have never traveled with a pack train. Arising at the first streak of dawn, one man cooked the breakfast while the other drove in the horses. These were allowed to graze free at every camping place, each horse having a cowbell around its neck, only Loco being hobbled, for he had a fashion of wanoff on an exploring expedition of his own and leading all the other horses with him. The horses were liable to be anywhere within two miles of camp, and it was necessary to get behind them to drive them in. Four miles over these mountains would be considered a pretty good day's work in the East. Out here it merely gave one an appetite for his breakfast. If you get behind a pack of well-trained horses they will usually walk right straight to camp, but on occasions I have walked, thrown stones, and cussed from seven until twelve before I managed to get them in. Sometimes a bear will run off a pack of horses. This happened to us once, and it took two days to track them to the head of a canyon fifteen miles off, and then we had to break Loco all over again.

Breakfast and packing together would take an hour, so we seldom got started before seven o'clock. One of us rode first to pick out the trail, then followed the four packhorses and the man in the rear, whose duty it was to keep them in the trail and going along. Some days the trail was fine, running along the grassy south hillsides with fine views of the snowcapped ranges, rivers, lakes, and glaciers; on others it was one continual struggle over fallen logs, boulders, through ice-cold rivers swifter than the Niagara rapids, and around bluffs so high that we could scarcely distinguish the outlines of the trees below. Suppose for a minute that you have the job of keeping the horses in the trail. You ride behind the last horse, lazily watching the train. You do not hurry them as they stop for an instant to catch at a whiff of bunch grass beside the trail. Two miles an hour is all the speed you can hope to make. Suddenly one horse will leave the trail enticed by some particularly green grass a little to one side, and leaning over in your saddle you pick up a stone and hurl it at the delinquent, and he falls into line again. Then everything goes well until suddenly one of the packhorses breaks off on a faint side trail going for all he is worth. You dig in your spurs and follow him down the mountainside over rocks and down timber until he comes to a stop half a mile below in a thicket of quaking aspen. You extricate him and drive him back. The next thing you know one of the horses starts to buck and you notice that his pack is turning; then everything starts at once. The pack slides between the horse's legs, he bucks all the harder, the frying pan comes loose, a side pack comes off, and the other horses fly in every direction. Perhaps in an hour you have corralled the horses, repacked the cause of your troubles, and are hitting the trail again. In another day's travel the trail may lead over down timber and big boulders and for eight solid hours you are whipping the horses to make them jump the obstructions, while your companion is pulling at the halters.

Rustling with a pack train is a soul-trying occupation. Where possible we always aimed to go into camp about three in the afternoon. Then the horses got a good feed before dark—they will not feed well at night—and we had plenty of time to make a comfortable camp and get a good supper. We seldom pitched our tent on these one-night camps unless the weather looked doubtful, preferring to make a bed of pine boughs near the fire. The blankets were laid on top of a couple of pack sheets and the tent over all.

For several days we had been traveling thus, looking for a pass across a long snowcapped mountain range that barred our way to the north. Finally we found a pass between two large peaks where we thought

we could get through, so we started up. When we got up to timberline
the wind was blowing so hard that we could not sit on our horses. It
would take up large stones the size of one's fist and hurl them down
the mountainside. It swept by us cracking and roaring like a battery
of rapid-fire guns. To cross was impossible, so we backtracked a mile
to a spot where a little creek crossed the trail, made camp and waited.
It was three days before the wind went down enough to allow us to
cross.

The mountain sheep had made a broad trail through the pass, and
it was easy to follow, being mostly over shale rock. That afternoon,
descending the other side of the range, we camped just below timber
line by a little lake of the most perfect emerald hue I have ever seen.
The lake was about a mile long. At its head a large glacier extended
way up toward the peaks. On the east was a wall of bright red rock,
a thousand feet high, while to the west the hillside was covered with
dwarf pine trees, some of them not over a foot high and full-grown
at that. Below our camp the little stream, the outlet of the lake,
bounded down the hillside in a succession of waterfalls. A more beautiful picture I have yet to see. We stayed up late that night watching
it in the light of the full moon and thanked our lucky stars that we
were alive. It was very cold; we put on all the clothes we owned and
turned in under seven blankets. The heavens seemed mighty near
indeed, and the stars crackled and almost exploded with the still silver
mountains sparkling all around. We could hear the roar of the waterfalls below us and the bells of the horses on the hillside above. Our
noses were very cold. Far off a coyote howled, and so we went to
sleep—and instantly it was morning.

I arose and washed in the lake. It was my turn to cook, but first of
all I got my telescope and looked around for signs of game. Turning
the glass to the top of the wooded hillside, I saw something white
moving, and getting a steady position, I made it out to be the rump
of a mountain sheep. Looking carefully I picked out four others. Then
I called Bill. The sheep were mine by right of discovery, so we traded
the cook detail and I took my rifle and belt, stripped to trousers, moccasins, and shirt, and started out, going swiftly at first to warm up in
the keen mountain air. I kept straight up the hillside until I got to
the top and then started along the ridge toward the sheep. As I crossed
a little rise I caught sight of them five hundred yards ahead, the band
numbering about fifty. Some were feeding, others were bedded down
in some shale. From here on it was all stalking, mostly crawling through
the small trees and bushes which were hardly knee-high. Finally, getting within 150 yards, I got a good, steady, prone position between
the bushes, and picking out the largest ram, I got the white Lyman
sight nicely centered behind his shoulder and very carefully and grad-

ually I pressed the trigger. The instant the gun went off I knew he was mine, for I could have gotten in another shot even if I had wished it. The ram I had fired at was knocked completely off its feet, but picked himself up instantly and started off with the others; but after he had run about a hundred yards I saw his head drop and, turning half a dozen somersaults, he rolled down the hill and I knew I had made a heart shot. His horns measured sixteen and a half inches at the base, and the nose contained an enormous bump, probably caused in one of his fights for the supremacy of the herd.

I dressed the ram and then went for the horses. Bill, by this time, had everything packed up, so after going up the hill and loading the sheep on my saddle horse, we started down the range for a region where it was warmer and less strenuous and where the horsefeed was better. That night we had mountain sheep ribs—the best meat that ever passed a human's mouth—and I had a head worth bringing home. A sixteen and a half inch head is very rare in these days. I believe the record head measured about nineteen inches. I remember distinctly, however, on another hunt in the Lillooet district of British Columbia, finding in the long grass of a valley the half-decayed head of an enormous ram. I measured the pith of the skull where the horn had been and it recorded eighteen inches. The horn itself must have been at least twenty one inches. The ram probably died of old age or was unable to get out of the high altitude when the snow came.   We journeyed on and on, having a glorious time in the freedom of the mountains. We were traveling in a circle, the diameter of which was about three hundred miles. One day we struck an enormous glacier and had to bend way off to the right to avoid it. For days as we traveled that glacier kept us company. It had its origin way up in a mass of peaks and perpetual snow, being fed from a dozen valleys. At least six moraines could be distinctly seen on its surface, and the air in its vicinity was decidedly cool. Where we first struck it, it was probably six miles wide, and I believe it was not a bit less than fifty miles long. We named it Chilko glacier, because it undoubtedly drained into a large lake of that name near the coast. At this point we were not over two hundred miles from the Pacific Ocean.

As the leaves on the aspen trees started to turn we gradually edged around and headed toward our starting point, going by another route, however, trusting to luck and the careful map we had been making to bring us out somewhere on the Scumscum River above the post. The days were getting short now and the nights very cold. We had to travel during almost all the daylight and our horses started to get poor. The shoes we had taken for them were used up by this time, and we had to avoid as much as possible the rocky country. We traveled fast for a month until we struck the headwaters of the Scumscum;

then knowing that we were practically safe from being snowed up in the mountain, we made a permanent camp on a hillside where the horsefeed was good and started to hunt and tramp to our hearts' delight, while our horses filled up on the grass. We never killed any more game than we could use, which was about one animal every ten days. In this climate meat will keep for a month if protected from flies in the daytime and exposed to the night air after dark.

We were very proud of our permanent camp. The tent was pitched under a large pine tree in a thicket of willows and quaking aspen. All around it was built a windbreak of logs and pine boughs, leaving in front a yard, in the center of which was our camp fire. The windbreak went up six feet high, and when a fire was going in front of the tent we were as warm as though in a cabin, no matter how hard the wind blew. Close beside the tent was a little spring, and half a mile away was a lake full of trout from fifteen pounds down. We spent three days laying in a supply of firewood. Altogether it was the best camp I ever slept in. The hunting within tramping distance was splendid. We rarely hunted together, each preferring to go his own way. When we did not need meat we hunted varmints, and I brought in quite a number of prime coyote pelts and one wolf. One evening Bill staggered into camp with a big mountain lion over his shoulders. He just happened to run across it in a little pine thicket. That was the only one we saw on the whole trip, although their tracks were everywhere and we frequently heard their mutterings in the still evenings. The porcupines at this camp were unusually numerous. They would frequently get inside our windbreak and had a great propensity for eating our soap. Lion, the hound, would not bother them; he had learned his lesson well. When they came around he would get an expression on his face as much as to say, "You give me a pain."

The nights were now very cold. It froze every night, and we bedded ourselves down with lots of skins and used enormous logs on the fire so that it would keep going all night. We shot some marmots and made ourselves fur caps and gloves and patched up our outer garments with buckskin. And still the snow did not come.

One day while out hunting I saw a big goat on a bluff off to my right and determined to try to get him for his head, which appeared through my telescope to be an unusually good one. He was about half a mile off when I first spied him, and the bluff extended several miles to the southwest like a great wall shutting off the view in that direction. I worked up to the foot of the bluffs and then along; climbing up several hundred feet I struck a shelf that appeared to run along the face at about the height I had seen the goat. It was ticklish work, for the shelf was covered with slide rock which I had to avoid disturbing, and then too, in places it dwindled to a ledge barely three feet wide with about five hundred feet of nothing underneath. After about four hundred yards of this work I heard a rock fall above me and looking up saw the billy leaning over an outrageous corner looking at me. Aiming as nearly as I could straight up, I let drive at the middle of the white mass. There was a grunt, a scramble, and a lot of rocks, and then down came the goat, striking in between the cliff and a big boulder and not two feet from me. I fairly shivered for fear he would jump up and butt me off the ledge, but he only gave one quiver and lay still. The 330-grain bullet entering the stomach had broken the spine and killed instantly. He was an old grandfather and had a splendid head, which I now treasure very highly. I took the head, skin, fat, and some of the meat back to camp that night, having to pack it off the bluff in sections. The fat rendered out into three gold pans full of lard. Goat fat is excellent for frying, and all through the trip it was a great saving on our bacon.

Then one night the snow came. We heard it gently tapping on the tent, and by morning there were three inches in our yard. The time had come only too soon to pull out, which we did about ten o'clock, bidding good-bye to our permanent camp with its comfortable windbreak, its fireplace, table, and chairs. Below us the river ran through a canyon, and we had to cross quite a high mountain range to get through. As we ascended, the snow got deeper and deeper. It was almost two feet deep on a level on top of the range. We had to go down a very steep hogback and here had trouble in plenty. The horses' feet balled up with snow, and they were continually sliding. A packhorse slid down on top of my saddle horse and started him, I was on foot in front and they knocked me down, and the three of us slid until stopped by a fallen tree. Such a mess I never saw. One horse was on top of another. The pack was loose, and frozen ropes tangled up with everything. It took us half an hour to straighten up the mess, and the frozen lash ropes cut our hands frightfully. My ankle had become slightly strained in the mix-up, and for several days I suffered agonies with it. There was no stopping—we had to hit the trail hard or get snowed in. One day we stopped to hunt. Bill went out while I nursed my leg. He brought in a fine seven-point buck.

Speaking of the hunt he said: "I jumped the buck in a flat of down timber. He was going like mad about a hundred yards off when I first spied him. I threw up the old rifle and blazed away five times before he tumbled. Each time I pulled I was conscious that the sights looked just like that trademark of the Lyman sight showing the running deer and the sight. When I went over to look at the buck I had a nice little bunch of five shots right behind the shoulder. Those Lyman sights are surely the sights for a hunting rifle." Bill was one of the best shots on game I ever saw. One day I saw him cut the heads off of three grouse in trees while he sat in the saddle with his horse walking uphill. Both our rifles did mighty good work. The more I use a rifle the more I become convinced of the truth of the saying, "Beware of the man with one gun." Get a good rifle to suit you exactly. Fix the trigger pull and sights exactly as you wish them and stick to that gun as long as it will shoot accurately, and you will make few misses in the field.

Only too soon we drove our pack train into the post. As we rode up, two men were building a shack. One of them dropped a board, and we nearly jumped out of our skins at the terrific noise. My! how loud everything sounded to our ears, accustomed only to the stillness of those grand mountains. We stayed at the post three days, disposing of our horses and boxing up our heads and skins, and then pulled out for civilization. Never again will such experiences come to us. The day of the wilderness hunter has gone for good. And so the hunt of our lives came to an end.

OUTDOOR LIFE
DECEMBER 1906

An anthology of hunting stories would never be complete without a true bear-attack story, and this one will chill you to the marrow. What's worse than being attacked by one Alaska brown bear? Being attacked by two *Alaska brown bears, of course. And that's what happens here. The story will make you squeamish, but it will also make you smarter the next time you hunt in bear country.*

Nightmare Hunt

by ROLLIN BRADEN
as told to MARGUERITE REISS

MY hunting buddy, Darrel Rosin, chided me as we pushed aside the high brush on the narrow path leading back to the cabin.

"Thought you told me these bears up here go after moose nose like kids after ice cream," Darrel kidded. "Here we've been on this moose hunt for two weeks and nary the sign of a bear. Just doesn't stack up."

Whether we had seen them or not, we were in bear country. It was the tag end of the moose season in southern Alaska, fifty miles south of Soldotna, two hundred miles south of Anchorage.

I was getting anxious about our lack of success as the end of our trip drew near. Finally, my dad, Wes, and my brother, Wayne, managed to get their moose on the same day, but neither Darrel nor I scored.

On one of the last days of our moose hunt, Darrel and I started off through the high willows that surrounded our camp. We had our minds set on adding two more moose carcasses to those already hanging in the tree near the cabin.

Darrel figured that he'd get his from a platform we had built twenty feet up in a tall spruce tree four years earlier. It was a terrific lookout, commanding a splendid view across the thick brush, spruce stands, and tundra bogs.

Darrel let it be known that he was going to get his moose if it took him all day—and it nearly did. At 5 P.M., I heard a shot from Darrel's Ruger 77.

"Got him!" I heard Darrel yell. "At one hundred yards."

It was a little after 7 P.M. when we finished dressing his kill and were starting back to the cabin to stow our meat ax, saw, and rope.

The spruce shadows were, for me, depressingly long. Darrel had gotten his moose, but I was still empty-handed. I was thinking of using up the last half hour or so of twilight to locate a bull that I knew had been with the rest of the bulls we'd taken.

If I couldn't get him tonight, I'd get him at first light tomorrow. Only one day of the season remained.

I stepped just a couple of feet away from Darrel and stopped, listening. Though I couldn't explain it, the silence cloaking the wilderness seemed somehow different. But then, the whole two weeks of September 1985 had been different.

I checked my compass and shoved it in a rear pocket of my hunting pants. I thought to myself that Dad and Wayne were just about finishing their spaghetti dinner a couple of miles down the road at the cabin of our friend, Lou Clarke. I also was thinking how spooky everything seemed out here in the deep twilight and vast wilderness. It was then that I heard a faint rustling in the brush a hundred feet or so away.

"It's your moose," Darrel called out. "Go get him, buster."

That rustling was almost a summons. That was my moose. I had to get him—now. Somehow I wanted to be alone when I got him.

"Go on ahead," I told Darrel. "I'm going back to meet him. What'll you bet he's a seventy-incher?"

"Shout 'whoopee' when you get him," Darrel hollered, waving me off and continuing toward the cabin.

Now the adrenaline was flowing through me—but good. I was as anxious and fired up as I had been on previous hunting trips when I got my eight moose. Each year, it seemed, those moments before the kill got more and more tense and anxious. I cut back the way we had come, angling northward in the direction of the intermittent rustling. Everything seemed fine. I kept low, crouching, on the lookout for anything that moved, testing each step for noise before I shifted my entire weight, and listening for sounds up ahead.

Realizing that the bull might be closer to me than I'd figured earlier, I geared up mentally for sudden action at close range. Another deep and eerie silence settled, and quieting my anxious thoughts wasn't easy. A spine-tingling sensation swept over me—the feeling that whatever I had been watching for in the thick brush up ahead had been, or maybe was, watching me. I didn't dare move fast.

I was waiting for the rustling sound, picturing a hefty bull, a moose with the longed-for seventy-inch rack, a critter far bigger than Dad's or Wayne's or all the eight moose I had taken in other years.

Suddenly, in a sound that came to me like the crack of summer lightning, underbrush snapped a couple of hundred feet away. I stared in the direction of the noise and heard another branch crack, only this time it was much louder. Slowly, just forty feet ahead, I saw the brush beginning to part. My breath stopped in my throat and I gasped as the leaves split apart like a green stage curtain revealing two of the fastest, biggest brown bears I'd ever seen, charging right at me.

"My God!" I heard myself stammer.

In a flash, I took stock. I had a few seconds—no more—to shoot at the half-growling, half-grunting, charging beasts. One was barrelling half a length in front of the other. I yelled, but they kept right on coming—their ugly brown faces glistening in the twilight, the rolling fur on their backs undulating like waves on the ocean.

Their huge jaws were open, revealing rows of razor-sharp teeth plainly visible at 30 feet. Their big heads reared up when they saw me, their tongues hanging out. They neither hesitated nor slowed down. Now there was no time for fear or paralysis. Each bear must have been several feet tall, weighing four hundred pounds or more. In that split second, they looked to me like monsters from outer space.

It is amazing how much agility comes with reflex in a life-or-death situation. I whirled to the right, hoping that my .338-calibur Ruger 77 would do the job.

I shot from the waist. The crack of my rifle seemed to reverberate for miles. I looked ahead. "My God," I thought, "nothing's changed." The bears were glaring, still charging toward me. I'm a crack shot but, this time, when it really mattered, I missed. Besides, when two are coming, which one do you aim for? The bullet hit a tree.

Now plainly visible were the ugly, yellow, razor spikes of teeth protruding from drooling jaws. I froze. Time seemed to stop, and I remember glancing at the beasts' claws for just a second. Before I could chamber another round, they'd be on me. I spun on my heels; now my back was to them and I was braced for their first blows. I dropped my rifle and threw my hands over my face, shielding my eyes. As I did this, the bears lunged. I felt a staggering blow against my back and then a force like a team of linebackers struck my shoulders, knocking me down. Sharp sticks cut my lips and weeds jammed in my mouth. My nose and forehead were wedged flat against the forest moss. Then, a ton of weight like the wheels of a car pinned down my back. I could hear strange, thick, guttural animal sounds and the sound of spasmodic breathing.

What I decided then was wrong—I know it now, but I wasn't thinking clearly at the time. I had been thrashing my arms and legs, but
it suddenly occurred to me that my struggle was futile. "Why fight?"
I asked myself. "You're dead already. Why resist?" At that moment,
one of the bears started chewing my ear after knocking my cowboy
hat off.

Something in me advised: "Play dead. Bears are supposed to get
disinterested and leave. But you've got to lie perfectly still." Still? "Dear
God, how?" a voice within me screamed. I jammed my thumbs down
into the earth as the first of countless agonizing needles began piercing
my buttocks and up and down my spine. Now, the slashing attack
moved higher.

Horror swept me as I felt pressure, like a foot, near my ear. Then
the real agony—I felt one of the beasts yanking my head up to get a
better grip on my neck. Stifling a scream, I ground my mouth into
the ground.

The grating sound intensified. Instead of letting up, the bears began
getting more ferocious. My entire body was being shoved and shaken
with tremendous animal power. My knees were being stomped and
ground down into the brush. One of the beasts was working on my
back, the other on my skull. Then, they traded places. The sequence
of events is hard to sort out, though. My mental pictures of the agony
are mercifully blurred.

I fought to keep from moving or twitching. Something in me seemed
to be ordering me to lie still, motionless, but my body rebelled and
my left leg twitched sharply. Every time there was movement, it was
followed by a burst of more needles of shooting pain. I had a mental
image of one of the bears clamping its open jaw around the entire
top of my head, attempting to crush in the bones, but not quite succeeding. I heard the animals panting in my ears. I figured that I was
in the throes of death. Death from bleeding. Death from shock.

They chewed on my head and back for what seemed hours, or days.
Then they stopped abruptly to rest. I sprawled absolutely motionless
and silent, my heart thumping wildly. I could feel my pulse pounding
in my wrists and temples.

"LAY still," I warned myself. "Don't move. You've lost a lot of blood.
Try to run and they'll flatten you and finish the job. If you as much
as twitch, you're done for."

I stiffened my knees to hold them firm, but the effort brought
movement that instantly caught the bears' attention and brought both
of them roaring to a standing position. Then they settled back and I
could see them several yards away, their piglike eyes glaring at me.

Miraculously, I was still alive—but for how long? How many arteries and blood vessels can rupture before you bleed to death? How many slashes can you take and still remain perfectly motionless?

Somehow, it comforted me to think about what I had been told all my life: After they kill, bears will refuse to immediately devour a human meal. They have been known to gulp down a moose kill, but you can count on them moving off without completely devouring the remains of a man. Sometimes, they return to cover the meat with leaves and twigs, but they go away for days until decomposition progresses to a certain stage. Bears have been known to relish rancid meat. But a fresh kill? They usually walk off as if it were poison.

I'll never forget the wave of relief and thankfulness that swept over me when the creatures were no longer on my back, jabbing and pulling.

"Are they gone?" a voice inside me asked. "Look and see."

Saliva clogged my mouth and throat. Slowly, I turned my head to the left. My face was caked with blood-soaked dirt, so I wiped my eyes and tried to look into the distance. That was all those waiting bears needed. Roaring, they were back at me, pouncing with new ferocity. One of them clamped its fangs on my shoulder, sending sharp teeth deep into muscle as pain zigzagged down my side, down my leg, to my toes. Now they began in earnest to rip the flesh at the back of my skull.

Despite the intense pain, the only thing on my mind was my children.

"Dear God," I begged. "Let me live. I want to see Max and Melinda again. God, let me live."

Things seemed to go blank for a moment and the scene wavered. Then, as if I were detached from the horror now enveloping me, a part of me began lecturing to the other part. I heard myself say, "Go limp . . . repeat over and over: I am still, still as death. I will let them chew. I will not move . . . I will play dead . . . play dead . . . let it happen . . . let them have me. . ."

"I can't" a part of me resisted.

"Yes, you can. Repeat: I will let them chew. I will not move. I will play dead." My inner voice seemed to be repeating the admonitions over and over.

I do not know how many minutes or seconds this eerie confab went on. I had long since lost track of how much time had passed. Tremors of pain were cutting into my chest now. A new and terrible fear seized me as the bears moved from my back to other parts of my body and alongside my lungs.

Then, in one moment, all of life seemed to ebb and stand still. Gone was the slurping, pulling, grunting, crunching, licking. Silence. Dead silence. "How," I wondered, "can something so huge move off so fast and so silently?"

But I knew they were nearby, sitting only yards away, their eyes watching for the slightest movement, their ears tensed for the slightest sound from my body. I forced myself not to look, not to raise my head, not to move so much as a finger or an eyelash. Now, all was deep, agonizing silence. Nothing moved. From my limbs, neck, and face, blood seeped silently into the dirt. My body seemed frozen, glued down, a part of the earth. Motionless, I listened. Now there was no rustling, no footsteps, no dry twigs breaking.

"Dear God," I thought, "Do I dare raise my head? Will they come at me again?"

I kept my eyes closed tight and a kind of peace filtered through the pain. I saw the little church that I attended in Soldotna. I saw my dad and mom. I saw my sister JoAnn and my brothers. I was with them and suddenly, somehow, I got the courage to lift my head just a little bit so I could look around.

The bears were gone. But how far? Were they lurking just behind that clump of spruce trees, ready to charge again? I had no idea where the bears were, but I told myself that, if they came back, I'd let them finish me off and end my suffering. I didn't want any more of that awful pain. But they weren't around, and somehow I had to find the strength to get away.

"Try getting up," I told myself. "See if you can stand without falling." Was I brain-damaged in the attack? I had to be able to think. If a lot of my brain was gone, would I be rational? Could I trust my thinking?

Fighting back the pain, I somehow was able to get on my feet. I realized then that my legs hadn't been broken. I lifted my hands to feel my head. My hand slid under my scalp as under a hat. I took my binoculars off over my head, unbuttoned my wool shirt with one hand, and slipped down my suspenders to strip off my shirt. There was no way I could let go of my head and remove my shirt without the loosened skin sliding out of place.

"I've got to get out of here fast," I kept thinking, "But which way?" New blood poured down my cheeks, soaking my pants and shirt.

Despite all this, I felt no revulsion, just an aching hope that somehow I might get my shirt tied around my head to hold everything in place until I could get help. I could see partially, but every movement I made seemed to increase the bleeding and to bring on greater weakness.

"Dear Lord," I prayed, "all the trees look the same. Show me which way to go. Help me to choose the right direction."

Maybe, I thought, the bears are still lurking around.

"Help me," I muttered aloud. "Help me." Then I yelled, "Darrel! Darrel! Help."

I started to run. To this day I don't know how, but I pushed the tall grass aside, stumbling, screaming. "Darrel! Help!"

Darrel heard my yelling. He cut back into the woods in the direction of my voice and then stopped dead in his tracks.

"Dear God!" he said as he saw me. "Oh, my God!"

I thought he was going to faint, but he helped me back to the cabin. Dad and Wayne were there when we arrived.

Someone gave me a mirror. I couldn't believe that the awfully mangled creature I saw was me. The entire back of my head, ear to ear, had been opened and lifted. The scalp was falling to the front like a slipped wig. A piece of scalp was missing. Punctures in my shoulder were so deep that I thought my lungs might be pierced. My back and legs were covered with gashes and bites. The bears' teeth had punctured through more than three inches of buttocks flesh. My head had been chewed badly. Sticks, grass, dirt, and bear saliva were in the wounds. My favorite watch, the one I liked because it was thin and easy on the hunt, was crunched through the dial. It had stopped at exactly 7:33 P.M.

Working swiftly, Darrel made a tourniquet out of a towel and tightened it around my head. Dad, meanwhile, cleaned the blood from my face and body.

The guys flung a mattress into the trailer and I climbed in. The trailer was hooked into our four-wheeler. By now, the pain was beginning to break through my consciousness as the protecting shock wore away.

Wayne was driving, and he frantically spun the wheels in his haste to get us out of the cabin and through the woods to our pickup truck parked six miles away. Once we got to the truck, we would drive sixty miles to Soldotna, where there would be a doctor and a plane to take me to Providence Hospital in Anchorage, two hundred miles away.

The white bath towel that the guys had given me had turned bright red. The pain in one of my buttocks was so great that I shifted my body in the trailer. It was too much effort to reach into my wool pants pocket to see what was jabbing me whenever we hit a bump. (I later found out that it was a chewing tobacco can.)

Conversation was sparse as we drove to the pickup truck. Darrel seemed to be feeling guilty about having not responded when he heard my shout and the shot I fired. But, at the time, Darrel thought that I had gotten my moose and was yelling "whoopee."

"I was so happy for you," he said. "I threw my hat in the air and hollered, 'Yiii-eee! Another moose bit the dust.' If only I had known."

What none of us knew was that more surprises were still in store. We got to the pickup only to find that we had to change a flat tire. Our troubles continued at the airline counter in Soldotna. There were no planes in the airport, so one was ordered to be flown out of Anchorage.

I arrived in the emergency room of Providence Hospital at 3 A.M. My physician, Dr. Jim Scully of Anchorage, spent five hours applying two hundred stitches and flushing and picking pine needles from my skull.

Rollin Braden spent eight days in the hospital, four of them in intensive care. He survived the ordeal in record time and without disfigurement. On September 25, 1985, he celebrated his thirty-first birthday.

Bear Facts

Alaska brown bears will attack, maul, and kill humans, according to Bill Taylor, game biologist with the Alaska Department of Fish and Game. They are rarely reported to have devoured a person, however.

These bears are known to maul and kill while protecting a food cache or their young. The cubs are born in December and January, kept in the den for two years with the sow and, when they are 2 and one-half years old, dismissed by the sow, who returns to breeding.

The bears that mauled Rollin Braden, according to Taylor's estimates, weighed about four hundred pounds each, were about seven feet in length, and were probably four-year-old siblings (still young enough to "hang out" together, yet not old enough to breed, which bears do at about five years of age).

"My guess is that they were trying to protect food in the area," said Taylor. "With their keen sense of smell, they were certainly aware of the gut piles. Even if replete with food, they would claim the gut piles for future feeding, normally by covering them with leaves and dragging limbs and twigs to cover the moose kill until it was preferred. The species has been known to eat the very rottenest of foods, but these animals have also been known to kill and eat a moose on the spot."

Taylor said he could not understand why the bears had not claimed the gut piles or made any effort to protect them.

"It is possible they were guarding other meat," he said.

OUTDOOR LIFE
NOVEMBER 1985

Jim Carmichel is the shooting editor of Outdoor Life, *and I believe he has the best job on the staff. He spends about ninety percent of his waking hours shooting guns and flying off on hunting trips. The remaining ten percent, he gives to* Outdoor Life *in writing time. If I sound jealous, you're right. So when Jim told me that this fifteen-foot crocodile nearly did him in one night in a sixteen-foot dugout canoe on a river in Africa, I really wasn't too upset.*

The Croc That Wouldn't Die

by JIM CARMICHEL

THE horror story began when we headed our sixteen-foot fiberglass inboard/outboard runabout into the mouth of the Senkwi River and quietly cruised upstream. The Senkwi has another name—a long African name that I can neither spell nor pronounce. But when translated, it tells of a fearsome god that dwells where there is no sun and whose slobber is filled with such deadly creatures that everything it touches is killed and devoured. The legend behind the name tells how the god's deadly slobber gushes out of the earth and flows from a mountain, spreading death across the land, until it meets and is conquered by the benevolent god of the Zambezi River.

The river of death no longer flows into the mighty Zambezi but into Lake Kariba, which was formed by the damming of the Zambezi, but the putrid waters that spill into the man-made sea are still full of the devil's own creatures.

Beyond the first bend in the river of death, the world transforms itself into the prehistoric. Trees do not bloom or bear leaf, having been raped by a blight that twisted them into bare roosts for sulking vultures and carrion-eating water birds. Great shaggy nests of dead grass, as large as a native hut, sag from the gnarled snags of tree limbs, and long-beaked birds cry out with cackling wails.

Little vegetation grows along the river. The banks are mostly bare earth and mud, dotted with shapeless stone and rimmed with a rock wall, all blending into a brown landscape. There is no game, but we know that wild animals had been there at one time because skulls and other bones lay scattered along the banks as if a recent flood had cleansed the river's depths of its dead.

Such a place demands silence, and little was said as we slowly cruised upstream. Oomo and Jason, the two black Africans, who normally smiled and talked to each other continuously, were silent, watchful, and clearly apprehensive without knowing why. Neither of them lived nearby, and they had not heard the legend of the river. Soon, though, they would have their own story of the river to tell their grandchildren. Before the safari ended, both told me that they would never go up that river again.

As we rounded each bend in the river, there was a splash a few hundred yards ahead and a quiet ripple radiated from shore.

"Crocs," Rowbotham would say, his voice tight.

I'd seen crocodiles before in Sudan's Nile swamps and in French Equatorial Africa. In Botswana I had witnessed an ear-shattering battle between a croc and a baboon. The baboon's troop mates had viciously attacked the crocodile, but the hard-scaled reptile never loosened its jawlock on the unfortunate primate. It simply slid beneath the water and that was the end of the baboon.

The crocodiles I'd seen before had never impressed me as being especially wary, but these crocs were so wild that there was little chance of getting a good look at one before it slid into the water and disappeared.

"Are they always this wild?" I asked Mike Rowbotham, our professional hunter.

"Oh, yes," he answered, "they're spooky. It's tough to get a shot at one. They're more wary than any game animal."

That did it. Until that moment, I'd never had any real desire to hunt crocodiles but learning that they were hard to bag presented a challenge.

"Mike, I've got to shoot a croc," I announced. Rowbotham raised his eyebrows for a long moment and then gazed into the deathly green water as if silently struggling with himself. Then the cloud passed from his face, and he grinned with characteristic good humor. "Okay, Jim, we'll get one." Upstream, a silent form stirred the water's surface for an instant and then disappeared, radiating ripples across the slow current.

It was June of 1984, wintertime south of the Equator, and I was on safari in Zimbabwe, the game-rich African nation once known as Rhodesia. My hunting pal was Jack Atcheson, the North American outfitter, and our professional hunter was the well-known Mike Row-botham, operator of Hunter's Tracks PTY, a leading safari outfitter.

Jack and I wanted better-than-average trophies and during the preceding few weeks, he and I had been hunting in South Africa. We had taken half a dozen contenders for listing in the Rowland Ward Record Book, including the shy, bush-dwelling nyala antelope. Now, we were hunting leopard, kudu, and reedbuck, which tend to grow especially big in northern Zimbabwe. I had already killed a better-than-good Cape buffalo and part of it had been hung for leopard baits. Sometimes it takes a few days for the baits to get ripe enough to appeal to a leopard, so we were passing the days looking for the odd trophy or cruising Lake Kariba's shores and watching herds of elephants that came to drink and socialize.

The day after our first trip up the Senkwi River, the weather turned chill and remained cool for several days, spoiling our chances of finding a crocodile in a shootable position. More at home in the water than on land, they come ashore mainly to bask in the sun, but with the sun hidden by clouds and the air cooler than normal, they cradled themselves in the warmth of the sluggish river.

Several times that week, we saw crocs in the water, as many as a dozen at a time. Their snouts and eyes barely broke the water's surface and they looked like floating slabs of rotten wood. A few times I was only a few feet from the creatures and a killing shot through the eye and into the brain would have been simple. But shooting a croc in the water is usually a waste because they will sink immediately and no one wants to go diving for a crocodile in its home territory.

While we were watching a group of floating crocs, an unsuspecting coot landed in their midst and swam toward one of the motionless snouts. What happened next is as difficult to describe as the speed with which darkness fills a room when the light is switched off. The water boiled for an instant and then there was nothing but a gentle whirlpool. The coot simply vanished.

Despite their sharp, interlocking teeth, each one as long and as thick as a man's thumb, crocodiles do not kill by biting, or chewing their victims. The teeth are only a means of taking a grip on the prey. They kill a large animal by rolling over and over in the water. The fantastic turbulence and wrenching tears flesh and breaks bones until the dead or nearly dead victim goes down the gullet. They don't chew their food and don't need to because their powerful gastric juices digest the meal very quickly. With smaller creatures, the croc simply gets a good grip and submerges, drowning the prey, or the jaws may kill instantly when they take hold.

A more efficient and more remorseless killing machine does not exist in all of nature. So precisely honed are their killing techniques

and instincts that millions of years have wrought no evolutionary im-
provements. They are as they were at the dawn of creation—as patient,
as watchful, as swift, and just as incapable of pity.

By comparison, even the great white shark is second-class. The croc
is infinitely more efficient because it *thinks about killing* and uses practiced stealth to catch its victims. And it can do this on land as well as
in the water. A crocodile can sprint fast enough to grab an antelope
before the victim gets up speed enough to escape.

Morning and evening we checked our leopard baits, but the only
trophy taken was a tremendous record-class kudu bull Jack Atcheson
shot after a long and determined stalk. After nearly a week of slow
hunting, dawn was clear with a promise of a warm day. While checking
a leopard bait hung near the top of a rock ledge, we spotted a huge
kudu bull on the thickly brushed plain below, and after a nerve-rasping
game of hide and seek, I finally got a shot. It was my biggest kudu
ever, and the kill put the whole camp in a festive mood.

By noon the temperature was in the seventies and the day was right
for crocodile hunting.

"How about it, Mike?" I asked over lunch. "Today's my lucky day.
Let's go back up that weird river and try to bust one of those crocs."

For a moment Mike looked grim while he considered the possibil-
ities. Then he shrugged off whatever was bothering him, grinned,
and said it was a great day to kill a croc.

Knowing from past experience that it was useless to try approaching
sunning crocodiles on the bank in a boat, we worked out a simple
plan. We left Jason downstream with the boat, and the rest of us skirted
the river on foot. By staying hidden behind the standing snags and
logs that lay along the river's bank we hoped to stalk within range.

The plan worked perfectly. After a mile or so of skirting the river,
we topped a low hill and found ourselves looking down on a marshy
floodplain. At first the place seemed void of life, but after a quick
look, Mike crouched behind the rotted shell of a tree and motioned
all of us to do likewise. I peered cautiously from behind a stump
through binoculars and spotted a sleeping croc, then another, and
another. Lying along the opposite bank, there must have been twelve
or fifteen. They were hard to see because the sun had dried their
hides so that they blended perfectly with the foul black river mud.
Their hides were not rich and glossy like a crocodile handbag but dull
and caked with mud and slimy moss. They were hideously ugly but
possessed a hypnotic quality that made it difficult not to look at them.

Some professional hunters become so obsessed by hunting crocodiles
that they neglect their families, friends, and businesses for months at
a time. If a man must fight inner demons, no symbol of them is more
fitting than the crocodile.

Mike crawled to the stump where I was hiding and whispered, "If we all try to get closer, one of the crocs will spot us and spook the lot. Jack and I will stay here while you try to get close enough for a shot. Take your time and stay low. Remember—you have to bust the brain with the first shot or the croc will be in the water in a flash."

The usual advice about bullet placement on a crocodile is, "Hit him behind the smile." A croc's mouth ends in an upward crook that looks like a cruel smile. This crook is more or less on a vertical line with the eye. Somewhere along this line is what passes for a brain, a target not much bigger than a walnut. If you study a croc's head, you'll see that there isn't much space for a brain. The entire skull was designed for killing, not for thinking. Hitting a big crocodile anywhere except the brain is pretty much a wasted effort. Unless you can blow one apart with a howitzer, their reaction to a body shot is almost no reaction at all. It takes death a long time to catch up with a reptile, so despite the crocodile's considerable size, the only vulnerable spot is a tiny target which has to be hit just right or the animal will be lost to die later at the bottom of the water.

I had only one rifle on this safari, a custom-made .338 Winchester Magnum built on a '98 Mauser action by the David Miller Company of Tucson, Arizona. This masterpiece has become my favorite big-game rifle because it never changes zero. The first shot is always dead on target if I do my part. My handload was a 250 grain Nosler Partition bullet over 69 grains of 4350 and a CCI Magnum primer. This combination churns up about 2,550 feet per second at the muzzle, more than enough horsepower to punch the Nosler bullet all the way through a Cape buffalo. It had done just that earlier on this safari.

Crawling on the hard-baked earth, I zigzagged from stump to stump until I was within about two hundred yards of the sleeping crocodiles. There I found a tree carcass big enough to hide behind. After getting into a sitting position, I slipped the rifle's sling behind my elbow and pulled it tight. Rested alongside the dead tree, the rifle was so steady that the cross hairs scarcely jiggled as they settled on the nearest crocodile's head.

"Hold on," I told myself, "take your time and get a real trophy." Until then I hadn't given much thought to what a trophy crocodile should look like. They don't have antlers or tusks like an elephant or a mane like a lion, so how do you judge? The only difference so far as I could see was sheer body size, so I resolved to shoot the biggest one. That turned out to be a simple choice because the one that lay at the river's edge with its tail still in the water was easily twice as big as any of the others. Luckily, the biggest croc was also the closest and was lying broadside so that I had a clear view of its grim smile. For a moment the cross hairs vibrated on the crocodile's head, then they were still and the bullet crossed the river. The big croc's tail violently lashed the water a time or two and then was dead still. The only motion I could see was a growing spot of thin red—behind the smile.

"Well done, Jim. That's one more good croc," Rowbotham said as he joined me. He studied the beast through his dusty binoculars to make doubly sure it was dead. "Oomo, run back and fetch Jason and the boat," he called, "let's see if we can get that devil back to camp."

A half hour later, during which time the croc had not twitched, we crossed the river in the boat and I had my first close-up look at my trophy. It was absolutely incredible. No animal I've ever bagged or seen was as awesome. "It's one of the biggest crocs I've ever seen," Rowbotham exclaimed. That's when I realized I had shot a monster croc.

"This is unbelievable," I said. "I think it's the best trophy I've ever taken, better even than an elephant with hundred pound tusks." The croc measured fourteen and a half feet from nose tip to tail tip and more than sixteen feet over the curve.

With Jack's video camera recording the scene, I walked around the beast, lifting and flexing its prehistoric feet, not believing, even with the evidence before me, that such a creature could exist, now or at any time. There was no bullet hole in the skull, only an inch-long crack where the .338 slug had blasted its way toward the brain. Incredibly, there was no exit wound. The same load that could drill completely through a Cape buffalo had been stopped by the crocodile's head.

"Open its mouth so I can get a shot of the teeth," Jack requested, aiming his camera at the creature's blunt snout. Slipping my fingers between the teeth I got a grip on the jagged upper jaw and heaved it wide. Teeth rimmed the mouth like spikes of broken glass imbedded in the top of a wall. The mouth's lining was white and fleshy, like that of a snake. The whiteness was spotted by watery reptile blood. The throat was choked by a clotting puddle of blood, dripping from the place where its brain had been. Even in death, the crocodile looked as though it still possessed a will to kill.

"Now that you've got the beast in hand, what do you plan to do with it?" Mike asked.

"I want the hide tanned and mounted with the head on," was my quick answer. "If I can get it in my house, I'll leave it outside to scare away stray dogs and peddlers."

"Well, the thing must weigh three-quarters of a ton. We'll have to tow it back to camp with the boat," Mike said.

"Too risky, Mike. I don't want to lose it," I told him. "We've got to figure out a way to get it in the boat, even if we have to skin it here."

"I think we can get the whole thing in the boat," Jack Atcheson told us. "I've been manhandling elk and moose for years, and I know a couple of tricks that might help us get the croc into the boat."

With Jack directing, we cut stout poles, and with two men to the pole, we levered the croc out of its slimy bed. After considerable grunting and cussing in a variety of languages, we heaved the croc's head and forelegs over the boat's bow. The massive head was too slippery to grasp, so Mike rigged a rope bridle around the head and snout that provided secure handholds. As it turned out, that was about the only smart thing we did all afternoon.

When the crocodile was about halfway in the boat, we relaxed our grip for a moment to take a breather before the final heave. At that moment the massive body expanded as if it were taking a deep breath, and the rear legs reached out in a jerky spasm. For a moment the feet ripped at the air, but then the claws caught the gunwale of the boat. With incredible strength, the croc forced its mass into the boat, leaving only the six-foot tail dangling over the bow. Then it was still again.

I think I was the first to speak. "Reptiles often do that. The nervous system doesn't get the message that it is dead for hours after the fact. That's why frogs' legs kick in the skillet."

Jack and Mike agreed with my assessment but the two Africans didn't seem at all convinced.

"Well, anyway, it was nice of the croc to help out. It saved us a lot of sweat," Mike said. "Let's get the tail in somehow and shove off for camp."

The crocodile's bulk almost completely filled the bow section and its snout filled the two-foot-wide walkway in the forward bulkhead on which the boat's steering wheel was mounted. There wasn't room to tuck the croc's tail in the bow compartment, so we bent it in a curve and secured it with a rope more or less aboard. Then a new problem presented itself. The great weight forward almost put the bow under water. A few inches lower and the boat would sink.

This problem was eased to some extent when the five of us climbed into the rear of the boat, leveling it to some degree, though the boat floated bow down until we gained enough speed to lift it. More or less level, we cruised down the river into the vastness of Lake Kariba.

Even with the added weight slowing the boat, I figured we would make it to camp before dark. There was nothing to worry about, and there were plenty of camp workers to unload the crocodile. After sun-downers and a warm shower to wash away the stinking river slime, we'd have a good time at dinner telling crocodile stories.

The first sign of serious trouble was a small but steady stream of water that rippled around our feet on the deck from bow to stern.

My guess was that the trickle was only water flowing out of the crocodile and that it would eventually stop, but a few minutes later the
trickle became a tide. I went forward and crawled over the crocodile,
to find out where the water was coming from. I discovered that both
bow storage wells were flooded and overflowing, apparently from
water washing under the gunwale cowling.

Jason was running the boat, and when I announced what was happening his reaction was to slow the engine. Deprived of its planing
lift, the boat's bow dived beneath the waves and we would have sunk
right there had it not been for Mike Rowbotham. He grabbed the
throttle from the terrified Jason and punched the engine to full power.
The bow lifted just an inch or two above the lake's surface. But even
then we still had one hell of a problem. We were a half mile from
shore in a rapidly sinking boat. Could we make it? I didn't think we
could and began a mental inventory of our options.

The whole problem of course was the crocodile, but there was no
possibility of getting it out of the boat in the time we had left. The
two Africans were in utter panic and probably couldn't swim. Were
there life jackets aboard, I wondered. Clearly Jack would lose his ex-
pensive video equipment, and the depths would also claim my David
Miller rifle, worth at least $5,000 and Mike's double-barreled Charles
Boswell rifle, worth more thousands. What bothered me most, more
than the boat, the rifles, and the equipment, was that I would lose
the crocodile. I really *wanted* that crocodile.

I didn't look at the shore, only at the water as it crept up over the
gunwales and splashed inside, and at Mike's hand on the throttle. He
was wringing the last foot-pound of energy from the overloaded engine. We couldn't make it, I knew, but now I could see the bottom of
the lake—five feet deep, three feet,—maybe we could make it! We
made it! The boat crunched to a stop on the gravel shore, the engine
still screaming.

A half hour later, with the boat bailed dry, we nervously eased back
into the main channel and headed for home camp. Not much was
said about what had happened. We all knew how close we had been
to disaster, possibly even tragedy, and when you come that close, there
isn't much to say. I sat on the engine cowling, holding my rifle and
studying the hideous design of the crocodile's head.

And one eye opened.

Considering the scare we'd just had, the idea of a live crocodile in
the boat struck me as hilarious. The situation was made even more
ridiculous by Jason's proximity to the croc. No more than ten inches
separated the monster's teeth from Jason's bare feet and legs.

"Look, Jason," I said, pointing at the open eye and already laughing
at what I thought the African's reaction would be.

For a long moment Jason didn't react at all. He just stood there regarding the red glowing orb with all the solemn detachment of a cow pondering a flower. Then the crocodile's other eye opened and Jason levitated onto the gunwale and monkey-walked aft to the farthest corner of the boat, leaving the controls untended and the throttle wide open.

I lunged for the wheel, brushing by the croc's snout. My movement apparently aroused the croc. It lunged at me, and it would surely have had my leg had it not been for the rope looped around its snout. Even so, the loop was slack enough for the croc to open its mouth about four inches, showing its ugly teeth. There was a gurgling roar, and I had no doubt that it was coming after me. Its feet scratched on the deck as it struggled to squeeze through the walkway in the bulkhead. Fortunately, it wriggled and scratched into the opening and wedged itself tighter. How long the bulkhead would have held against the croc's overwhelming strength I can't say, but, with a final roar, the beast's head slumped to the deck and was still, its eyes closed.

Dead at last?

Stepping cautiously, fearful of arousing the croc again, Jason returned to the boat's controls and we moved on toward camp. The crocodile's return from the dead had given us all a bad turn and had there been a bottle of whiskey on board it wouldn't have lasted much longer than a butterfly in a blast furnace. What would have happened if the croc had demolished the bulkhead was plain enough. Even with its mouth tied, its thrashing would surely have capsized the boat. There were many ways it could kill, but perhaps it was really dead at last and the rest of the trip would be safe.

And then the boat's engine quit. Out of gas.

There we were in the middle of Lake Kariba, our boat stopped, with the sun sinking fast, and with a monster crocodile that wouldn't stay dead. Happily, there was a spare can of gas on board, which Jason poured into the main tank, but with the fuel line sucked dry, the engine wouldn't fire. For tense, heart-pounding minutes, the starter motor groaned without effect and then, inevitably, buzzed to a stop. The battery was dead and we were trapped in the smothering darkness of a moonless tropical night.

Oomo had found a paddle and was digging at the water with determination, but the shore was an hour or more away at our slow speed, and there would be more hours of walking to camp. Hiking through the watering places of a variety of animals in the dark is not congenial exercise. There would be lions there, and leopards, elephants, and Cape buffalo. And snakes.

While I was thinking these thoughts, Jason was digging through some gear in the stern of the boat and presently made a joyous announcement: "Look, See new battery, see!" His black face was invisible in the darkness but his smile shone like a beacon.

Then Jack Atcheson's years of hunting experience came to our assistance. During all the years I've known Jack, I've never ceased to be amazed at the things he carries in his ever-present knapsack. A flashlight I would have expected, but when he dug deep and came out with a set of battery jumper cables, we all nearly dropped our teeth. It's hard not to like Jack Atcheson, especially at such moments.

Looking up to thank my lucky stars, I was dazzled by a shooting star, and then another. "Look, Jack," I said, "there's a meteor shower. No wait, those aren't meteors, they're stars spinning around us."

The cause of the celestial phenomenon was Oomo at work with the paddle. Having no idea how to use a paddle, he was simply clawing at the water from one corner of the stern. This caused us to spin. We'd been so occupied with our problems that we had failed to notice the considerable RPMs Oomo had achieved.

"Knock it off, Oomo," Mike told him. "If you want to be useful, put your mouth over the gas tank pipe and blow as hard as you can. That will force some gas into the carburetor so we can get started."

So with Oomo balancing himself on the gunwale and blowing into the fuel tank, Jack holding the jumper cables, Jason grinding the starter, Mike cursing our luck, and me wondering where I'd gone wrong, we bobbed and drifted in the black waters of Lake Kariba. Despite Oomo's hearty blowing, the fuel line remained empty, so we had to do something else. Our next effort was to uncover the engine, remove the air filter, and hope to fire the engine by pouring gasoline directly into the carburetor.

Of course, this would not normally be a very smart way to deal with a sluggish engine in a crowded boat, but we had other disasters on our minds, so the thought of an explosion wasn't all that disturbing. Just to be a little safer, however, I crouched down behind the upturned engine cowling when Jason hit the starter. The engine caught for a second but sputtered and stopped. "Pour more gas in the carburetor," Mike ordered, "it wants to start."

Again I crouched behind the cowling, scarcely noticing that my backside was only inches from the croc's mouth, and again the engine sputtered and died. The effort was repeated a dozen times, each time more despairing than the last, when suddenly the fuel pump went to work and the engine rumbled to life. Again we were off toward camp and hoping for a stiff drink and a hot, if late, meal. Surely nothing else could go wrong.

"Shine your light on the croc, Jack," I asked, "let's see how it's doing." I can't remember exactly what made me want to see the croc just then, but I'll never forget what happened next. The instant Jack's flashlight beam hit the monster, two things became terrifyingly clear. Its eyes were open again and the rope around its snout was gone. Startled into instant life by the light, the crocodile roared mightily, opening its mouth wide. Bloody slime streamed out of its mouth between the teeth. Again Jason was in the stern, leaving the throttle open and the wheel untended so that we careened across the water.

"Grab the wheel, Mike," I yelled, "I'm going to shoot him again." But as I fed a round into the rifle's chamber, a feeling of helplessness possessed me. I couldn't do much. I'd blown its brain to mush. Where else could I shoot it? Was it unkillable?

The only possibility was to put the muzzle behind the creature's head and blow the spine apart. But to do that, I'd have to shoot almost straight down. If the bullet exited, would it make a hole in the boat big enough to sink it? The croc kept inching toward me by squeezing through the walkway in the bulkhead. I was backed against the engine cowling and could retreat no farther. The croc's teeth were less than two feet away and coming closer.

"Shoot, shoot, shoot," voices pleaded. Jason and Oomo were hanging over the stern, ready to let go when the monster broke through the bulkhead. They were willing to give themselves to the black lake rather than to the crocodile.

I felt like a schoolboy facing the town bully in a fight I knew I'd lose. "Okay," I shouted, "if it gets this far, I'm going to shoot, no matter what." With the rifle's muzzle I traced a line six inches in front of the snapping mouth. That had a calming effect on everyone, for a moment, even the crocodile closed its mouth and backed off a couple of inches.

"Hold the light steady, Jack," I said, "I think I see the rope." There was a loop of rope under the crocodile's chin. Could I reach it? I snagged the loop with the muzzle of the rifle and slowly worked the rope free. Finally the rope was in my hands but too tangled to be of any use. I untied knot after knot in the wet rope until there was enough to tie a noose. Next, I slipped the noose over the croc's snout and used the rifle to push the rope rearward.

"Get around behind the croc's head, Mike," I whispered, afraid to speak loudly. "When I throw you the rope, pull it tight. That will keep his mouth closed so we can hog-tie him."

"Just throw me the rope," Mike answered, already scrambling around on the gunwale of the boat. "I'll hold his head up so he can't open his mouth."

And for the next half hour, we traveled with Mike astride the giant reptile like a rodeo rider, holding its mouth closed and head back. In camp at last, we called for reinforcements, and after considerable struggling, succeeded in locking the crocodile's mouth closed with heavy wire.

News of a giant crocodile travels fast in the African bush. By noon the next day, a considerable crowd of natives had collected to see the monster. Even then, the croc was still twitching and trying to move. An old black man puffed thoughtfully at his gourd pipe and, shaking his head, spoke softly in his native tongue.

"What did he say?" I asked.

"He says it takes them a long time to die."

OUTDOOR LIFE
MAY 1985

Patrick McManus is Outdoor Life's *humorist, and his monthly column "The Last Laugh" is read by millions. I picked this story, "The Hunting Lesson," for a reason. We can all identify with Pat, his buddy Retch Sweeny, and poor Sidney Fipps. They remind me of the old story of the novice who does very well at trap and skeet for the first time. The pros hanging around the clubhouse know why this happens all too often. "Wait till he finds out how hard those clay birds are to hit," an old campaigner will say, "then I bet he won't hit so many." And that's how it was with poor Sidney.*

The Hunting Lesson

by PATRICK F. McMANUS

OVER the years it has been my distinct honor and pleasure to introduce numerous persons to the sport of hunting the white tail deer. It is odd, however, that a man can have a thousand successes and one failure, and it will be the failure that sticks in his mind like a porky quill in a hound's nose. Thus it is with my single failure, one Sidney Fipps. Even now, five years later, I torment myself with the question of where I went wrong. How did I slip up with Fipps?

The affair started off innocently enough. One fall day, with none of my regular hunting partners available for the following weekend, I strolled next door to Sidney's house to invite him to go deer hunting with me. I found him digging up bulbs in the garden, and greeted him informally, namely by sneaking up behind him and dumping a basket of moldering leaves over his head. Not one to enjoy a good joke on himself, Sidney growled malevolently as he shook the soggy leaves from his balding dome and thrust blindly at me with the garden trowel.

"Sidney," I said, holding him at bay with a rake handle, "I am about to give you the opportunity of a life-time. How would you like to go deer hunting with me?"

"Not much," he replied, digging some leaf mold from an ear. "In fact, my desire to go hunting with you is so small as to escape detection by any means known to science!"

"Don't like hunting, huh?" I said. "Well, many people who have never been exposed to the sport feel that way about it. Listen, I can teach you all about hunting. One weekend out with me, and you'll come back loving it."

"No," Sidney snarled.

"If nothing else, you'll enjoy getting out in the crisp mountain air. It will invigorate you."

"No! No! *No!*"

"Sid, I just know you'll enjoy the camaraderie of the hunting camp, the thrill of the pursuit, the . . ."

"No, I tell you, no! *Go home!*"

". . . the free meat and. . ."

"Free meat?"

"Sure. Just think of packing away all those free venison steaks and chops and roasts in the freezer."

"Free meat. Venison's pretty tasty too. I tasted it once. Yeah, I wouldn't mind getting a bunch of free meat. Then, too, as you say, there's the hunting camp camaraderie, the crisp mountain air, and the thrill of pursuit. But I'm willing to put up with all that stuff if I can get some free meat."

I would have patted him on the shoulder, but I didn't want to get my hands all dirty with leaf mold. "I can see right now you have the makings of a true sportsman," I told him.

"So, how do I get this free deer?" Sidney asked.

"Well, you just go out with me and get it. Of course, there are a few odds and ends you'll need to pick up down at Duffy's Sporting Goods."

"Like what?"

"Oh, let's see. You'll want a rifle, of course. Outfitted with scope and sling. A couple boxes of shells. Seems to me there's something else. A knife! You need a good hunting knife. And a whetstone. I nearly forgot the whetstone. That should be about it. You have a good pair of insulated boots don't you? No? Oh, wool pants, you'll need wool pants and some good wool socks and a wool shirt and a down parka and some thermal underwear and an orange hunting vest and a red cap. Heck, that should do it. Good, you're making a list. Did I say gloves? Get some gloves. Oh, binoculars! And first-aid kit. And a survival kit, with a daypack to carry it in. Rope, you'll need a length of rope for dragging your free deer out of the mountains with. We could use my tent, of course, but it has a rip in the roof on the guest's side. You might want to buy a tent. A sub-zero sleeping bag, did I mention that? You'll probably want an insulated sleeping pad, too.

Down booties are awfully nice to slip into when you take off your hunting boots, but they're optional. Then there's the grub, and that's it."

"Hmmmm," Sidney said, studying his list. "Just how big are these free deer, anyway?"

"Plenty big enough," I said.

"Geez," he said, "I don't know how I can afford to buy all the stuff on this list."

"Take some advice from an old experienced hunter," I said. "Mortgage the house."

The day after Sidney purchased his gear, I took him out to the gun club range and we sighted in his rifle. He grouped his last five shots right in the center of the bull's-eye. Then I showed him my technique of scattering shots randomly around the target because, as I explained, you never know which way the deer might jump just as you pull the trigger.

"How long before I learn to do that?" Sidney asked.

"Years," I said. "It's not something you master overnight."

The day before the hunt, my old friend Retch Sweeney called up and said he would be able to make it after all.

"How come he's going?" Sidney snapped when I told him the news. They are not exactly bosom buddies.

"He's between jobs," I said.

"I didn't know he ever worked," Sidney growled. "When did he get laid off?"

"1957."

I explained to Sidney the absolute necessity of being ready on time the following morning. "We'll pick you up at your house at two sharp. Got that? *Two sharp!*

"Right," he said.

"Don't bother about breakfast. We can grab a quick bite at Gerty's Truck Stop just before we turn off the highway and head up to our hunting area. Now remember, *two sharp!*"

We picked Sidney up the next morning at exactly 4:15. He was furious. Naturally, Retch and I were puzzled. Then it occurred to me that since this was Sidney's first hunt, he didn't realize that when hunters say "two sharp," they mean "some time around four."

"Stop whimpering and toss your gear in back," Retch said kindly. "You better not have forgot nothin' either, because we're not turnin' around and comin' back for it! Now put your rifle in the rack next to mine."

"What do you mean, next to yours?"

"That ol' .30-06 right there. . . . Say, I wonder if you fellas mind swingin' by my house again. Just take a few minutes."

After Retch had picked up his rifle and I had returned to my house for my sleeping bag and then we had gone back to Retch's for his shells, it was five o'clock by the time we got out to the highway.

"Aren't we going to be awfully late with all these delays?" Sidney asked. "What time will we start hunting?"

Retch and I looked at each other and laughed. "Why, man, we're already hunting!" Retch said. "This is it. Gettin' there is half the fun."

We drove along in darkness for an hour, with Retch and me entertaining Sidney with bawdy jokes and detailed accounts of other hunting trips. "It was a tough shot, looked impossible to me at first," Retch was saying. "The deer was going away from me at an angle and . . ."

I held up my hand for silence. "Okay, now we got to get serious. We're coming to the most difficult and dangerous part of the trip. We get through this ordeal and we should be okay. It'll be easy going by comparison from then on. Now I want you guys to watch yourselves. If you start to feel faint or queezy, Sid, let Retch or me know, and we'll help you out."

"Cripes!" Sidney said, nervously. "What do we have to do, climb a sheer cliff or something?"

"Worse," I said. "We're going to eat breakfast at Gerty's Truck Stop."

Dawn had long since cracked and spilled over the mountains by the time we arrived at our hunting spot. Retch looked out the window and groaned.

"What are you groaning for?" I asked. "I'm the one that had Gerty's chile pepper omelette."

"It's not that," Retch said. "I see fresh tracks in the snow all over the place. If we'd been here an hour earlier, we'd have nailed us some deer."

"Listen," I said. "Did we come out to nail deer or to go hunting today? If we're hunting, we have to get up two hours late, forget a bunch of stuff we have to go back for, and then stop for breakfast at Gerty's. You know how it's done."

"Yeah, sorry, I forgot for a second when I saw the tracks," Retch said. "I got carried away. Who cares about nailing deer right off, for Pete's sake!"

"I do!" Sidney whined. "I got $2500's worth of gear with me and I want to get my free deer!"

It was clear that Sidney had a lot to learn about hunting, so I lost no time in starting on his first lesson. I put him on a stand and told him that Retch and I would sweep around the far side of the ridge and drive some deer past him. "We'll be back in an hour," I told him. "Don't move!"

Retch and I returned three hours later and found Sidney still on the stand. We tilted him over against a tree for safety until we got a fire going to thaw him out. "How come you didn't move around?" I asked him.

"Y-you t-told me to stay on the st-stand. You said y-you would be b-back in an hour, and for me not to m-move."

"I'm sorry, I should have explained," I said. "When a hunter says he'll be back in an hour, that means not less than three hours. Furthermore, nobody ever stays on a stand like he's told to. As soon as the other hunters are out of sight, he beats it off to some other place where he's sure there's a deer but there never is. That's standard procedure. I guess I should have mentioned it to you."

"Yeah," Retch said. "Anyway, next time you'll know. It takes a while to catch on to deer hunting. Well, we might as well make camp. We ain't gonna get no deer today."

"Oh, I got one!" Sidney said. "See, he's lying over there behind that log. He was too big for me to move by myself. Right after you fellows left, he came tearing along the trail there, and I shot him."

"Oh, oh!" I said. "Better go have a look, Retch."

Retch walked over to the deer, looked down, shook his head, and walked back. "We're in for it now," he told me.

"How bad is it?" I asked.

"Six points."

"Cripes!" I said.

"Did I do it wrong?" Sidney asked.

"We'll have to wait and see," I said.

Sidney thought for a moment, then smiled. "Gee, wouldn't it be funny if I was the only one to get a deer and it was my first trip and all, and you guys were teaching me how to hunt. Not that I would ever mention it to the guys down at Kelly's Bar & Grill, but. . . . Is six points good? Say, let me tell you how I got him. It was a tough shot, looked impossible to me at first. The deer was going away from me at an angle, and. . . ."

"It's going to be worse than I thought," Retch said.

"Yeah," I said. "Ol' Sidney learns fast."

From The Grasshopper Trap *by Patrick F. McManus. Copyright 1985 by Patrick F. McManus. Reprinted by permission of Henry Holt and Company.*

I'm still trying to figure out why Robert Ruark had this terrible, almost irrational fear of the Cape buffalo. Because it's ugly? Because it's mean? Because it kills hunters and natives? I don't know. I do know that whenever Ruark wrote about buffaloes, he was at his best. Lots of things happen to Ruark in this tale. In fact, he discovers what he must do when two hundred buffaloes come bearing down on him. This story is from Ruark's book Horn of the Hunter, *a classic work about the author's earliest experiences hunting in Africa.*

I'm Afraid of M'Bogo

by ROBERT RUARK

SOME people say I look a little like Ernest Hemingway used to look when he was younger. At least I have a mustache. At least I read the man when I was much less aged and learned a lot thereby. I also followed his habits. He liked Cuba. So did I. We used to drink together, before the war, in different parts of the Floridita Café, which Constante runs off the square in Havana. I never spoke to Hemingway, who would be sitting behind the potted palm in the corner of the café, peering like a nearsighted professor over his glasses and reading the *Diario,* drinking the best daiquiris in the world, and looking very wise and school masterish.

I liked the *cangrejos moros* that the maestro liked, and I liked all the food next door at the Zaragozana, and I liked his good friends around the town. I liked how he wrote and what he had done and the things he was interested in. I liked it that he had been to Africa, where I had not been. I liked it that he had seen bulls that I had not seen, and that he had married women I had not married. Also that he had divorced women I had not enjoyed the opportunity of divorcing.

But I was very young and full of pride. I was too proud to walk twenty feet to talk to Papa. I was too proud to ask Constante to introduce me. I couldn't go over to this man and say that I was a writer too. Not especially since I toiled for the same firm that had paid Papa's way through Paris when he was learning to work with a typewriter. I was very possibly making more money at that time than he was making when he was learning how it felt to be young in Paris.

But you cannot just walk up to Ernest Hemingway and say, "*Que tal*, Papa, I am a writer too," or "I am a *turísta* who admires your stuff." So for two weeks I sat and looked at the *gran maestro* and wished something would happen so we could have a drink together, because there were so many things I wanted to ask him. Nothing happened.

The time passed and a war came and I got mixed up in the gunnery end of that one and made several experiments into fear. I became an authority on fear, real fear and imagined fear. We were hit once by a German and again by lightning. We dodged mines and got bombed and watched friends disintegrate. That was real fear. A worse fear was seeing a naval battle at night—a battle that did *not* actually happen—and seeing a German E-boat run through the ranks of a convoy while being bombed by a plane, and learning that although everybody saw it there wasn't any E-bpat there and no plane was bombing the E-boat that wasn't actually there anyhow.

Then the war was over and I began to write again and I went back to the Africa I knew now and loved and went to Spain and Mexico and saw bullfights. I shot quail and drank whisky and went back to Australia to see if the women were still pretty, and they were. I shot Nauru deer in the high hills of Kiawe Nui on Molokai and pheasants in Connecticut and ducks in Louisiana. I busted a general out of Italy and chased a hoodlum out of Havana and imagined myself to be a hell of a fellow, always in the Hemingway pattern.

One day I looked around and realized that I was in Tanganyika, shooting lions with the same basic string of blacks that Hemingway had used fifteen years before. I had a handsome white hunter, just like the late Francis Macomber had a handsome white hunter, and a pretty wife I hoped wasn't going to shoot me in the head for convenience. I hoped I wasn't going to acquire gangrene or get chewed up, either. I am not Gregory Peck.

This day I was crawling after buffalo, which I did not really want to do. I am bitterly afraid of buffalo, the big, rope-muscled wild ox with horns like steel girders and a disposition to curdle milk. I had walked through a swamp that was full of water and snakes and rhinos. I had crawled and stumbled over two young mountains to reach a herd of buffalo that I didn't really want to associate with. I had already shot a buffalo and figured that was one thing I wouldn't have to do any more of. But Selby has a mad affection for the *mbogo*, a sort of perverse love and a completely unmanageable fascination for the big beasts. We had come back to the high plains under the Rift escarpment by Kiteti, back from the fruitless kudu expedition, back for one more try at rhino. And there was no rhino. But on the steep side of one of the hills reaching up to the escarpment there was a sprinkling of tiny black worms.

Adam, the Wakamba gunbearer, pointed. *"Mbogo,"* he said, and I could already feel my stomach start to knot. It was the same feeling I used to get when the lookout on the bow would reach for the phones and ring the bridge. "Periscope," he would say. "Periscope bearing so-and-so many degrees off the starboard bow," as if he were pleased at having done me a favor.

Harry looked at the buffalo through the glasses.

"There's a damned good bull in that herd," he said. "Better than the one you've got by six inches at least. I think we'd best go and collect him."

I didn't say anything. I just prayed inside me and hoped we would not have to crawl too far in order to scare me to death. I don't know what there is about buffalo that frightens me so. Lions and leopards and rhinos excite me but don't frighten me. But that buff is so big and mean and ugly and hard to stop, and vindictive and cruel and surly and ornery. He looks like he hates you personally. He looks like you owe him money. He looks like he is hunting you. I had looked at a couple of thousand of him by now, at close ranges, and I had killed one of him, and I was scareder than ever. He makes me sick in the stomach, and he makes my hands sweat, and he dries out my throat and my lips.

These buff were a herd of about two hundred, feeding up the edge of the hills below the escarpment and following a vague trail that meandered up the side and led eventually straight over the top. They were about two miles away, and it was walking all the way, walking when you could and crawling when you couldn't, and slipping on the loose stones and fighting through the wait-a-bit thorn, puffing and blowing and sweating and cursing in the hot sun in the middle of the day. And finally wiggling along on your belly, pushing the big gun ahead of you, sweat cascading and burning into your eyes, with your belly constricted into a tight hard kernel and your hands full of thorns and your heart two-blocked into your throat. And then the final, special Selby technique of leaping to your feet and dashing with a whoop into the middle of the herd, running at the bull, and depending on that thirty-second bewilderment to hold the buffalo stiff, like cattle, before you shot and hoped you hit him good so you wouldn't have to follow him into that awful thick bush he was certain to head for. And wait for you in it.

We crossed the mountains and were in the crawling, wiggling stage now. We had a good wind and the buff were just a few hundred yards ahead, looking blue-black and clean, as mountain buffalo are, instead of scabby and scaly and mud-splotched like the lowland fellows, or rusty red and scrubby like the herd that hung around Majimoto and Manyara. There were two good bulls—the old herd chieftain with a fine sweep of deeply rutted, heavy horns, and a younger gentleman, almost as good, who would be pushing the old boy out of the mob one of these days. Harry and I presumed to save him the trouble of a fight.

You judge a buffalo by the configuration and curl of horn as well as by the distance between his horn tips, and also by the depth of the horn boss as it rides his forehead, and by the degree of close-fitting joining of the two segments of boss as it comes together like a part in the middle of an Italian hoofer's head. Our bloke was very much all right on all counts. The boss covered his skull like a helmet, and the dividing line was as tight as a piece of string. The horns were shaped very well, not crooking in too much, and worn down evenly at the tips. He would be forty-eight inches or better between and forty-eight inches between those tips is a lot of buffalo. My first fellow was only forty-three and a bit, and he was impressive enough for me.

We were in the herd now, creeping on our bellies and pulling ourselves forward by digging elbows into sharp rocks. The buffalo were grazing unconcernedly all around us. The herd bull was lying down, resting, and there were a couple of cows obscuring him. It is a difficult sensation to describe, to be surrounded by two hundred animals weighing from eighteen hundred to twenty-five hundred pounds each, animals as testy and capricious of temper as stud fighting bulls, capable of killing you just as dead accidentally in a stampede as on purpose in a charge.

A buffalo close up is not handsome. His body is bulky, short-legged, and too long for symmetry. He smells of mud and dung and old milk. His patchy hide is scabby and full of flat ticks. Bits of his own excrement cling to him. Dirty moss grows on his horns, which are massive enough to bust everything up inside you if he even hits you a slight swipe with the flat, and sharp enough to put a hole in you big enough to hide a baseball bat in, and dirty enough to infect an army. He has the big bull's cloven hoofs, for he is a true unaltered ox and the progenitor of the Spanish fighting bull, and he delights to dance on your carcass until there is nothing much around but spatters of blood and tatters of flesh. Even his tongue is a weapon. It is as rough and harsh as a wood rasp. If you climb a tree or an anthill on the *mbogo* he will crane his ugly neck and lick the meat off you for as far up as he can reach. His tongue erodes your flesh as easily as a child licks the point off an ice-cream cone.

As I crawled along just behind Selby, with Adam and Kidogo following me, I was thinking these things. I knew a lot about buffalo by now. I knew how fast they are, despite their apparently lumbering gallop, how swiftly they can turn, how they stop cold on a dime, and how they go through bush at a spurt—bush that an elephant wouldn't recommend. I knew how much lead they would soak and keep coming, especially after being wounded. You may kill him easily with one bullet, but if you don't, the next fourteen .470s serve mostly as a minor irritant. And you cannot run away from a wounded buffalo. You have to stand and take him as he is, shooting at his nostrils as he comes at you with his head high and his horns swept back, his neck stretched and his cold eyes unblinking at you. You shoot for the nose and hope it gets into the brain, because if you shoot too high the bullets bounce off his massive horn boss like rubber balls off walls in a New York stickball game. And if he keeps on coming, like the one that got up on Bob Maytag a few months before, he comes with a hole under one eye and a hole under the other, and then somebody like Selby had best have one serious slug left to shoot him at four or five feet and catch him when he falls. When this one fell with his eye finally shot out they picked fifteen 500-grain bullets out of his carcass, all of them enough to kill him separately, but the first fourteen unable to kill him collectively.

A leopard will possibly claw up more people and is faster and tougher to hit when he lies back on your trail and begins to stalk you, but you can change his charge with a shotgun blast and he dies very easily, as all cats with thin hides and delicate bones and soft flesh die. You can change an elephant's mind, too, by shooting him in the face, and you can change a rhino's mind by shooting him anywhere that he's biggest. But the reason my friend *Mbogo* is generally rated as the toughest piece of all the African furniture is that he is a single-minded type. You got to kill him to discourage him. He scents very good and sees very far and hears marvelously. He keeps the egrets around to eat his ticks off him but not because he needs them for anything but ticks and society. The rhino and his tickbird sentries are another matter. The *faro* uses birds for eyes, and the ticks come in as a bonus for the bird-dog job they do for the rhino. The buff really fancies the snowy egrets because their white plumage looks nice and decorative on his black back. They are the only pretty thing about him.

GOD, as I was crawling and creeping and cursing and sweating, how I remembered all the buffalo I had met and the first one I had shot. Maybe the reason I was so sensitive about buff was that I took two stampedes and a dozen stalks before I finally shot one, and I had been in three more stampedes since. *This bloody Selby*, I said. *Him and his*

fascination for this awful animal. Him and his get-up-and-run-yelling tech-
nique of making the last fifty yards at a gallop, standing and shooting in the
middle of the herd while the animals snort and explode past you, not wanting
to run over you but not caring if they do run over you. They wall their eyes
with mad panic and stream past you, each one bigger than a pair of
Brahman bulls, each one with two inches of skin thickness to cover
the steel cables that make his muscles an armor plating, each one with
enough obscene vitality to run for five miles shot through the heart.

As I crept along on by belly I remembered *Mbogo Moja,* the first
one. We had stalked across a swamp and I was bitterly out of breath,
the stomach muscles jumping and a piercing pain in the chest and a
great tremble in the fingers that wasn't a fear-shake but a nervous
reaction to fatigue. We walked as far as we could walk, with the long
withes of grass tripping you at every step, and then here suddenly
was an old bull and his *askari*—an expelled herd bull, driven off from
the cows by his son, with a neophyte to run his errands for him and
learn all his wisdom so that someday he could go back and kick the
bejesus out of the reigning bull who had driven Papa off from his
wives and his family security.

So we crawled this one, too, like you creep geese in Louisiana, stopping and freezing occasionally when the *askari* raised his head to stare
at you with a colder stare than any actress ever wasted on an enemy.

This *askari* was mighty nervous. He felt that everything wasn't happy.
He kept feeding away, edging off to the nastiest patch of thornbush
in Tanganyika, with the starting of the Serengeti reserve on the other
side of the swamp. If the one we shot got hurt and went across he
would not only be sick and angry and venomous in his sickness, but
he would also be illegal.

We crept to a bush and froze behind it, and there were the animals,
fifty yards away and moving steadily out of range. Harry had his hand
palm down behind him, and suddenly he lifted it in a curling beckon.
I crawled, still blowing, up to his shoulder. He turned his head slightly
and whispered.

"We're not going to get any closer," he said. "That *askari* is nervous
and leading the old boy away. You better bust him now, although he's
too far off for my pleasure. Try to take him just where his neck comes
down into his chest."

Selby, when he is working with dangerous animals, always wears
two stalks of extra bullets sticking like cigarettes from his right hand.
Harry had said: *Do what I do.* I had two stalks of extra bullets sticking
out between the second and third fingers of *my* right hand. At this
time it had not occurred to me that Selby was left-handed.

I got up on one knee and sighted low into the old bull's chest, and
the heavy Westley-Richards settled handily in balance and I squeezed

off the trigger, and then the bull was gone and I was on the ground, my nose full of cordite fumes and my head full of chimes. Away off somewhere a gun exploded, and then there came a mournful bellow as morose as a hunting horn, a cow's horn, lonesome-sounding in the Carolina woods when a Negro cropper is lost and blowing hard on the horn to keep himself from being frightened blond until he finds the dirt road again.

Selby was standing now, spraddle-legged, with his hands on his hips and looking down at me.

"For Christ sake," he said, jerking his head toward the wood. "*One* of you ought to get up."

From this I assumed the buffalo was down too. It appeared that *right-handed* shooters are not supposed to store their spare ammunition in their shooting hand. In the effort to emulate Selby it never occurred to me that the guy was a natural southpaw, and that bullets contained in a shooting hand would ride back against the second trigger and touch off the other barrel simultaneously, loosing 150 grains of cordite against your face.

"You all right?" Harry asked. "What happened?"

"Both barrels," I said. "At once. Dropped me. Did I hit him?"

"You knocked him tail over tin cup," Harry said. "He turned completely over. Then he got up and departed."

"I thought I heard somebody else shoot," I said. "Away over yonder."

"Me," Selby said. "This bugger was flat out for the bush. I'd not taken the time to check his blood pressure, you know. I didn't know how good you hit him. I thought I'd best break his back before he got stuck into that patch of bush. Very nasty in there. Actually I shouldn't have bothered. Hear that bellow? He's dying now. You'll find you got his heart. They don't bellow from a spine shot. Hope you don't mind, old boy, but once in a while a little collaboration saves all hands a lot of trouble. I know how to pull a sick one out of the bush. But it's just that I don't fancy it as a recreation."

We walked up to the buffalo. He was dying, bellowing, making mournful sounds, and trying to drag himself toward us.

"Slip one bullet into the gun," Harry said. "I still don't trust that sear. Take him just behind the horns in the back of the head. You know what I always keep saying. The dead ones kill us."

I slid a single bullet into the right-hand barrel of the .470 and squinted carefully at the back of this boy's neck, where the muscle roll humped out like the back of the neck on a retired prize fighter. I was gun-shy. I pulled instead of squeezing, but the bullet went in and poor old *Mbogo* stretched his neck forward to its full length. Blood crept out of his nostrils and he was dead. Dead and ugly. Uglier dead than alive, and four times as ferocious.

Adam and Kidogo unsheathed a *panga* and a sharp skinning knife and started the postmortem. They took out a rib section, which they would eat themselves, and they removed the heart and the kidneys and the liver. They snipped the fat from around his intestines, and we finally burrowed into his chest cavity in the interests of science.

This *mbogo* had accepted a .470 bullet, five hundred grains of hard-nose bullet powered by seventy-five grains of cordite. He had taken it through the jugular and into the heart, where it smashed all the major arteries and crushed the whole top of the heart. It had ranged backward through him and destroyed the lungs. When we opened him up about ten gallons of black lung blood gushed out. Yet he had gotten up off the ground with this terrible wound and taken off as blithely for the bush as if we had pinked him in the fanny with a .22.

"Nobody ever believes it," Harry said. "Sometimes I don't. But these creatures are damned near indestructible. Look there at the mess you made with that bloody cannon. And remember that he was two hundred yards away and rolling off like a steam engine when I popped his spine for him and put him down. He'd have gone half a mile and still had enough gas left to scare us green when he came from a piece of bush not big enough to hide a hare."

"I don't ever want to shoot another one," I said. "This is all the *mbogo* I need this day, or any other. Like the *memsaab* says: '*Hapana taka piga mbogo lio*'. Nor any other day. Any man with one buffalo doesn't need another. It's like what David Green says. A man with a Rumanian for a friend doesn't need an enemy. David's a Rumanian."

"You'll shoot another," Harry said. "You will always hunt buff. It's a disease. You've killed a lion and you don't care whether you ever take another. But you will hunt buffalo until you are dead, because there is something about them that makes intelligent people into complete idiots. Like me. They are the only beast in Africa that can make my stomach turn like it rolls over when you've had too much grog and don't know whether the bed will stay there for you. You'll hunt more *mbogo*, all right. Kidogo! *Taka headskin kwa bwana*."

THAT was a long time ago as we measure time in Africa. That was practically in another century. There was another lion and a leopard and a cheetah and all sorts of the common stuff and some rhino we didn't get and some kudu that we butched and a lot of travel in between it. There was a stampede in between it. Like yesterday.

WE were driving back to the camp in the latish afternoon, with the oryx and the cheetah done now and out of the way. Where the road dips low and the hills begin to slide down away from the escarpment there is a big swamp, a long, wide flat, full of high reeds, with the hills moving up on the other side into a tiptilted half bowl of land. This was just a few miles away from Kiteti, where the camp was pitched and where the hippo grunted in the front yard. This was two turns in the road and one baobab tree away from camp and a *bathi* and one of Dr. Ruark's nutritious deliciouses, the bone-building gin.

The sun had slipped a little in the sky and the evening nip was coming into the air when Harry slowed the Rover to an easy stop. Across the marsh, only a quarter mile away, the big fat black worms were crawling down the hill.

"*Mbogo,*" Harry said. "My sainted aunt, *what* a head on the big fellow."

They were probably the same herd that I was working on this moment, and thinking about now, but out of focus a few miles and feeding very quietly down the side of the hill and into the swamp. I was bitter enough.

"I know," I said. "*Kwenda.* Let us go and collect it. Let us struggle through the marsh and go and collect it. By all means. *Pese pese.*"

"Right," Harry said. "I was just going to mention that possibly we should go and collect it. Haven't much time, though. Past five now. What we do we will have to do in a hurry. *Kwenda. Pese pese.*"

We fought through the high grasses, in some spots eight and ten feet tall, and treacherously mucky underfoot. We slipped and sloshed and stumbled and fell and bogged. The mosquitoes were in very good form. By the time we'd got across the swamp the buff had all fed down off the slope and were in the grass. We scouted carefully around them. You could see where they fed by where the egrets fluttered, zooming up into the sky and returning to settle on the animals' backs. One time we got too close on the way across. An old bull, his horns worn down by use to fists, was feeding out from the main mob and I almost tripped over him. Again the wind was right and he never cared that we were there. Big knob-billed geese flew over us and honked. Teals dipped and whizzed around us. We hit the far shore finally, wet and bug-bitten, and and stumbled along its rocky outcrop to a big thorn tree. Harry went up it like a monkey. He could see from there. He could see very well from there. He was up the tree a long time.

He came down.

"How are your legs feeling?" he said. "Are you up to a bit of a sprint?"

"As up as I'm ever apt to be," I said. "Where are we running and from whom?"

"Look," he said soberly. "I don't kid you much. There are two hundred buffalo out there in that high grass. They are feeding down toward the neck of the marsh. We have to get back the same way we came. It's wet in there and sticky. There are going to be about five hundred yards where we have to run. We have to run in order to get past two hundred buffalo. If the wind twists and they catch a scent of us they may stampede. Charge they won't. You know this. But in that high grass, if they all start running we won't be visible to them until they're already swarming over us. That's why I want to know if you're willing to chance a run for it."

"What happens if they do take off?" I asked Harry. "What do you do when two hundred buff come bearing down on you?"

"I would *try* to shoot one," Harry said. "I would try to shoot one so we could climb up on him so's the others could see us and run around us. It would call for a bit of lucky shooting to drop one so we could use him in a hurry. You've seen how hard they are to stop."

It was nearly six when we headed back through the marsh where the car was and camp was and booze was. Off to the right as we slipped through the reeds you could hear the buffalo chewing and snorting and grunting. You could see the egrets and hear them squawk. We were doing fine and were nearly out of the thigh-high water and into the muck when we walked right up on the back of an outgrazing bull buffalo. He let out a large bellow and took off, galloping awkwardly, out to stir up the animals and alert the town. You could hear the sudden loud, harsh rustle in the reeds when he alerted the town.

"Run," Selby said in the smallest and most distinct voice I ever heard a man use. "Run. That way."

We ran. We ran through the stinking ooze, tripping over the long grasses, hearts hitting hard in chests and breath gasping in rattles, and over to the right other things were running. Two hundred buffalo were running. They weren't scenting us because we were still down-wind, but old Uncle Wilbur with the knobby horns had passed the word and two hundred buffalo were galloping like a spread formation on a football field. They ran and we ran. You couldn't see them run because the grass was twice as tall as they were, but you could hear them breaking it down as they pounded steadily through it.

We reached some reasonably high ground and some shorter grass. As we hit it fifty buffalo, the right wing of the spread, passed just aft of us at full gallop, something under fifty feet behind us. I was completely winded. Harry was short of breath. We still had the black boys with us.

"Jesus loving God," Harry said.

I didn't say anything. Kidogo said something in Nandi. Adam said something in Wakamba.

"I'd not like to have to do that again," Harry said. "Bit of a near thing there at the end."

We walked toward the other shore. I was walking slowly. Harry was out in front by twenty feet. All of a sudden his cupped hand reached out and drew me up to him. This one I wasn't really anxious to believe.

The damned buffalo had run the length of the marsh and had turned in formation and charged again, this time straight into our scent. They were standing like a Roman battalion, feet firmly rooted, heads proudly high, and noses sniffing, no more than twenty yards in front of Selby. I came up behind him on the run.

"Him on the left, by the cow," Selby said. "That one. The good one. Not the first one. The second bull."

I was gasping like a boasted fish when I threw the .470 up just as the entire batallion wheeled to run the other way. I went for the big fellow's rear end, having read somewhere that if you shot at the root of the tail you either broke his back or discommoded his kidneys. The gun said bang and the buff went away and there was no whunk after the sound of the shot. It was almost dark now.

"Thank the Lord," Selby said reverently.

"Thank the Lord what?" I said peevishly.

"Thank the Lord you didn't hit him," Selby said. "Or else we'd have to go and find him in the dark."

"This has been quite a day," I said.

"*Ndio, bwana,*" Kidogo said, although he had not been asked.

Virginia was waiting for us when we came into the camp in the soft black night, the fires going cheerfully and what seemed to be a gin bottle on the table.

"I don't know why you let me do these things," I said. "Why the hell don't you keep me home like any decent wife would if she loved her husband?"

Virginia looked at us, thorn-torn, wet to the waist, tsetse-bit, mosquito-chewed, suicidally tired, sunburned, and out of humor.

"Buffalo again," she said. "Idiots."

I was thinking about this as we crawled into the middle of the herd, the herd of buffalo I didn't want anything else to do with ever, ever again.

We had to pause for a long time behind a big thornbush, waiting for the herd bull to get up and for the cows to move away off from in front of him. I got some little breath back and summed the situation. A big fat tsetse was biting me on the bite another big fat tsetse had created as an art form earlier. The sweat was running down in solid sheets, the salt of it burning my eyes. Grass seeds were secreted in my socks and chewing on my ankles like bugs. I had more thorns in my crown than any man needs. This was costing me a minimum of a hundred dollars a day after transportation.

At this particular moment an old cow with an evil expression, a cow I had not seen, looked right over the bush I was hiding behind. She looked at me cynically and hostilely.

"Woof!" the old cow said. "Garrumph!"

I got up on my feet. I had the gun with me.

"God *damn* Ernest Hemingway," I said bitterly, and when the bull lurched up, crooked-kneed, I walloped him. The bull went down. He got up again. "God *damn* Ernest Hemingway," I said again. "This has gone far enough." I squeezed on the bull again, and the gun was jammed. Then I heard Harry shoot, and the bull went over. He got up. He took off. All the buffalo took off. It was sort of like crossing Park Avenue against a light. Animals went past us like taxicabs.

"We killed him all right," Selby said. "We turned him over twice. Why don't we have a cigarette and give him a little chance to get slightly sick before we go after him?"

The cigarette tasted brassy in my mouth. Harry was looking cheerful again. The boys were not. Nor was I. I had a hunch a compliment was coming. It came.

"Well," Harry said, "let's go and pull him out by the tail."

This was the compliment. This, the accolade. This was what I had been waiting for. When a dangerous animal is wounded, especially a buffalo, the professional generally sends the client back to the car, with a gunbearer to hold his hand, while the hunter goes into the thick brush and earns his pay by finishing off the angry animal the client has wounded. If the client is a very good and deserving client, the hunter may ask him politely if he'd like to go along and share the fun. If the client is a very, very good client, he gets a compliment.

"Let's go get him," Harry said, as if he assumed there was no question about it. I gave him a brilliant answer and hated myself for it.

"Okay," I said.

We checked the loads on the rifles and we dived into the bush. Adam and Kidogo were spooring ahead of us, crouched, sniffing like dogs on a scent. There were lots of places in the bush for buffalo to be, grown-over dongas and patches of tangled impossibilities where any buffalo in his senses would stop and wait for killable people to come by. The bloody dung and bright gouts of heart blood always led into a cul-de-sac and always led out again. This was a peculiar buffalo. He never stopped once to bleed and sulk and build his hatred into a fever. He moved. He was a traveling man.

I found out all about me on this little *shauri*. I found out more about

me than I found out in three years of war. I found out that I was a
very brave man, because a man as scared as I was, poking my way
through that bush and spreading the underbrush ahead of me with
a gun barrel while two black innocents worked as bird dogs and trusted
me to finally face the issue of a bull buffalo bursting out of bush at
under twenty yards—I found out just how far you can carry fear. I
found out at what point just ordinary fear is overcome by the fear of
fear, and where it charged into cold determination.

JU-88s, scream and all, never scared me like walking cautiously and
slowly through this Tanganyikan bush, tracking, searching each clump
of grass and blob of trees for twenty-five hundred pounds of vindictive
force and evil plotting. Submarines and ghosts and footpads and buzz
bombs never scared me like this—never scared me into a glandular
panic in which myself walked outside myself and observed the other
myself at work, cold and competent and functional out of pride of
trust by two blacks and an English schoolboy.

We tracked this bull for three hours and over three miles of mountain and bush. Sometimes you would go for several hundred yards
without a single holly berry of blood to tell you what you were chasing.
We sometimes found a sudden spatter of the pinker lung blood. Then
we would find nothing at all and would be forced to recast our steps,
working backward on the trail until we picked up the old blood trail,
and heading in a new direction. Harry and I walked this boy up to
tangled retreats that he had to be in and wasn't in, but we had to sort
him out of it as though he was in it.

For three hours my safety was off the gun and it was carried at
half-port. For three hours I was mentally and psychologically girded
to stand flat-footed and spraddle-legged and shoot this ton of fury
until there wasn't anything else left to shoot him with. For three hours
I was nerve-edged to a sort of super-perception, perception where
every sound, every scent, every blade of grass, every rustle of breeze,
every upturned stone and disturbed piece of earth meant something
with a sick and angry buffalo on the end of it.

We found him dead.

I hated him for not being alive, for not charging, for not making
me prove out loud what I had already proved inside me.

He was lying dead like a damned old cow in a pasture, under the
shade of an acacia. The flies were already at him. He had taken my
bullet and Harry's through the lower heart and he had gone the three
miles in the three hours and he had not even contemplated standing
to make a fight. He was an unworthy enemy and he had degraded
me by working me up to this point of desperate courage and had then
cheated me of the opportunity to prove my courage. He had cheated
the two black boys of a chance to scuttle and sprawl in the sudden

rush of fierceness, while their *bwanas* did with guns what white *bwanas* are supposed to do. Here he was, dead, carrion, a hunk of meat, a slow trickle dried on his nostrils, looking beautiful in the horn department and just as dead as the Democrats, for more years than the Democrats will be dead. The buzzards were coming down.

"*Hapana*," Adam said, looking disgusted.

"*Ehhh*," Kidogo said.

"Bloody fraud," Selby said. "Never knew one before who wouldn't at least entertain the idea of standing and fighting. This one didn't. Never even paused long enough for the blood to collect in a pool."

"God *damn* Ernest Hemingway *and* Francis Macomber," I said.

This was a big buff and a handsome buff, but the littler one, the uglier one, is the one I got hanging on the wall.

It's hard to say who started writing outdoor literature, but one would be hard put to claim that Frank Forester didn't have something to do with it in a big way. His real name was Henry William Herbert, but millions of readers only knew him as Frank Forester. Most of his work appeared in the mid-1850s. I can't think of too many outdoor writers who can claim that sort of longevity. Read this and you'll know why.

The Warwick Woodlands

by FRANK FORESTER

MUCH as I had heard of Tom Draw, I was, I must confess, taken altogether aback when I, for the first time, set eyes upon him. I had heard Harry Archer talk of him fifty times as a crack shot; as a top sawyer at a long day's fag; as the man of all others he would choose as his mate, if he were to shoot a match, two against two—what then was my astonishment at beholding this worthy, as he reared himself slowly from his recumbent position? It is true, I had heard his so-briquet, "Fat Tom," but, Heaven and Earth! Such a mass of beef and brandy as stood before me, I had never even dreamt of. About five feet six inches at the very utmost in the perpendicular, by six or— "by'r lady"—nearer seven in circumference, weighing, at the least computation, two hundred and fifty pounds, with a broad jolly face, its every feature—well formed and handsome, rather than otherwise— mantling with an expression of the most perfect excellence of heart and temper, and over-shadowed by a vast mass of brown hair, sprinkled pretty well with gray! Down he plumped from the counter with a thud that made the whole floor shake, and with a hand outstretched, that might have done for a Goliath, out he strode to meet us.

"Why, hulloa! hulloa! Mr. Archer," shaking his hand till I thought he would have dragged the arm clean out of the socket—"How be you, boy? How be you?"

"Right well, Tom, can't you see? Why confound you, you've grown twenty pound heavier since July!—but here, I'm losing all my manners!—this is Frank Forester, whom you have heard me talk about so often! He dropped down here out of the moon, Tom, I believe! at least I thought about as much of seeing the man in the moon, as of meeting *him* in this wooden country—but here he is, as you see, come all the way to take a look at the natives. And so, you see, as you're about the greatest curiosity I know of in these parts, I brought him straight up here to take a peep! Look at him, Frank—look at him well! Now, did you ever see, in all your life, so extraordinary an old devil?—and yet, Frank, which no man could possibly believe, the old fat animal has some good points about him—he can walk *some!* shoot, as he says, *first best!* and drink—good Lord, how he can drink!"

"And that reminds me," exclaimed Tom, who with a ludicrous mixture of pleasure, bashfulness, and mock anger, had been listening to what he evidently deemed a high encomium; "that *we* haven't drinked yet; have you quit drink, Archer, since I was to York? What'll you take, Mr. Forester? Gin? yes, I have got some prime gin! You never sent me up them groceries though, Archer; well, then, here's luck! What, Yorkshire, is that you? I should ha' thought now, Archer, you'd have cleared that lazy Injun out afore this time!"

"Whoy, measter Draa—what 'na loike's that kind o'talk?—coom coom now, where'll Ay tak t' things tull?"

"Put Mr. Forester's box in the bedroom off the parlor—mine upstairs, as usual," cried Archer. "Look sharp and get the traps out. Now, Tom, I suppose you have got no supper for us?"

"Cooper, Cooper! you snooping little devil," yelled Tom, addressing his second hope, a fine dark-eyed, bright-looking lad of ten or twelve years; "Don't you see Mr. Archer's come?—away with you and light the parlor fire, look smart now, or I'll cure you! Supper—you're always eat! eat! eat! or, drink! drink!—*drunk!* Yes! supper; we've got pork! and chickens—"

"Oh! damn your pork," said I, "salt as the ocean I suppose!" "And double damn your chickens," chimed in Harry, "old superannuated cocks which must be caught *now,* and then beheaded, and then soused into hot water to fetch off the feathers; and save you lazy devils the trouble of picking them. No, no, Tom! get us some fresh meat for tomorrow; and for tonight let us have some hot potatoes, and some bread and butter, and we'll find beef; eh, Frank? and now look sharp, for we must be up in good time tomorrow, and, to be so, we must to bed betimes. And now, Tom, are there any cock?"

"Cock! yes, I guess there be, and quail, too, pretty plenty! quite a

smart chance of them, and not a shot fired among them this fall, anyhow!"

"Well, which way must we beat tomorrow? I calculate to shoot three
days with you here; and, on Wednesday night, when we get in, to
hitch up and drive into Sullivan, and see if we can't get a deer or two!
You'll go, Tom?"

"Well, well, we'll see anyhow; but for tomorrow, why, I guess we
must beat the 'Squire's swamp hole first; there's ten or twelve cock
there, I know; I see them there myself last Sunday; and then acrost
them buckwheat stubbles, and the big bog meadow, there's a *drove* of
quail there; two or three bevys got in one, I reckon; leastwise I counted
thirty-three last Friday was a week; and through Seer's big swamp,
over to the great spring!"

"How *is* Seer's swamp? too wet, I fancy," Archer interposed, "at
least I noticed, from the mountain, that all the leaves were changed
in it, and that the maples were quite bare."

"Pretty fair, pretty fair, I guess," replied stout Tom, "I harnt been
there myself though, but Jem was down with the hounds arter an old
fox t'other day, and sure enough *he said* the cock kept flopping up
quite thick afore him; but then the critter *will* lie, Harry; he *will* lie
like thunder, you know; but somehow I concaits there be cock there
too; and then, as I was saying, we'll stop at the great spring and get
a bit of summat, and then beat Hell Hole; you'll have sport there for
sartin! What dogs have you got with you, Harry?"

"Your old friends, *Shot* and *Chase,* and a couple of spaniels for thick
covert!"

"Now, gentlemen, your suppers are all ready."

"Come, Tom," cried Archer; "you must take a bite with us—Tim,
bring us in three bottles of champagne, and lots of ice, do you hear?"

And the next moment we found ourselves installed in a snug parlor,
decorated with a dozen sporting prints, a blazing hickory fire snapping
and sputtering and roaring in a huge Franklin stove; our luggage
safely stowed in various corners, and Archer's double gun case
propped on two chairs below the window.

An old-fashioned round table, covered with clean white linen of
domestic manufacture, displayed the noble round of beef which we
had brought up with us, flanked by a platter of magnificent potatoes,
pouring forth volumes of dense steam through the cracks in their
dusky skins; a lordly dish of butter, that might have pleased the appetite of *Sisera;* while eggs and ham, and pies of apple, mincemeat,
cranberry, and custard, occupied every vacant space, save where two
ponderous pitchers, mantling with ale and cider, and two respectable
square bottles, labelled "Old Rum" and "Brandy—1817," relieved the
prospect. Before we had sat down, Timothy entered, bearing a horse

bucket filled to the brim with ice, from whence protruded the long necks and split corks of three champagne bottles.

"Now, Tim," said Archer, "get your own supper, when you've finished with the cattle; feed the dogs well tonight; and then to bed. And hark you, call me at five in the morning; we shall want you to carry the game bag and the drinkables; take care of yourself, Tim, and good night!"

"No need to tell him that," cried Tom, "he's something like yourself; *I tell* you, Archer, if Tim ever dies of thirst, it must be where there is nothing wet but water!"

"Now hark to the old scoundrel, Frank," said Archer, "hark to him pray, and if he doesn't out eat both of us, and out drink anything you ever saw, may I miss my first bird tomorrow—that's all! Give me a slice of beef, Frank; that old Goth would cut it an inch thick, if I let him touch it; out with a cork, Tom! Here's to our sport tomorrow!"

"Uh; that goes good!" replied Tom, with an oath, which, by the apparent gusto of the speaker, seemed to betoken that the wine had tickled his palate—"that goes good! that's different from the darned red trash you left up here last time."

"And of which you have *left* none, I'll be bound," answered Archer, laughing; "my best Latour, Frank, which the old infidel calls trash."

"It's all below, every bottle of it," answered Tom: "I wouldn't use such rotgut stuff, no, not for vinegar. 'Taint half so good as that red sherry you had up here oncet; that was poor weak stuff, too, but it did well to make milk punch of; it did well instead of milk."

"Now, Frank," said Archer, "you won't believe me, *that I know;* but it's true, all the same. A year ago, this autumn, I brought up five gallons of exceedingly stout, rather fiery, young, brown sherry—draught wine, you know!—and what did Tom do here, but mix it, half and half, with brandy, nutmeg, and sugar, and drink it for milk punch!"

"I did *so,* by the eternal," replied Tom, bolting a huge lump of beef, in order to enable himself to answer—"I did *so,* and good milk punch it made, too, but it was too weak! Come, Mr. Forester, we harn't drinked yet, and I'm kind o' gittin dry!"

And now the mirth waxed fast and furious—the champagne speedily was finished, the supper things cleared off, hot water and Starke's Ferintosh succeeded, cheroots were lighted, we drew closer in about the fire, and, during the circulation of two tumblers—for to this did Harry limit us, having the prospect of unsteady hands and aching heads before him for the morrow—never did I hear more genuine and real humor, than went round our merry trio.

Tom Draw, especially, though all his jokes were not such altogether as I can venture to insert in my chaste paragraphs, and though at times his oaths were too extravagantly rich to brook repetition, shone forth resplendent. No longer did I wonder at what I had before deemed Harry Archer's strange hallucination; Tom Draw *is* a decided genius—rough as a pine knot in his native woods—but full of mirth, of shrewdness, of keen mother wit, of hard horse sense, and last, not least, of the most genuine milk of human kindness. He is a rough block; but, as Harry says, there is solid timber under the uncouth bark enough to make five hundred men, as men go now-a-days *in cities!*

At ten o'clock, thanks to the excellent precautions of my friend Harry, we were all snugly berthed before the whiskey, which had well justified the high praise I had heard lavished on it, had made any serious inroads on our understanding, but not before we had laid in a *quantum* to ensure a good night's rest.

Bright and early was I on foot the next day, but before I had half dressed myself I was assured, by the clatter of the breakfast things, that Archer had again stolen a march upon me; and the next moment my bedroom door, driven open by the thick boot of that worthy, gave me a full view of his person—arrayed in a stout fustian jacket—with half a dozen pockets in full view, and Heaven only knows how many more lying *perdu* in the broad skirts. Kneebreeches of the same material, with laced half boots and leather leggins, set off his stout calf and well-turned ankles.

"Up! up! Frank," he exclaimed, "it is a morning of ten thousand; there has been quite a heavy dew, and by the time we are afoot it will be well evaporated; and then the scent will lie, I promise you! make haste, I tell you, breakfast is ready!"

Stimulated by his hurrying voice, I soon completed my toilet, and entering the parlor found Harry busily employed in stirring to and fro a pound of powder on one heated dinner plate, while a second was undergoing the process of preparation on the hearthstone under a glowing pile of hickory ashes.

At the side table, covered with guns, dog whips, nipple wrenches, and the like, Tim, rigged like his master, in half boots and leggins, but with a short roundabout of velveteen, in place of the full-skirted jacket, was filling our shot pouches by aid of a capacious funnel, more used, as its odor betokened, to facilitate the passage of gin or Jamaica spirits than of so sober a material as cold lead.

At the same moment entered mine host, togged for the field in a huge pair of cowhide boots, reaching almost to the knee, into the tops of which were tucked the lower ends of a pair of trousers, containing yards enough of buffalo cloth to have eked out the mainsail of a North River sloop; a waistcoat and single-breasted jacket of the same material, with a fur cap, completed his attire; but in his hand he bore a large decanter filled with a pale yellowish liquor, embalming a dense mass of fine and wormlike threads, not very different in appearance from the best vermicelli.

"Come, boys, come—here's your bitters," he exclaimed; and, as if to set the example, filled a big tumbler to the brim, gulped it down as if it had been water, smacked his lips, and incontinently tendered it to Archer, who, to my great amazement, filled himself likewise a more moderate draught, and quaffed it without hesitation.

"That's good, Tom," he said, pausing after the first sip; "that's the best I ever tasted here; how old's that?"

"Five years!" Tom replied: "five years last fall! Daddy Tom made it out of my own best apples—take a horn, Mr. Forester," he added, turning to me—"It's *first best* cider sperits—better a darned sight than that Scotch stuff you make such an etarnal fuss about, toting it up here every time, as if we'd nothing fit to drink in the country!"

And to my sorrow I did taste—old apple whiskey, with Lord knows how much snakeroot soaked in it for five years! They may talk about gall being bitter; but, by all that's wonderful, there was enough of the *amari aliquid* in this *fonte*, to me by no means of *leporum*, to have given an extra touch of bitterness to all the gall beneath the canopy; and with my mouth puckered up, till it was like anything on earth but a mouth, I set the glass down on the table; and for the next five minutes could do nothing but shake my head to and fro like a Chinese mandarin, amidst the loud and prolonged roars of laughter that burst like thunderclaps from the huge jaws of Thomas Draw, and the subdued and half-respectful cachinnations of Tim Matlock.

By the time I had got a little better, the black tea was ready, and with thick cream, hot buckwheat cakes, beautiful honey, and—as a stand by—the still venerable round, we made out a very tolerable meal.

This done, with due deliberation Archer supplied his several pockets with their accustomed load—the clean-punched wads in this—in that the Westley Richards' caps—here a pound horn of powder—there a shot-pouch on Syke's lever principle, with double mouthpiece—in another, screwdriver, nipple wrench, and the spare cones; and, to make up the tale, dog whip, dram bottle, and silk handkerchief in the sixth and last.

"Nothing like method in this world," said Harry, clapping his low-crowned broad-brimmed mohair cap upon his head; "take my word for it. Now, Tim, what have you got in the bag!"

"A bottle of champagne, sur," answered Tim, who was now employed slinging a huge fustian game bag, with a net-work front, over his right shoulder, to counterbalance two full shot belts which were already thrown across the other—"a bottle of champagne, sur—a cold roast chicken—t' Cheshire cheese—and t' pilot biscuits. Is your dram bottle filled wi' t' whiskey, please sur?"

"Aye, aye, Tim. Now let loose the dogs—carry a pair of couples and a leash along with you; and mind you, gentlemen, Tim carries shot for all hands; and luncheon—but each one finds his own powder, caps, etc.; and any one who wants a dram, carries his own—the devil a-one of you gets a sup out of my bottle, or a charge out of my flask! That's right, old Trojan, isn't it?" with a good slap on Tom's broad shoulder.

"Shot! Shot—why Shot! don't you know me, old dog?" cried Tom, as the two setters bounded into the room, joyful at their release— "good dog! good Chase!" feeding them with great lumps of beef.

"Avast! there Tom—have done with that," cried Harry; "you'll have the dogs so full that they can't run."

"Why, how'd you like to hunt all day without your breakfast—hey?"

"Here, lads! here, lads! wh-e-ew!" and followed by his setters, with his gun under his arm, away went Harry; and catching up our pieces likewise, we followed, nothing loth, Tim bringing up the rear with the two spaniels fretting in their couples, and a huge black thorn cudgel, which he had brought, as he informed me, "all t' way from bonny Cawoods."

It was as beautiful a morning as ever lighted sportsmen to their labors. The dew, exhaled already from the long grass, still glittered here and there upon the shrubs and trees, though a soft fresh south-western breeze was shaking it thence momently in bright and rustling showers; the sun, but newly risen, and as yet partially enveloped in the thin gauzelike mists so frequent at that season, was casting shadows, seemingly endless, from every object that intercepted his low rays, and checkering the whole landscape with that play of light and shade, which is the loveliest accessory to a lovely scene; and lovely was the scene, indeed, as e'er was looked upon by painter's or by poet's eye— how then should humble prose do justice to it?

Seated upon the first slope of a gentle hill, midway of the great valley heretofore described, the village looked due south, toward the chains of mountains which we had crossed on the preceding evening, and which in that direction bounded the landscape. These ridges, cultivated halfway up their swelling sides, which lay mapped out before our eyes in all the various beauty of orchards, yellow stubbles, and rich pastures dotted with sleek and comely cattle, were rendered yet more lovely and romantic by here and there a woody gorge, or rocky chasm, channeling their smooth flanks and carrying down their tributary rills to swell the main stream at their base. Toward these we took our way by the same road which we had followed in an opposite direction on the previous night—but for a short space only—for having crossed the stream by the same bridge which we had passed on entering the village, Tom Draw pulled down a set of bars to the left, and strode out manfully into the stubble.

"Hold up, good lads!—whe-ew—whewt!" and away went the setters through the moist stubble, heads up and sterns down, like foxhounds on a breast-high scent, yet under the most perfect discipline; for at the very first note of Harry's whistle, even when racing at the top of their pace, they would turn simultaneously, alter their course, cross each other at right angles, and quarter the whole field, leaving no foot of ground unbeaten.

No game, however, in this instance, rewarded their exertions; and on we went across a meadow, and two other stubbles, with the like result. But now we crossed a gentle hill, and at its base came on a level tract, containing at the most ten acres of marsh land, overgrown with high coarse grass and flags. Beyond this, on the right, was a steep rocky hillock, covered with tall and thrifty timber of some thirty years' growth, but wholly free from underwood. Along the left-hand fence ran a thick belt of underwood, sumach and birch, with a few young oak trees interspersed; but in the middle of the swampy level, covering at most some five or six acres, was a dense circular thicket composed of every sort of thorny bush and shrub, matted with catbriers and wild vines, and overshadowed by a clump of tall and leafy ashes, which had not as yet lost one atom of their foliage, although the underwood beneath them was quite sere and leafless.

"Now then," cried Harry, "this is the 'Squire's swamp hole!' Now for a dozen cock! hey, Tom! Here, couple up the setters, Tim; and let the spaniels loose. Now Flash! now Dan! down charge, you little villains!" and the well-broke brutes dropped on the instant. "How must we beat this cursed hole?"

"You must go through the very thick of it, concarn you!" exclaimed Tom; "at your old work already, hey? trying to shirk at first!"

"Don't swear so! you old reprobate! I know my place, depend on it," cried Archer; "but what to do with the rest of you!—there's the rub!"

"Not a bit of it," cried Tom—"here, Yorkshire—Ducklegs—here, what's your name—get away you with those big dogs—atwixt the swamp hole, and the brush there by the fence, and look out that you mark every bird to an inch! You, Mr. Forester, go in there, under that butternut; you'll find a blind track there, right through the brush—keep that 'twixt Tim and Mr. Archer; and keep your eyes skinned, do! there'll be a cock up before you're ten yards in. Archer, you'll go right through, and I'll—"

"You'll keep well forward on the right—and mind that no bird crosses to the hill; we never get them, if they once get over. All right! In with you now! Steady, Flash! steady! hie up, Dan!" and in a moment Harry was out of sight among the brushwood, though his progress might be traced by the continual crackling of the thick underwood.

Scarce had I passed the butternut, when, even as Tom had said, up flapped a woodcock scarcely ten yards before me, in the open path, and rising heavily to clear the branches of a tall thornbush, showed me his full black eye, and tawny breast, as fair a shot as could be fancied.

"Mark!" halloaed Harry to my right, his quick ear having caught the flap of the bird's wing, as he rose. "Mark cock—Frank!"

Well—steadily enough, as I thought, I pitched my gun up! covered my bird fairly! pulled!—the trigger gave not to my finger. I tried the other. Devil's in it, I had forgot to cock my gun! and ere I could retrieve my error, the bird had topped the bush, and dodged out of sight, and off—"Mark! mark!—Tim!" I shouted.

"Ey! ey! sur—Ay see's um!"

"Why, how's that, Frank?" cried Harry. "Couldn't you get a shot?"

"Forgot to cock my gun!" I cried; but at the selfsame moment the quick sharp yelping of the spaniels came on my ear. "Steady, Flash! steady, sir! Mark!" But close upon the word came the full round report of Harry's gun. "Mark! again!" shouted Harry, and again his own piece sent its loud ringing voice abroad. "Mark! now a third! mark, Frank!"

And as he spoke I caught the quick rush of his wing, and saw him dart across a space, a few yards to my right. I felt my hand shake; I had not pulled a trigger in ten months, but in a second's space I rallied. There was an opening just before me between a stumpy thick thornbush which had saved the last bird and a dwarf cedar; it was not two yards over; he glanced across it; he was gone, just as my barrel sent its charge into the splintered branches.

"Beautiful!" shouted Harry, who, looking through a cross glade, saw the bird fall, which I could not. "Beautiful shot, Frank! Do all your work like that, and we'll get twenty couple before night!"

"Have I killed him!" answered I, half doubting if he were not quizzing me.

"Killed him? of course you have; doubled him up completely! But look sharp! there are more birds before me! I can hardly keep the dogs down, now! There! there goes one—clean out of shot of me, though! Mark! mark, Tom! Gad, how the fat dog's running!" he continued. "He sees him! Ten to one he gets him! There he goes—bang! A long shot, and killed clean!"

"Ready!" cried I. "I'm ready, Archer!"

"Bag your bird, then. He lies under that dock leaf, at the foot of yon red maple! That's it; you've got him. Steady now, till Tom gets loaded!"

"What did you do?" asked I. "You fired twice, I think!"

"Killed two!" he answered. "Ready, now!" and on he went, smashing away the boughs before him, while ever and anon I heard his cheery voice, calling or whistling to his dogs, or rousing up the tenants of some thickets into which even he could not force his way; and I, creeping, as best I might among the tangled brush, now plunging half thigh deep in holes full of tenacious mire, now blundering over the moss-covered stubs, pressed forward, fancying every instant that the rustling of the briers against my jacket was the flip-flap of a rising woodcock. Suddenly, after bursting through a mass of thorns and wild vine, which was in truth almost impassable, I came upon a little grassy spot quite clear of trees, and covered with the tenderest verdure, through which a narrow rill stole silently; and as I set my first foot on it, up jumped, with his beautiful variegated back all reddened by the sunbeams, a fine and full-fed woodcock, with the peculiar twitter which he utters when surprised. He had not gone ten yards, however, before my gun was at my shoulder and the trigger drawn; before I heard the crack I saw him cringe; and, as the white smoke drifted off to leeward, he fell heavily, completely riddled by the shot, into the brake before me; while at the same moment, whir-r-r! up sprung a bevy of twenty quail, at least, startling me for the moment by the thick whirring of their wings, and skirring over the underwood right toward Archer. "Mark, quail!" I shouted, and, recovering instantly my nerves, fired my one remaining barrel after the last bird! It was a long shot, yet I struck him fairly, and he rose instantly right upward, towering high! high! into the clear blue sky, and soaring still, till his life left him in the air, and he fell like a stone, plump downward!

"Mark him! Tim!"

"Ey! ey! sur. He's a de-ad un, that's a sure thing!"

At my shot all the bevy rose a little, yet altered not their course the least, wheeling across the thicket directly round the front of Archer, whose whereabouts I knew, though I could neither see nor hear him. So high did they fly that I could observe them clearly, every bird well defined against the sunny heavens. I watched them eagerly. Suddenly one turned over; a cloud of feathers streamed off down the wind; and then, before the sound of the first shot had reached my ears, a second pitched a few yards upward, and after a heavy flutter, followed its hapless comrade.

Turned by the fall of the two leading birds, the bevy again wheeled, still rising higher, and now flying very fast; so that, as I saw by the direction which they took, they would probably give Draw a chance of getting in both barrels. And so indeed it was; for, as before, long ere I caught the booming echoes of his heavy gun, I saw two birds keeled over, and almost at the same instant, the cheery shout of Tim announced to me that he had bagged my towered bird! After a little pause, again we started, and hailing one another now and then, gradually forced our way through brake and brier toward the outward verge of the dense covert. Before we met again, however, I had the luck to pick up a third woodcock, and as I heard another double shot from Archer, and two single bangs from Draw, I judged that my companions had not been less successful than myself. At last, emerging from the thicket, we all converged, as to a common point, toward Tim; who, with his game bag on the ground, with its capacious mouth wide open to receive our game, sat on a stump with the two setters at a charge beside him.

"What do we score?" cried I, as we drew near; "what do we score?"

"I have four woodcocks, and a brace of quail," said Harry.

"And I, two cock and a brace," cried Tom, "and missed another cock; but he's down in the meadow here, behind that 'ere stump alder!"

"And I, three woodcock and one quail!" I chimed in, naught abashed.

"And Ay'se marked doon three woodcock—two more beside yon big un, that measter Draa made siccan a bungle of—and all t' quail—every feather on um—doon i' t' bog meadow yonner—ooh! but we'se make grand sport o't!" interposed Tim, now busily employed stringing bird after bird up by the head, with loops and buttons in the game bag!

"Well done then, all!" said Harry. "Nine timberdoodles and five quail, and only one-shot missed! That's not bad shooting, considering what a hole it is to shoot in. Gentlemen, here's your health," and filling himself out a fair-sized wine-glass-full of Ferintosh, into the silver cup of his dram bottle, he tossed it off; and then poured out a similar libation for Tim Matlock. Tom and myself, nothing loth, obeyed the hint, and sipped our modicums of distilled waters out of our private flasks.

"Now, then," cried Archer, "let us pick up these scattering birds. Tom Draw, you can get yours without a dog! And now, Tim, where are yours?"

"T' first lies oop yonder in yon boonch of brachens, ahint t' big scarlet maple; and t' other—"

"Well! I'll go to the first. You take Mr. Forester to the other, and when we have bagged all three, we'll meet at the bog meadow fence, and then hie at the bevy!"

This job was soon done, for Draw and Harry bagged their birds cleverly at the first rise; and although mine got off at first without a shot, by dodging round a birch tree straight in Tim's face, and flew back slap toward the thicket, yet he pitched in its outer skirt, and as he jumped up wild I cut him down with a broken pinion and a shot through his bill at fifty yards, and Chase retrieved him well.

"Cleverly stopped, indeed!" Frank halloaed; "and by no means an easy shot! and so our work's clean done for this place, at the least!"

"The boy *can* shoot *some*," observed Tom Draw, who loved to bother

Timothy; "the boy *can* shoot *some,* though he *doos* come from York-shire!"

"Gad! and Ay wush Ay'd no but gotten thee i' Yorkshire, measter Draa!" responded Tim.

"Why! what if you had got me there?"

"What? Whoy, Ay'd clap thee iv a cage, and hug thee round t' feasts and fairs loike; and shew thee to t' folks at so mooch a head. Ay'se sure Ay'd mak a fortune o' t!"

"He has you there, Tom! Ha! ha! ha!" laughed Archer. "Tim's down upon you there, by George! Now, Frank, do fancy Tom Draw in a cage at Boroughbridge or Catterick fair! Lord! how the folks would pay to look at him! Fancy the sign board too! The Great American Man-Mammoth! Ha! ha! ha! But come, we must not stay here talking nonsense, or we shall do no good. Show me, Tim, where are the quail!"

"Doon i' t' bog meadow yonner! joost i' t' slack,* see thee, there!" pointing with the stout black-thorn; "amang yon bits o' bushes!"

"Very well—that's it; now let go the setters; take Flash and Dan along with you, and cut across the country as straight as you can go to the spring head, where we lunched last year; that day, you know, Tom, when McTavish frightened the bull out of the meadow, under the pin oak tree. Well! put the champagne into the spring to cool, and rest yourself there till we come; we shan't be long behind you.

Away went Tim, stopping from time to time to mark our progress, and over the fence into the bog meadow we proceeded; a rascally piece of broken tussocky ground, with black mud knee-deep between the hags, all covered with long grass. The third step I took, over I went upon my nose, but luckily avoided shoving my gun barrels into the filthy mire.

"Steady, Frank, steady! I'm ashamed of you!" said Harry; "so hot and so impetuous; and your gun too at the full cock; that's the reason, man, why you missed firing at your first bird, this morning. I never cock either barrel till I see my bird; and, if a bevy rises, only one at a time. The birds will lie like stones here; and we cannot walk too slow. Steady, Shot, have a care, sir!"

Never, in all my life, did I see anything more perfect than the style in which the setters drew those bogs. There was no more of racing, no more of impetuous dash; it seemed as if they knew the birds were close before them. At a slow trot, their sterns whipping their flanks at every step, they threaded the high tussocks. See! the red dog straightens his neck, and snuffs the air.

"Look to! look to, Frank! they are close before old Chase!"

Now he draws on again, crouching close to the earth. "Toho! Shot!"

*Slack—Yorkshire. Anglice, *Moist hollow.*

Now he stands! no! no! not yet—at least he is not certain! He turns his head to catch his master's eye! Now his stern moves a little; he draws on again.

There! he is sure now! what a picture—his black full eye intently glaring, though he cannot see anything in that thick mass of herbage; his nostril wide expanded, his lips slavering from intense excitement; his whole form motionless, and sharply drawn, and rigid, even to the straight stern and lifted foot, as a block wrought to mimic life by some skillful sculptor's chisel; and, scarce ten yards behind, his liver-colored comrade backs him—as firm, as stationary, as immovable, but in his attitude, how different! Chase feels the hot scent steaming up under his very nostril; feels it in every nerve, and quivers with anxiety to dash on his prey, even while perfectly restrained and steady. Shot, on the contrary, though a few minutes since he too was drawing, knows nothing of himself, perceives no indication of the game's near presence, although improved by discipline, his instinct tells him that his mate has found them. Hence the same rigid form, still tail, and constrained attitude, but in his face—for dogs *have* faces—there is none of that tense energy, that evident anxiety; there is no frown upon his brow, no glare in his mild open eye, no slaver on his lip!

"Come up, Tom; come up, Frank, they are all here; we must get in six barrels; they will not move; come up, I say!"

And on we came, deliberately prompt, and ready. Now we were all in line: Harry the center man, I on the right, and Tom on the left hand. The attitude of Archer was superb; his legs set a little way apart, as firm as if they had been rooted in the soil; his form drawn back a little, and his head erect, with his eye fixed upon the dogs; his gun held in both hands, across his person, the muzzle slightly elevated, his left grasping the trigger guard; the thumb of the right resting upon the hammer, and the forefinger on the trigger of the left-hand barrel; but, as he had said, neither cocked. "Fall back, Tom, if you please, five yards or so," he said, as coolly as if he were unconcerned, "and you come forward, Frank, as many; I want to drive them to the left, into those low red bushes; that will do: now then, I'll flush them; never mind me, boys, I'll reserve my fire."

And, as he spoke, he moved a yard or two in front of us, and under his very feet, positively startling me by their noisy flutter, up sprang the gallant bevy: fifteen or sixteen well-grown birds, crowding and jostling one against the other. Tom Draw's gun, as I well believe, was at his shoulder when they rose; at least his first shot was discharged before they had flown half a rood, and of course harmlessly: the charge must have been driven through them like a single ball; his second barrel instantly succeeded, and down came two birds, caught in the act of crossing. I am myself a quick shot, *too* quick if anything, yet my first barrel was exploded a moment after Tom Draw's second; the other followed, and I had the satisfaction of bringing both my birds down handsomely; then up went Harry's piece—the bevy being now twenty or twenty-five yards distant—cocking it as it rose, he pulled the trigger almost before it touched his shoulder, so rapid was the movement; and, though he lowered the stock a little to cock the second barrel, a moment scarcely passed between the two reports, and almost on the instant two quail were fluttering out their lives among the bog grass.

Dropping his butt, without a word, or even a glance to the dogs, he quietly went on to load; nor indeed was it needed: at the first shot they dropped into the grass, and there they lay as motionless as if they had been dead, with their heads crouched between their paws; nor did they stir thence till the tick of the gunlocks announced that we again were ready. Then lifting up their heads, and rising on their forefeet, they sat half-erect, eagerly waiting for the signal:

"Hold up, good lads!" and on they drew, and in an instant pointed on two several birds. "Fetch!" and each brought his burthen to our feet; six birds were bagged at that rise, and thus before eleven o'clock we had picked up a dozen cock, and within one of the same number of fine quail, with only two shots missed. The poor remainder of the bevy had dropped, singly, and scattered, in the red bushes, whither we instantly pursued them, and where we got six more, making a total of seventeen birds bagged out of a bevy twenty strong at first.

One towered bird of Harry's, certainly killed dead, we could not with all our efforts bring to bag; one bird Tom Draw missed clean, and the remaining one we could not find again; another dram of whiskey, and into Seer's great swamp we started: a large piece of woodland, with every kind of lying. At one end it was open, with soft black loamy soil, covered with docks and coltsfoot leaves under the shade of large but leafless willows, and here we picked up a good many scattered woodcock; afterward we got into the heavy thicket with much tangled grass, wherein we flushed a bevy, but they all took to tree, and we made very little of them; and here Tom Draw began to slow and labor; the covert was too thick, the bottom too deep and unsteady for him.

Archer perceiving this, sent him at once to the outside; and three times, as we went along, ourselves moving nothing, we heard the round reports of his large caliber. "A bird at every shot, I'd stake my life," said Harry, "he never misses cross shots in the open"; at the same instant a tremendous rush of wings burst from the heaviest thicket: "Mark! partridge! partridge!" and as I caught a glimpse of a dozen large birds fluttering up, one close upon the other, and darting away as straight and nearly as fast as bullets, through the dense branches of a cedar brake, I saw the flashes of both Harry's barrels, almost simultaneously discharged, and at the same time over went the objects of his aim; but ere I could get up my gun the rest were out of sight. "You must shoot, Frank, like lightning, to kill these beggars; they are the ruffed grouse, though they call them partridge here: see! are they not fine fellows?"

Another hour's beating, in which we still kept picking up, from time to time, some scattering birds, brought us to the spring head, where we found Tim with luncheon ready, and our fat friend reposing at his side, with two more grouse, and a rabbit which he had bagged along the covert's edge. Cool was the Star champagne; and capital was the cold fowl and Cheshire cheese; and most delicious was the repose that followed, enlivened with gay wit and free good humor, soothed by the fragrance of the exquisite cheroots, moistened by the last drops of the Ferintosh qualified by the crystal waters of the spring. After an hour's rest, we counted up our spoil; four ruffed grouse, nineteen woodcocks, with ten brace and a half of quail beside the bunny, made up our score—done comfortably in four hours.

"Now we have finished for today with quail," said Archer, "but we'll get full ten couple more of woodcock; come, let us be stirring; hang up your game bag in the tree, and tie the setters to the fence; I want you in with me to beat, Tim; you two chaps must both keep the out-side—you all the time, Tom; you, Frank, till you get to that tall thun-der-shivered ash tree; turn in there, and follow up the margin of a wide slank you will see; but be careful, the mud is very deep, and dangerous in places; now then, here goes!"

And in he went, jumping a narrow streamlet into a point of thicket, through which he drove by main force. Scarce had he got six yards into the brake, before both spaniels quested; and, to my no small won-der, the jungle seemed alive with woodcock; eight or nine, at the least, flapped up at once, and skimmed along the tongue of coppice toward the high wood, which ran along the valley, as I learned afterward, for full three miles in length—while four or five more wheeled off to the sides, giving myself and Draw fair shots, by which we did not fail to profit; but I confess it was with absolute astonishment that I saw two of those turned over, which flew inward, killed by the mar-velously quick and unerring aim of Archer, where a less thorough sportsman would have been quite unable to discharge a gun at all, so dense was the tangled jungle. Throughout the whole length of the skirt of coppice, a hundred and fifty yards, I should suppose at the utmost, the birds kept rising as it were incessantly—thirty-five, or, I think, nearly forty, being flushed in less than twenty minutes, although comparatively few were killed, partly from the difficulty of the ground, and partly from their getting up by fours and fives at once. Into the high wood, however, at the last we drove them; and there, till daylight failed us, we did our work like men. By the cold light of the full moon we wended homeward, rejoicing in the possession of twenty-six couple and a half of cock, twelve brace of quail—we found another bevy on our way home and bagged three birds almost by moonlight—five ruffed grouse, and a rabbit. Before our wet clothes were well changed, supper was ready, and a good blowout was followed by sound slumbers and sweet dreams, fairly earned by nine hours of incessant walking.

It was not yet broad daylight when Harry Archer, who had, as was usual with him on his sporting tour, arisen with the lark, was sitting in the little parlor I have before described, close to the chimney corner, where a bright lively fire was already burning, and spreading a warm cheerful glow through the apartment.

The large round table, drawn up close to the hearth, was covered with a clean though coarse white cloth, and laid for breakfast, with two cups and saucers, flanked by as many plates and eggcups, although as yet no further preparations for the morning meal, except the presence of a huge homemade loaf and a large roll of rich golden-hued butter, had been made by the neat-handed Phillis of the country inn. Two candles were lighted, for though the day had broken, the sun was not yet high enough to cast his rays into that deep and rock-walled valley, and by their light Archer was busy with the game bag, the front of which he had finished netting on the previous night.

Frank Forester had not as yet made his appearance; and still, while the gigantic copper kettle bubbled and steamed away upon the hearth, discoursing eloquent music, and servant after servant bustled in, one with a cold quail pie, another with a quart jug of cream, and fresh eggs ready to be boiled by the fastidious epicures in person, he steadily worked on, housewife and saddler's silk, and wax and scissors ready to his hand; and when at last the door flew open, and the delinquent comrade entered, he flung his finished job upon the chair, and gathered up his implements with:

"Now, Frank, let's lose no time, but get our breakfasts. Halloa! Tim, bring the rockingham and the tea chest; do you hear?"

"Well, Harry, so you've done the game bag," exclaimed the other, as he lifted it up and eyed it somewhat superciliously—"Well, it is a good one certainly; but you are the queerest fellow I ever met, to give yourself unnecessary trouble. Here you have been three days about this bag, hard all; and when it's done, it is not half as good a one as you can buy at Cooper's for a dollar, with all this new-fangled machinery of loops and buttons, and I don't know what."

"And you, Master Frank," retorted Harry, nothing daunted, "to be a good shot and a good sportsman—which, with some few exceptions, I must confess you are—are the most culpably and wilfully careless about your appointments I ever met. I don't call a man half a sportsman, who has not everything he wants at hand for an emergency, at half a minute's notice. Now it so happens that you cannot get, in New York at all, anything like a decent game bag—a little fancy-worked French or German jigmaree machine you can get anywhere, I grant, that will do well enough for a fellow to carry on his shoulders, who goes out *robin gunning*, but nothing for your man to carry, wherein to keep your birds cool, fresh, and unmutilated. Now, these loops and buttons, at which you laugh, will make the difference of a week at least in the bird's keeping, if every hour or so you empty your pockets—wherein I take it for granted you put your birds as fast as you bag them—smooth down their plumage gently, stretch their legs out, and hang them by the heads, running the button down close to the neck of each. In this way this bag, which is, as you see, half a yard long, by a quarter and a half a quarter deep, made double, one bag of fustian, with a net front, which makes two pockets—will carry fifty-one quail or woodcock, no one of them pressing upon, or interfering with, another, and it would carry sixty-eight if I had put another row of loops in the inner bag; which I did not, that I might have the bottom vacant to carry a few spare articles, such as a bag of Westley Richards' caps, and a couple of dozen of Ely's cartridges."

"Oh! that's all very well," said Frank, "but who the deuce can be at the bore of it?"

"Why be at the bore of shooting at all, for that matter?" replied Harry—"I, for one, think that if a thing is worth doing at all, it is worth doing *well*—and I can't bear to kill a hundred or a hundred and fifty birds, as our party almost always do out here, and then be obliged to throw them away, just for want of a little care. Why, I was shooting summer cock one July day two years ago—there had been heavy rain in the early morning, and the grass and bushes were very wet—Jem Blake was with me, and we had great sport, and he laughed at me like the deuce for taking my birds out of my pocket at the end of every hour's sport, and making Timothy smooth them down carefully, and bag them all after my fashion. Egad I had the laugh though, when we got home at night!"

"How so," asked Frank, "in what way had you the laugh?"

"Simply in this—a good many of the birds were very hard shot, as is always the case in summer shooting, and all of them got more or less wet, as did the pockets of Jem's shooting jacket, wherein he persisted in carrying his birds all day—the end was, that when we got home at night, it having been a close, hot, steamy day, he had not one bird which was not more or less tainted—and, as you know of course, when taint has once begun, nothing can check it."

"Ay! ay! well that indeed's a reason; if you can't buy such a bag, especially!"

"Well, you cannot then, I can tell you! and I'm glad you're convinced for once; and here comes breakfast—so now let us to work, that we may get on our ground as early as may be. For quail you cannot be too early; for if you don't find them, while they are rambling on their feeding ground, it is a great chance if you find them at all."

"But, after all, you can only use up one or two bevies or so; and, that done, you *must* hunt for them in the basking time of day, after all's done and said," replied Frank, who seemed to have got up somewhat paradoxically given that morning.

"Not at all, Frank, not at all," answered Harry—"that is if you know your ground; and know it to be well stocked; and have a good marker with you."

"Oh! this is something new of yours—some strange device fantastical—let's have it, pray."

"Certainly you shall; you shall have it *now* in precept, and in an hour or two in practice. You see those stubbles on the hill—in those seven or eight fields there are, or at least should be, some five bevies; there is good covert, good *easy* covert all about, and we can mark our birds down easily; now, when I find one bevy, I shall get as many barrels into it as I can, mark it down as correctly as possible, and then go and look for another."

"What! and not follow it up? Now, Harry, that's mere stuff; wait till the scent's gone cold, and till the dogs can't find them? 'Gad, that's clever, anyway!"

"Exactly the reverse, friend Frank; exactly the reverse. If you follow up a bevy, of *quail* mark you, on the instant, it's ten to one almost that you don't spring them. If, on the contrary, you wait for half an hour, you are sure of them. How it is, I cannot precisely tell you. I have sometimes thought that quail have the power of holding in their scent, whether purposely or naturally—from the effect of fear perhaps contracting the pores, and hindering the escape of the effluvia—I know not, but I am far from being convinced even now that it is not so. A very good sportsman, and true friend of mine, insists upon it that birds give out no scent except from the feet, and that, consequently, if they squat without running they cannot be found. I do not, however, believe the theory, and hold it to be disproved by the fact that dead birds do give out scent. I have generally observed that there is no difficulty in retrieving dead quail, but that, wounded, they are constantly lost. But, be that as it may, the birds pitch down, each into the best bit of covert he can find, and squat there like so many stones, leaving no trail or taint upon the grass or bushes, and being of course proportionally hard to find; in half an hour they will begin, if not disturbed, to call and travel, and you can hunt them up, without the slightest trouble. If you have a very large tract of country to beat, and birds are very scarce, of course it would not answer to pass on; nor ever, even if they are plentiful, in wild or windy weather, or in large open woods; but where you have a fair ground, lots of birds and fine weather, I would always beat on in a circuit, for the reason I have given you. In the first place, every bevy you flush flies from its feeding to its basking ground, so that you get over all the first early, and *know* where to look afterward; instead of killing off one bevy, and then going blundering on, at blind guesswork, and finding nothing. In the second place, you have a chance of driving two or three bevies into one brake, and of getting sport proportionate; and in the third place, as I have told you, you are much surer of finding marked birds after an hour's lapse, than on the moment."

"I will do you the justice to say," Forester replied, "that you always make a tolerably good fight in support of your opinions; and so you have done now, but I want to hear something more about this matter of holding scent—facts! facts! and let me judge for myself."

"Well, Frank, give me a bit more of that pie in the mean time, and I will tell you the strongest case in point I ever witnessed. I was shooting near Stamford, in Connecticut, three years ago, with C—— K——, and another friend; we had three as good dogs out, as ever had a trigger drawn over them. My little imported yellow and white setter, Chase, after which this old rascal is called—which Mike Sandford considered the best-nosed dog he had ever broken—a capital young pointer dog of K——'s, which has since turned out, as I hear, superlative, and P——'s old and staunch setter Count. It was the middle of a fine autumn day, and the scenting was very uncommonly good. One of our beaters flushed a bevy of quail very wide of us, and they came over our heads down a steep hillside, and all lighted in a small circular hollow, without a bit of underbrush or even grass, full of tall thrifty oak trees, of perhaps twenty-five years' growth. They were not much out of gunshot, and we all three distinctly saw them light; and I observed them flap and fold their wings as they settled. We walked straight to the spot, and beat it five or six times over, not one of our dogs ever drawing, and not one bird rising. We could not make it out; my friends thought they had treed, and laughed at me when I expressed my belief that they were still before us, under our very noses. The ground was covered only by a deep bed of sere decaying oak leaves. Well, we went on, and beat all round the neighborhood within a quarter of a mile, and did not find a bird, when lo! at the end of perhaps half an hour, we heard them calling—followed the cry back to that very hollow; the instant we entered it, all the three dogs made game, drawing upon three several birds, roaded them up, and pointed steady, and we had half an hour's good sport, and we

were *all* convinced that the birds had been there *all* the time. I have
seen many instances of the same kind, and more particularly with
wing-tipped birds, but none I think so tangible as this!"

"Well, I am not a convert, Harry; but, as the Chancellor said, I
doubt."

"And that I consider not a little, from such a positive wretch as you
are; but come, we have done breakfast, and it's broad daylight. Come,
Timothy, on with the bag and belts; he breakfasted before we had
got up, and gave the dogs a bite."

"Which dogs do you take, Harry; and do you use cartridge?"

"Oh! the setters for the morning; they are the only fellows for the
stubble; we should be all day with the cockers; even setters, as we *must*
break them here for wood shooting, have not enough of speed or
dash for the open. Cartridges? yes! I shall use a loose charge in my
right, and a *blue* cartridge in my left; later in the season I use a *blue*
in my right and a *red* in my left. It just makes the difference between
killing with both, or with one barrel. The *blue* kills all of twenty, and
the *red* all of thirty-five yards further than loose shot; and they kill
clean!"

"Yet many good sportsmen dislike them," Frank replied; "they say
they ball!"

"They do not *now,* if you load with them properly; formerly they
would do so at times, but that defect is now rectified—with the *blue*
and *red* cartridges at least—the *green,* which are only fit for wildfowl,
or deer shooting, will do so sometimes, but very rarely; and they will
execute surprisingly. For a bad or uncertain rifle shot, the *green* cartridge with SG shot is the thing—twelve good-sized slugs, propelled
with force enough to go through an inch plank, at eighty yards, within
a compass of three feet—but no wad must be used, either upon the
cartridge or between that and the powder; the small end must be
inserted downward, and the cartridge must be chosen so that the wad
at the top shall fit the gun, the case being two sizes less than the caliber.
With these directions no man need make a mistake; and, if he can
cover a bird fairly, and is cool enough not to fire within twenty yards,
he will never complain of cartridges, after a single trial. Remember,
too, that *vice versa* to the rule of a loose charge, the *heavier* you load
with powder, the *closer* will your cartridge carry. The men who do not
like cartridges are—you may rely upon it—of the class which prefers
scattering guns. I always use them, except in July shooting, and I shall
even put a few *red* in my pockets, in case the wind should get up in
the afternoon. Besides which, I always take along two buckshot cartridges, in case of *happening,* as Timothy would say, on some big var-
mint. I have four pockets in my shooting waistcoat, each stitched off
into four compartments—each of which holds, *erect,* one cartridge—

you cannot carry them loose in your pocket, as they are very apt to break. Another advantage of this is, that in no way can you carry shot with so little inconvenience, as to weight; besides which, you load one third quicker, and your gun *never* leads!"

"Well! I believe I will take some today—but don't you wait for the Commodore?"

"No! He drives up, as I told you, from Nyack, where he lands from his yacht, and will be here at twelve o'clock to luncheon; if he had been coming for the morning shooting, he would have been here ere this. By that time we shall have bagged twenty-five or thirty quail, and a ruffed grouse or two; besides driving two or three bevies down into the meadows and the alder bushes by the stream, which are quite full of woodcock. After luncheon, with the Commodore's aid, we will pick up these stragglers, and all the timberdoodles!"

In another moment the setters were unchained, and came careening, at the top of their speed, into the breakfast room, where Harry stood before the fire, loading his double gun, while Timothy was buttoning on his left leggin. Frank, meanwhile, had taken up his gun, and quietly sneaked out of the door, two flat irregular reports explaining, half a moment after, the purport of his absence.

"Well, now, Frank, that *is*"—expostulated Harry—"that *is* just the most snobbish thing I ever saw you do; ain't you ashamed of yourself now, you genuine cockney!"

"Not a bit—my gun has not been used these three months, and something *might* have got into the chamber!"

"Something *might not,* if when you cleaned it last you had laid a wad in the center of a bit of greased rag three inches square and rammed it about an inch down the barrel, leaving the ends of the linen hanging out. And by running your rod down you could have ascertained the fact, without unnecessarily fouling your piece. A gun has no right ever to miss fire *now;* and never *does,* if you use Westley Richards' caps, and diamond gunpowder—putting the caps on the *last thing*— which has the further advantage of being much the safer plan, and seeing that the powder is up to the cones before you do so. If it is not so, let your hammer down, and give a smart tap to the under side of the breech, holding it uppermost, and you will never need a picker; or at least almost never. Remember, too, that the best picker in the world is a strong needle headed with sealing wax. And now that you have finished loading, and I lecturing, just jump over the fence to your right; and that footpath will bring us to the stepping-stones across the Ramapo. By Jove, but we shall have a lovely morning."

He did so, and away they went, with the dogs following steadily at the heel, crossed the small river dry-shod, climbed up the wooded bank by dint of hand and foot, and reached the broad brown corn stubble. Harry, however, did not wave his dogs to the right hand and left, but calling them in, quietly plodded along the headland, and climbed another fence, and crossed a buckwheat stubble, still without beating or disturbing any ground, and then another field full of long bents and ragwort, an old deserted pasture, and Frank began to grumble, but just then a pair of bars gave access to a wide fifty acre lot, which had been wheat, the stubble standing still knee-deep, and yielding a rare covert.

"Now we are at the far end of our beat, and we have got the wind too in the dogs' noses, Master Frank—and so hold up, good lads," said Harry. And off the setters shot like lightning, crossing and quartering their ground superbly.

"There! there! well done, old Chase—a dead stiff point already, and Shot backing him as steady as a rail. Step up, Frank, step up quietly, and let us keep the hill of them."

They came up close, quite close to the staunch dog, and then, but not till then, he feathered and drew on, and Shot came crawling up till his nose was but a few inches in the rear of Chase's, whose point he never thought of taking from him. Now they are both upon the game. See how they frown and slaver, the birds are close below their noses.

Whirr—r—r! "There they go—a glorious bevy!" exclaimed Harry, as he cocked his right barrel and cut down the old cock bird, which had risen rather to his right hand, with his loose charge—"blaze away, Frank!" Bang—bang!—and two more birds came fluttering down, and then he pitched his gun up to his eye again and sent the cartridge after the now distant bevy, and to Frank's admiration a fourth bird was keeled over most beautifully, and clean killed, while crossing to the right, at forty-six yards, as they paced it afterward.

"Now mark! mark, Timothy—mark, Frank!" And shading their eyes from the level sunbeams, the three stood gazing steadily after the rapid bevy. They cross the pasture, skim very low over the brush fence of the cornfield—they disappear behind it—they are down! no! no! not yet—they are just skirting the summit of the topped maize stalks—now they are down indeed, just by that old ruined hovel, where the cat-briers and sumach have overspread its cellar and foundation with thick underwood. And all the while the sturdy dogs are crouching at their feet unmoving.

"Will you not follow those, Harry?" Forester inquired—"there are at least sixteen of them!"

"Not I," said Archer, "not I, indeed, till I have beat this field—I expect to put up another bevy among those little crags there in the corner, where the red cedars grow—and if we do, they will strike down the fence of the buckwheat stubble—that stubble we must make good, and the rye beside it, and drive, if possible, all that we find before us to the cornfield. Don't be impatient, and you'll see in time that I am in the right."

No more words were now wasted; the four birds were bagged without trouble, and the sportsmen being in the open, were handed over on the spot to Tim; who stroked their freckled breasts, and beautifully mottled wing coverts and backs, with a caressing touch, as though he loved them; and finally, in true Jack Ketch style, tucked them up severally by the neck. Archer was not mistaken in his prognostics—another bevy had run into the dwarf cedars from the stubble at the sound of the firing, and were roaded up in right good style, first one dog, and then the other, leading; but without any jealousy or haste.

They had, however, run so far, that they had got wild, and, as there was no bottom covert on the crags, had traversed them quite over to the open, on the far side—and, just as Archer was in the act of warning Forester to hurry softly round and head them, they flushed at thirty yards, and had flown some five more before they were in sight, the feathery evergreens for a while cutting off the view—the dogs stood dead at the sound of their wings. Then, as they came in sight, Harry discharged both barrels very quickly—the loose shot first, which evidently took effect, for one bird cowered and seemed about to fall, but gathered wing again, and went on for the present—the cartridge, which went next, although the bevy had flown ten yards further, did its work clean, and stopped its bird. Frank fired but once, and killed, using his cartridge first, and thinking it in vain to fire the loose shot. The remaining birds skimmed down the hill, and lighted in the thick bushy hedgerow, as Archer had foreseen.

"So much for Ely!" exclaimed Harry—"had we both used two of them, we should have bagged four then. As it is, I have killed one which we shall not get; a thing that I most particularly hate."

"That bird will rise again," said Frank.

"*Never!*" replied the other, "he has one, if not two, shot in him, well forward—if I am not much mistaken, before the wing—he is dead now! but let us on. These we must follow, for they are on our line; you keep this side the fence, and I will cross it with the dogs—come with me, Timothy."

In a few minutes more there was a dead point at the hedgerow.

"Look to, Frank!"

"Ay! ay! Poke them out, Tim"; then followed sundry bumps and threshings of the briers, and out with a noisy flutter burst two birds under Forester's nose. Bang! bang!

"The first shot too quick, altogether," muttered Archer; "Ay, he has missed one; mark it, Tim—there he goes down in the corn, by jingo—you've got that bird, Frank! That's well! Hold up, Shot"—another point within five yards. "Look out again, Frank."

But this time vainly did Tim poke, and thrash, and peer into the bushes—yet still Shot stood, stiff as a marble statue—then Chase drew up and snuffed about, and pushed his head and forelegs into the matted briers, and thereupon a muzzling noise ensued, and forthwith out he came, mouthing a dead bird, warm still, and bleeding from the neck and breast.

"Frank, he has got my bird—and shot, just as I told you, through the neck and near the great wing joint—good dog! good dog!"

"The devil!"

"Yes, the devil! but look out man, here is yet one more point"; and this time ten or twelve birds flushed upon Archer's side; he slew, as usual, his brace, and as they crossed, at long distance, Frank knocked down one more—the rest flew to the cornfield.

In the middle of the buckwheat they flushed another, and, in the rye, another bevy, both of which crossed the stream, and settled down among the alders. They reached the cornfield, and picked up their birds there, quite as fast as Frank himself desired—three ruffed grouse they had bagged, and four rabbits, in a small dingle full of thorns, before they reached the corn; and just as the tin horns were sounding for noon and dinner from many a neighboring farm, they bagged their thirty-fourth quail. At the same moment, the rattle of a distant wagon on the hard road, and a loud cheer replying to the last shot, announced the Commodore who pulled up at the tavern door just as they crossed the stepping-stones, having made a right good morning's work, with a dead certainty of better sport in the afternoon, since they had marked two untouched bevies, thirty-five birds at least, beside some ten or twelve more stragglers into the alder brakes, which Harry knew to hold—moreover, thirty woodcock, as he said, at the fewest.

"Well! Harry," exclaimed Frank, as he set down his gun, and sat down to the table, "I must for once knock under—your *practice* has borne out your *precepts*."

The Quail

"Certainly this is a very lovely country," exclaimed the Commodore suddenly, as he gazed with a quiet eye, puffing his cigar the while, over the beautiful vale, with the clear expanse of Wickham's Pond in the middle foreground, and the wild hoary mountains framing the rich landscape in the distance.

"Truly, you may say that," replied Harry; "I have traveled over a large part of the world, and for its own peculiar style of loveliness, I must say that I never have seen anything to match with the vale of Warwick. I would give much, very much, to own a few acres, and a snug cottage here, in which I might pass the rest of my days, far aloof from the

Fumum et opes strepitumque Romae."

"Then, why the hell I don't I own a few acres?" put in ancient Tom; "I'd be right glad to know, and gladder yit to have you up here, Archer."

"I would indeed, Tom," answered Harry; "I'm not joking at all; but there are never any small places to be bought hereabout; and, as for large ones, your land is so confounded good, that a fellow must be a nabob to think of buying."

"Well, how would Jem Burt's place suit you, Archer?" asked the fat man. "You knows it—jist a mile and a half 'tother side Warwick, by the crick side? I guess it will have to be sold anyhow next April; least-ways the old man's dead, and the heirs want the estate settled up like."

"Suit me!" cried Harry, "by George! it's just the thing, if I recollect it rightly. But how much land is there?"

"Twenty acres, I guess—not over twenty-five, no how."

"And the house?"

"Well, that wants fixin' some; and the bridge over the crick's putty bad, too, it will want putty nigh a new one. Why, the house is a story and a half like; and it's jist an entry stret through the middle, and a parlor on one side on't, and a kitchen on the t'other; and a chamber behind both on 'em."

"What can it be bought for, Tom?"

"I guess three thousand dollars; twenty-five hundred, maybe. It will go cheap, I reckon; I don't hear tell o' no one lookin' at it."

"What will it cost me more to *fix* it, think you?"

"Well, you see, Archer, the land's ben most darned badly done by, this last three years, since old 'squire's ben so low; and the bridge, that'll take a smart sum; and the fences is putty much gone to rack; I guess it'll take hard on to a thousand more to fix it up right, like you'd like to have it, without doin' nothin' at the house."

"And fifteen hundred more for that and the stables. I wish to heaven I had known this yesterday; or rather before I came up hither," said Harry.

"Why so?" asked the Commodore.

"Why, as the deuce would have it, I told my broker to invest six thousand, that I have got loose, in a good mortgage, if he could find one, for five years; and I have got no stocks that I can sell out; all that I have but this, is on good bond and mortgage, in Boston, and little enough of it, too."

"Well, if that's all," said Forester, "we can run down tomorrow, and you will be in time to stop him."

"That's true, too," answered Harry, pondering. "Are you sure it can be bought, Tom?"

"I guess so," was the response.

"That means, I suppose, that you're perfectly certain of it. Why the devil can't you speak English?"

"English!" exclaimed Frank; "Good Lord! why don't you ask him why he can't speak Greek? English! Lord! Lord! Lord! Tom Draw and English!"

"I'll jist tell Archer what he warnts to know, and then see you, my dear little critter, if I doosn't English you some!" replied the old man, waxing wroth. "Well, Archer, to tell heaven's truth, now, I doos *know* it; but it's an *eternal* all-fired shame of me to be tellin' it, bein' as how I knows it in the way of business like. It's got to be selled by *vandoo* in April.

"Then, by Jove! I will buy it," said Harry; "and down I'll go to-morrow. But that need not take you away, boys; you can stay and finish out the week here, and go home in the Ianthe; Tom will send you down to Nyack."

"Sartain," responded Tom; "but now I'm most darned glad I told you that, Archer. I meant to a told you on't afore, but it clean slipped out of my head; but all's right, now. Hark! hark! don't you hear, boys? The quails hasn't all got together yit—better luck! Hush, A——, and you'll hear them callin'—whew-wheet! whew-wheet! whe-whe-whe;" and the old Turk began to call most scientifically; and in ten minutes the birds were answering him from all quarters, through the circular space of bog meadow, and through the thorny brake beyond it, and some from a large ragwort field further yet.

"How is this, Frank—did they scatter so much when they dropped?" asked Harry.

"Yes; part of them 'lighted in the little bank on this edge, by the spring, you know; and some, a dozen or so, right in the middle of the bog, by the single hickory; and five or six went into the swamp, and a few over it."

"That's it! that's it! and they've been running to try to get together," said the Commodore.

"But was too skeart to call, till we'd quit shootin'!" said Tom. "But come, boys, let's be stirrin', else they'll git together like; they keeps drawin', drawin', into one place now, I can hear."

No sooner said than done; we were all on foot in an instant, and ten minutes brought us to the edge of the first thicket; and here was the truth of Harry's precepts tested by practice in a moment; for they had not yet entered the thin bushes, on which now the red leaves hung few and sere, before old Shot threw his nose high into the air, straightened his neck and his stern, and struck out at a high trot; the other setter evidently knowing what he meant, though as yet he had not caught the wind of them. In a moment they both stood steady; and, almost at the same instant, Tom Draw's Dash, and A——'s Grouse, came to the point, all on different birds, in a bit of very open ground, covered with wintergreen about knee-deep, and interspersed with only a few scattered bushes.

Whir-r-r-r—up they got all at once! what a jostle—what a hubbub! Bang! bang! crack! bang! crack! bang! Four barrels exploded in an instant, almost simultaneously; and two sharp unmeaning cracks announced that, by some means or other, Frank Forester's gun had missed fire with both barrels.

"What the deuce is the matter, boys!" cried Harry, laughing, as he threw up his gun, after the hubbub had subsided, and dropped two birds—the only two that fell, for all that waste of shot and powder.

"What the deuce ails you?" he repeated, no one replying, and all hands looking bashful and crestfallen. "Are you all drunk? or what is the matter? I ask merely for information."

"Upon my life! I believe *I am!*" said Frank Forester. "For I have not loaded my gun at all, since I killed those two last snipe. And, when we got up from luncheon, I put on the caps just as if all was right— but all is right now," he added, for he had repaired his fault, and loaded, before A——or fat Tom had done staring, each in the other's face, in blank astonishment.

"Step up to Grouse, then," said Archer, who had never taken his eye off the old brown pointer, while he was loading as fast as he could. "He has got a bird, close under his nose; and it will get up, and steal away directly. That's a trick they will play very often."

"He haint got no bird," said Tom, sulkily. And Frank paused doubtful.

"Step up, I tell you, Frank," said Harry, "the old Turk's savage; that's all."

And Frank did step up, close to the dog's nose; and sent his foot through the grass close under it. Still the dog stood perfectly stiff; but no bird rose.

"I told you there warn't no quails there;" growled Tom.

"And I tell you there are!" answered Archer, more sharply than he often spoke to his old ally; for in truth, he was annoyed at his obstinate pertinacity.

"What do you say, Commodore? Is Grouse lying? Kick that tussock— kick it hard, Frank."

"Not he," replied A——; "I'll bet fifty to one, there's a bird there."

"It's devilish odd, then, that he won't get up!" said Frank.

Whack! whack! and he gave the hard tussock two kicks with his heavy boot, that fairly made it shake. Nothing stirred. Grouse still kept his point, but seemed half-inclined to dash in. Whack! a third kick that absolutely loosened the tough hassock from the ground, and then, whirr-r, from within six inches of the spot where all three blows had been delivered, up got the bird, in a desperate hurry; and in quite as desperate a hurry Forester covered it—covered it before it was six yards off! His finger was on the trigger, when Harry quietly said, "Steady, Frank!" and the word acted like magic.

He took the gun quite down from his shoulder, nodded to his friend, brought it up again, and turned the bird over very handsomely, at twenty yards, or a little further.

"Beautifully done, indeed, Frank," said Harry. "So much for coolness!"

"What do you say to that, Tom?" said the Commodore, laughing.

But there was no laugh in Tom; he only muttered a savage growl, and an awful imprecation; and Harry's quick glance warned A—— not to plague the old Trojan further.

All this passed in a moment; and then was seen one of those singular things that will at times happen; but with regard to quail only, so far as I have ever seen or heard tell. For as Forester was putting down the card upon the powder in the barrel which he had just fired, a second bird rose, almost from the identical spot whence the first had been so difficultly flushed, and went off in the same direction. But not in the least was Frank flurried now. He dropped his ramrod quietly upon the grass, brought up his piece deliberately to his eye, and killed his bird again.

"Excellent—excellent! Frank," said Harry again. "I never saw two prettier shots in all my life. Nor did I ever see birds lie harder."

During all this time, amidst all the kicking of tussocks, threshing of bog grass, and banging of guns, and, worst of all, bouncing up of fresh birds, from the instant when they dropped at the first shot, neither one of Harry's dogs, nor Tom's little Dash, had budged from their own charge. Now, however, they got up quickly, and soon retrieved all the dead birds.

"Now, then, we will divide into two parties," said Harry. "Frank, you go with Tom; and you come with me, Commodore. It will never do to have you two jealous fellows together, you won't kill a bird all day," he added, in a lower voice. "That is the worst of old Tom, when he gets jealous he's the very devil. Frank is the only fellow that can get along with him at all. He puts *me* out of temper, and if we both got angry, it would be very disagreeable. For, though he is the very best fellow in the world, when he is in a rage he is untameable. I cannot think what has put him out, now; for he has shot very well today. It is only when he gets behind hand, that he is usually jealous in his shooting; but he has got the deuce into him now."

By this time the two parties were perhaps forty yards apart, when Dash came to a point again. Up got a single bird, the old cock, and flew directly away from Tom, across Frank's face; but not for that did the old chap pause. Up went his cannon to his shoulder, there was a flash and a roar, and the quail, which was literally not twelve feet from him, disappeared as if it had been resolved into thin air. The whole of Tom's concentrated charge had struck the bird endwise, as it flew from him; and, except the extreme tips of his wings and one foot, no part of him could be found.

"The devil!" cried Harry, "that is too bad!"

"Never mind," said the Commodore, "Frank will manage him."

As he spoke a second bird got up, and crossed Forester in the same manner, Draw doing precisely as he had done before; but, this time, missing the quail clear, which Forester turned over.

"Load quick! and step up to that fellow. He will run, I think!" said Archer.

"Ay! ay!" responded Frank, and, having rammed down his charge like lightning, moved forward, before he had put the cap on the barrel he had fired.

Just as he took the cap out of his pocket between his finger and thumb, a second quail rose. As cool and self-possessed as it is possible to conceive, Frank cocked the left-hand barrel with his little finger, still holding the cap between his forefinger and thumb, and actually contrived to bring up the gun, somehow or other, and to kill the bird, pulling the trigger with his middle finger.

At the report a third quail sprang, close under his feet; and, still unshaken, he capped the right-hand barrel, fired, and the bird towered!

"Mark! mark! Tom—ma-ark Timothy!" shouted Harry and A——in a breath.

"That bird is as dead as Hannibal now!" added Archer, as, having spun up three hundred feet into the air, and flown twice as many hundred yards, it turned over, and fell plumb, like a stone, through the clear atmosphere.

"Ayse gotten that chap marked doon roight, ayse warrant un!" shouted Timothy from the hillside, where with some trouble, he was holding in the obstreperous spaniels. "He's doon in a roight laine atwixt 't muckle gray stean and yon hoigh ashen tree."

"Did you ever see such admirable shooting, though?" asked A——in a low voice. "I did not know Forester shot like that."

"Sometimes he does. When he's cool. He is not certain; that is his only fault. One day he is the coolest man I ever saw in a field, and the next the most impetuous; but when he *is* cool, he shoots splendidly. As you say, A——, I never saw anything better done in my life. It was the perfection of coolness and quickness combined."

"I cannot conceive how it *was* done at all. How he brought up and fired that first barrel with a cap between his thumb and forefinger! Why, I could not fire a gun so, in cold blood!"

"Nor could he, probably. Deliberate promptitude is the thing! Well, Tom, what do you think of that? Wasn't that pretty shooting?"

"It was so, pretty shootin'," responded the fat man, quite delighted out of his crusty mood. "I guess the darned little critter's got three barrels to his gun somehow; leastwise it seems to me, I swon, 'at he fired her off three times without loadin'! I guess I'll quit tryin' to shoot agin Frank, today."

"I told you so!" said Harry to the Commodore, with a low laugh, and then added aloud—"I think you may as well, Tom—for I don't believe the fellow will miss another bird today."

And in truth, strange to say, it fell out in reality nearly as Archer had spoken in jest. The whole party shot exceedingly well. The four birds, which Tom and the Commodore had missed at the first start, were found again in an old ragwort field, and brought to bay; and of the twenty-three quail which Forester had marked down into the bog meadow, not one bird escaped, and of that bevy not one bird did Frank miss, killing twelve, all of them double shots, to his own share, and beating Archer in a canter.

But that sterling sportsman cared not a stiver; too many times by far had he had the field, too sure was he of doing the same many a time again, to dislike being beaten once. Besides this, he was always the least jealous shot in the world, for a very quick one; and, in this instance, he was perhaps better pleased to see his friend "go in and win," than he would have been to do the like himself.

Exactly at two o'clock, by A——'s repeater, the last bird was bagged; making twenty-seven quail, forty-nine snipe, two ruffed grouse, and one woodcock, bagged in about five hours.

"So far, this is the very best day's sport I ever saw," said Archer; "and two things I have seen which I never saw before; a whole bevy of quail killed without the escape of one bird, and a whole bevy killed entirely by double shots, except the odd bird. You, A——, have killed three double shots—I have killed three—Tom Draw one double shot, and the odd bird; and Master Frank there, confound him, six double shots running—the cleverest thing I ever heard of, and, in Forester's case, the best shooting possible. I have missed one bird, you two, and Tom three."

"But Tom beant a goin' to miss no more birds, I can tell you, boy. Tom's drinked agin, and feels kind o'righter than he did—kind o' *first best!* You'd best all drink boys—the spring's handy, close by here; and after we gits down acrost the road into the big swamp, and Hell Hole, there arn't a drop o' water fit to drink, till we gits way down to Aunt Sally's big spring hole, jest to home."

"I second the motion," said Harry; "and then let us be quick, for the day is wearing away, and we have got a long beat yet before us. I wish it were a sure one. But it is not. Once in three or four years we get a grand day's sport in the big swamp; but for one good day we have ten bad ones. However, we are sure to find a dozen birds or so in Hell Hole; and a bevy of quail in the Captain's swamp, shan't we, Tom?"

"Yes, if we gits so far; but somehow or other I rather guess we'll find quite a smart chance o'cock. Captain Reed was down there a' Satterday, and he saw heaps on 'em."

"That's no sure sign. They move very quickly now. Here today and there tomorrow," said Archer. "In the large woods especially. In the small places there are plenty of sure finds."

"There harn't been nothing of frosts yet keen enough to stir them," said Tom. "I guess we'll find them. And there harn't been a gun shot off this three weeks there. Hoel's wife's ben down sick all the fall, and Halbert's gun busted in the critter's hand."

"Ah! did it hurt him?"

"Hurt him some—skeart him considerable, though. I guess he's quit shootin' pretty much. But come—here we be, boys, I'll keep along the outside, where the walkin's good. You git next me, and Archer next with the dogs, and A——inside of all. Keep right close to the cedars, A——; all the birds 'at you flushes will come stret out this aways. They never flies into the cedar swamp. Archer, how does the ground look?"

"I never saw it look so well, Tom. There is not near so much water as usual, and yet the bottom is all quite moist and soft."

"Then we'll get cock for sartain."

"By George!" cried A——, "the ground is like a honeycomb, with their borings; and as white in places with their droppings, as if there had been a snow fall!"

"Are they fresh droppings, A——?"

"Mark! Ah! Grouse! Grouse! for shame. There he is down. Do you see him, Harry?"

"Ay! ay! Did Grouse flush him?"

"Deliberately, at fifty yards off. I must lick him."

"Pray do; and that mercifully."

"And that soundly," suggested Frank, as an improvement.

"Soundly *is* mercifully," said Harry, "because one good flogging settles the business; whereas twenty slight ones only harass a dog, and do nothing in the way of correction or prevention."

"True, oh king!" said Frank, laughing. "Now let us go on; for, as the bellowing of that brute is over, I suppose 'chastisement has hidden her head.' "

And on they did go; and sweet shooting they had of it; all the way down to the thick deep spot, known by the pleasing sobriquet of Hell Hole.

The birds were scattered everywhere throughout the swamp, so excellent was the condition of the ground; scattered so much, that, in no instance did two rise at once; but one kept flapping up after another, large and lazy, at every few paces; and the sportsmen scored them fast, although scarcely aware how fast they were killing them. At length, when they reached the old creekside, and the deep black mud holes, and the tangled vines and leafy alders, there was, as usual, a quick, sharp, and decisive rally. Before the dogs were thrown into it, Frank was sent forward to the extreme point, and the Commodore out into the open field, on the opposite side from that occupied by fat Tom.

On the signal of a whistle from each of the party, Harry drove into the brake with the spaniels, the setters being now consigned to the care of Timothy; and in a moment, his loud "Hie cock! Hie cock! Pur-r-r—Hie cock! good dogs!" was succeeded by the shrill yelping of the cockers, the flap of the fast rising birds, and the continuous rattling of shots.

In twenty minutes the work was done; and it was well that it was done; for, within a quarter of an hour afterwards, it was too dark to shoot at all.

In that last twenty minutes twenty-two cock were actually brought to bag, by the eight barrels; twenty-eight had been picked up, one by one, as they came down the long swamp, and one Harry had killed in the morning. When Timothy met them, with the horses, at the big oak tree, half an hour afterward—for he had gone off across the fields, as hard as he could foot it to the farm, as soon as he had received the setters—it was quite dark; and the friends had counted their game out regularly, and hung it up *secundum artem* in the loops of the new game bag.

It was a huge day's sport—a day's sport to talk about for years afterward—Tom Draw does talk about it now!

Fifty-one woodcock, forty-nine English snipe, twenty-seven quail, and a brace of ruffed grouse. A hundred and twenty-nine head in all, on unpreserved ground, and in very wild walking. It is to be feared it will never be done any more in the vale of Warwick. For this, alas! was ten years ago.

When they reached Tom's it was decided that they should all return home on the morrow; that Harry should attend to the procuring his purchase money; and Tom to the cheapening of the purchase.

In addition to this, the old boy swore, by all his patron saints, that he would come down in spring, and have a touch at the snipe he had heard Archer tell on at Pine Brook.

A capital supper followed; and of course lots of good liquor, and the toast, to which the last cup was quaffed, was

LONG LIFE TO HARRY ARCHER, AND LUCK TO HIS SHOOTING BOX

to which Frank Forester added

"I wish he may get it."

And so that party ended; all of its members hoping to enjoy many more like it, and that very speedily.

THE WARWICK WOODLANDS
1850

Robert Elman is an old friend, but that has nothing to do with my selecting his story "God Bless the Running Deer" for this book. Bob is a good writer and a knowledgeable sportsman. Unfortunately, Bob, like most of us, has slumps of bad luck in the woods or on the water. He talks about one of those slumps here. Is he embarrassed or ashamed of messing up in the woods? Never! Rather than hiding these awkward moments, Bob shares them with us, and teaches us something about being a bit more human. It won't be so bad next time you miss a deer or lose a big bass. You'll handle it better, thanks to Bob.

God Bless the Running Deer

by ROBERT ELMAN

ONLY once have I shot a running deer, and it was a most important running deer. Having been forced to grow comfortable with my limitations—in much the same way that I have acquired a fond tolerance for the limitations of my neighbors, at least in small doses—I don't ordinarily shoot at wild-flushing pheasants or ducks that flare too wide of the blind. There are those who say the kill doesn't matter. They are fools or liars. I can laugh at misses, pass up easy shots when there is reason, and come home skunked but happy. All of that doesn't matter. The kill matters. And the manner of the kill matters. All else is trivial, for nothing else is final.

I have killed deer as they walked or trotted or started up from a last bed. I have killed a buck as it chewed its cud and another as it raised its head, curled its lips, flicked its tongue to savor every wafting molecule of estruating doe musk—flehmening, the biologists call it. Lusting, I say, as it died. But only once have I shot a running deer.

The summer when I was almost nine years old, my name was Running Deer. My parents had sent me to a summer camp where sometimes, I forgot my fat and inability to hit a ball while discovering that I could tell oak from maple leaves, squirrel tracks from raccoon tracks. As often as two or three times a day I secretly molted out of my dog-day ·cicada self, remaining outwardly a bulbous insect husk but inwardly transformed into a fleet Sioux brave tracking fearsome bears and fearful enemies. How intoxicating was the pungency of wet, moldering acorns and punk wood, and I signed my postcards to my mother: "Love, Running Deer."

Almost half a century later I stood over a young buck mule deer that lay on its right side, stone dead but with its motor reflexes whirring feebly like the prop of an old outboard motor that has just been turned off. The final sputter is disconcerting. The deer's forelegs, horizontal, touching only air, continued to rotate, feebly running as the deer lay still.

My wife and children and I long ago consumed the last morsel of that deer's flesh, and I took delight in sucking the marrow from a femur. All the same, the running deer will run in my mind forever. I would have it no other way. Its being is joined to mine for eternity. Remorse is not regret, and sympathy is something else entirely—as is remembrance, vital remembrance. I wonder if only the hunter can understand the compassion of the eater for the eaten. I wonder if only the hunter understands the apology and prayer offered by gracefully primitive tribes to the caribou or walrus before they joyfully spear it. Therein lies the sole metaphysical difference between me and the lion tearing out the paunch of a gazelle. Possibly there are additional differences between me and the more civilized gnawers of tender choplets sawn a month or two beforehand from a lamb's carcass hanging in a refrigerated abattoir. I can only wish them and myself *bon appétit.*

On the other hand, I'm not sufficiently analytical to make absolute statements about the need to hunt, or my other need—to tell stories about it. I can only say that this one needs telling because I suspect (my remembrance of the incidents being very clear) that it may touch the ghosts that run in the hunter's mind.

If this need of mine did not begin with the escape from myself when I tracked gray squirrels and made Camp Greylock's baseball diamonds disappear, then it must have begun a year or two later, when my family moved from New York City to a town called Summit, an up-and-coming bedroom community that kept itself very busy in those Second World War days by fighting valiantly to save the world for democracy while devising ways to keep more Jews and Italians from moving into town.

When our neighbors realized that their citadel had been infiltrated, that only their country club and their children's dance classes were legally off limits to us and they could not oust the enemy, they sent two missionaries to convert us. One was a Presbyterian minister who invited us to his church and gave me a tract about the joy of conversion.

The second was a frail, white-haired lady who had served for years at her older brother's mission somewhere in China. Her dress reached to her calves: white with a pink and robin's-egg print of flowers and bluebirds. The print made me feel sad and guilty. I had split a bluebird's skull with a slingshot, and I wanted to confess to her and ask forgiveness. She arrived at our house on my birthday—I never found out how she knew it was my birthday—and said she had a gift for me. It was a Bible.

I thanked her. She asked me to promise I would read some Psalms. I said I would. Then she explained to me, gently, hesitantly, that my older brother Jacky was burning in hell because he had not been baptized. It was hard to look at her—poor kind missionary lady, almost in tears, feeling so sorry for me. I was still grieving for Jacky, but I didn't cry in front of the lady. That night I struggled through the ninety-sixth Psalm before reading the last few pages of Jack London's *The Call of the Wild*. If my brother was burning in hell, he somehow managed an occasional furlough to visit me during the half-dreaming, half-awake interlude before the alarm clock rang in the morning.

"Been fishing?"

"No," I told him. "I'm a hunter now."

"Tigers?"

"Some. Mostly bears."

I was bursting with Jack London, Theodore Roosevelt, Zane Grey, Albert Payson Terhune. My dream life was composed of wilderness adventure and dogs. Not even sexual fantasies would supplant that fare for another couple of years.

I daydreamed my way through the sixth grade. Sometimes I saw myself running through the woods, accompanied by several deer. Sometimes I conjured up my brother Jacky when he didn't appear of his own accord, and once I tried to visualize my forebears and all of the world's other heathen stacked like corded firewood. About once every couple of weeks, Red or Charley—the school's best athletes—would be waiting on the school steps for me to come out and get whipped; and afterward I would walk way off beyond the golf course to the woods.

Not all the kids were Reds or Charleys. There were some who made friends despite their fathers' misgivings and their own. I haven't been in touch with any of them since my second year in high school, when we moved to another town. Some of them probably died in Korea. Losing touch with them was easy. I liked being alone; alone in the woods, with no one to laugh at what I knew was laughable, I could once again be Running Deer.

The summer after the sixth grade, my father gave me a BB gun, and once, pretending to be a great hunter, I actually sneaked up close enough to a woodchuck to kill it. It must have been a sick or injured woodchuck, but no matter. The first shot only stunned the animal. I wasn't upset. I put more BBs into its head until it was dead. Little boys perceive no agony but their own. Grown-ups contain the ghosts of agony inflicted, and those who kill may begin to understand about the manner of the kill. The understanding of parents is of a very different kind; I wanted to cook and eat the woodchuck, but they wouldn't hear of it. Afterward, I stopped hunting for a while because dead animals do nothing interesting. I had become preoccupied with the grace of garter snakes, the luxuriance of skunk cabbage, the quickness and music of pale green frogs.

I might have forgotten about hunting if I hadn't met a kid named Bobby Marvin, who wanted a friend like me and had nothing to lose— frail, freckled, asthmatic Bobby, the son of a schoolteacher but not what other teachers would call a good boy. More than once we skipped school together. He raised garter snakes (he liked them because they bore live young) and he gigged frogs, fished, ran a trapline for muskrats, and hunted squirrels with a loose-jointed old single-shot .22 rifle. A misfit, like me. He took me into the woods and taught me important things like how to examine bugs, skip stones on water, forget to be home on time.

My father gave me a Benjamin air rifle that was a lot more powerful than my BB gun. Eight strokes of its pump handle forced enough air into its compression chamber to send a pellet deep into a squirrel. I became good with it, shooting it in our yard, where I couldn't use Bobby's .22. I could stand under a tree and hit the head of a squirrel forty feet overhead. So could Bobby. I hope he still can, wherever he is. It was about then that a black man named George Jelks, who worked for my father, taught me how to cook squirrel and rabbit and raccoon, and showed me how a dog should hunt. I don't know whether he knew I loved him, and I don't believe I ever thanked him.

There were farms just outside of town then. One morning I sat alone at the edge of a woodlot bordering a cornfield, watching chipmunks load up their cheek pouches and dart home into crevices in a low stone fence. After a while I realized that all the chipmunks had disappeared. Then I saw a weasel working its way along the top of the stones like a rippling ribbon. Its long, thin body arched and then it pounced into a crevice. It was the first weasel I'd ever seen in the wild, and I was astonished that it was active after daylight. I sat for a long time but it never reappeared. Then I slowly realized that something else was moving close to me at the edge of the corn. I guess I must have heard a scratching. It was a hen pheasant pecking and poking like a barnyard chicken. Slowly, silently, I tugged a half-eaten sandwich of salami and rat cheese from my jacket pocket and took a bite. The hen paid no attention. She had settled down between rows of stubble and was sunning herself. I crumbled my bread and tossed crumbs in her direction.

She had to have seen me, smelled me, heard me, but she showed no interest and no fear. After a few minutes she stood up and pecked about, gradually working her way toward me. She was picking corn kernels, grit, and invisible specks of things off the moist earth. I never saw her pick a crumb of the bread. Why should she? Yet I told myself I had befriended a wild bird and was feeding her, that I was such a miraculous woodsman that wild creatures did not fear me. At any moment she would fly up to perch on my shoulder. When she was about six or eight feet from me, she turned, ran toward a row of stubble, nearly collided with a cornstalk, and bustled into the air with a great flapping of wings and venting of whitish excrement.

I still saw her as a wild creature I had befriended, but now she was also an elusive wild creature, my quarry, the woodchuck I had sneaked up on and the bear I had tracked in my dreams. That winter I set a Number 1 Victor Jump Trap very amateurishly on the sandy bank of a nearby creek, baited it for muskrat with a piece of apple, and caught one toe of a hen pheasant instead of a muskrat's foot. As I approached, the hen stood on her free leg, digging into the sand, trying to yank her other leg free. Abruptly she stopped pulling and just stood on her one leg, a bizarre statuette, her head cocked to the side, staring at me in terror with the eye that faced me, her wings slightly spread. Her long tail jabbed into the sand, the longest feather broken. There was no reason to think this was the same pheasant I had tried to feed, but I was sure it was. I was sure I recognized her. I tossed my jacket over her and tried to hug it down while stepping hard on the trap spring. It was my leather aviator's jacket, my best birthday present, but I didn't care if I tore it. I had to free her. She struggled frantically, throwing off the jacket, flapping her wings mightily, pecking at my face, trying to tear me with the talons of her free leg while thrashing about on her side. Then the trap opened just a little and I lost my balance and sat in the sand, showering myself with grit. She was gone. I laughed and waved. I had grit in my left eye, and just below it one of her scratches stung from lower lid to lower cheek. I was cold and muddy, but I would reach home before my parents did, and I would change my clothes. The scratches? Why tell them the story, not knowing how grown-ups would react? I could say I had tripped in some briers. I put on my jacket. With my sleeve I rubbed blood and mud from my cheek, and although I never could carry a tune I began whistling.

Years later, in British Columbia, I watched a grouse feign injury, hobbling across a logging road, dragging one wing piteously, to distract my attention from her chicks hiding in the brush. Another time, in New York, I saw a hen turkey fly off her nest at the base of a big pine, her wings thundering, when a fox came too close. Miraculously, I thought, the fox paid no attention to bird or nest. The fox was mousing and very soon went on its way, and the turkey came down out of the trees to settle again on her sixteen—*sixteen*—great buffy freckled eggs. Neither the fox nor the turkey knew I was there. Pheasant, grouse, turkey, fox, turkey eggs, I felt the same bond with them, they had become part of me and I had become part of their private universe: life, death, and joy hiding in the sand and brush. Who was it that wrote "Hope is the thing with feathers / that flutters in the soul . . ."? A fine poem. Emily Dickinson, I think. Does it matter? Is the immortality in the writer or the writing? Here in the woods it is not in the actor but in the act.

I suppose every pilgrim's progress hides a Slough of Despond, periods in every life when things go all awry. A period like that began for me one winter and lasted three years. That first winter I was living in a pleasant town, working for myself, and had no one but myself to blame. I decided I had better get me to the woods. St. Hubert, patron of huntsmen, tried it in 683 and was rewarded with a vision: in the Forest of Freyr he saw a mighty stag with a glowing crucifix between its antlers. Why, then, has God neglected to write out an ironclad guarantee that all such retreats will succeed? This one didn't for me.

One day I hunted grouse and moved not a bird, though my dog worked well. The woods are often full of sound, but not a squirrel crackled the leaves, not a catbird mewed nor a woodpecker rapped, and no breeze ruffled the boughs or creaked the trunks. That afternoon it rained. I like rain, but I didn't then, and the drops clung to my glasses and trickled down the back of my neck like slowly melting ice pellets.

A couple of nights later the temperature dropped and in the morning snow covered the ground. With Bob Stoutenburgh—a chortling prankster when caged in a house, a quiet friend in the woods—I went to kill a deer amid the gray hardwoods and green-black conifers of Pike County's Poconos. In the dark I found my stand at the base of a double-trunked tree, not bothering to clear away the leaves and twigs, as there would be no noise if I shifted my feet in the snow; just sitting on my day pack, leaning against the tree, warm enough in my down and wool, drowsing until daylight. I was awakened by a shot, off to my right and up the ridge, where Bob had his stand. Ordinarily I wouldn't have moved, but in the silencing snow I could get there fast. I found him dressing out a small buck with six-inch spike antlers. He wanted no help, and there was no need to drag the deer out to the road until later. He wiped his knife, washed his hands in the snow, sat down with me, and shared his coffee, which should have been therapy enough.

The little angers at an out-of-joint world should have loosened like caked snow sliding off spruce boughs in the sun. Instead the angers clung—not melting snow but wingless bugs probing the edges of concentration, crawling, tickling my scalp from inside, nibbling at my nerves. A wet, heavy snow began to fall. The flakes melted on my glasses and spattered on the objective lens of my riflescope. Naturally, goddamnit, I told myself, naturally I've got no lens caps.

Down below in the basin, hunters were moving deer. Even in the muffling snow we could hear a startled animal blundering through the woods toward us. It appeared abruptly—a fine, thick-necked, wide-antlered, blue-gray buck, walking straight toward me, then veering slightly, then pausing just behind a tree that blocked my view so that all I could see was a tree trunk with an antler jutting from each side of it: St. Hubert's crucifix grown monstrous. The buck moved clear of the tree and stopped again. Having seen or heard something alien to its world, it stood turning its head one way and then another, snow flecking its back with white, steam rising from its flanks. Nervously the deer raked the snow with its right forefoot. I am not a panicky hunter; I do not go catatonic with buck fever. But I cheeked the rifle and saw only a foggy blur through the wet scope. The deer wasn't forty yards away. I could have killed it with a shotgun. Sighting over the scope, I squeezed the trigger, and in the same instant the deer was gone and Bob howled in anguish. "Sweet Jeeeeeesus! You clipped bark three feet over his back." And—to hell with the details—that was the end of the hunt.

I leave superstition to the religious, and joke about jinxes. I felt the beginning of a long one coming on. We had some meat in the freezer, my wife and I, and enough income to get us through the winter, but I felt this jinx. I've read that ballplayers invariably, sooner or later, suffer from long slumps. I hope so.

The jinx brought on a lot of childhood memories, and mostly the sour kind. It was almost like being back in junior high or high school. We're told from infancy on about our sacred duty to fit in, to be team players—not misfits like Bobby Marvin and me. Bobby and me hunting frogs and squirrels: those memories were far from sour, yet they did not relieve the slump that I now recognized unequivocally as my jinx. Self-employment didn't require me to be much of a team player, but the achievements seemed trivial and the money came in erratically while the bills arrived in an unrelenting torrent. I accepted a job in Oklahoma and moved my family there. It didn't take long for everyone in the Oklahoma company to see that I might be capable but was not a team player. Funny thing about northeastern Oklahoma: no one was ever born there; they all come from Summit. Who says you can't go home again?

My new boss invited me on a deer hunt. He and I and several others met before daylight and drove to the woods. By the time we split up to take our stands I was feeling nervous and resentful, convinced that I was playing a command performance. I knew the boss didn't mean to do that to me, it just happened. Somehow he had given himself the impression that I was a Hunting Wizard. The Official Company Wizard of the Woods, I thought, shoved onstage to demonstrate. Demonstrate what? How to listen to a woodpecker's drumwork? How to watch a striped skunk waddle and undulate over a rocky ridge in the dawn light? How to go to sleep on stand or miss a buck at forty yards as I had the year before?

Alone on stand, I had the office with me, and the demons of my mind were in fine jeering form that day: "Hey, Hunting Wizard, they expect you to come out dragging a deer. How about that? Some smart-ass woodsman you turned out to be—an impresser of bosses, a fat-ass deskbound bumbler who gets lost in the woods, you simple turd, you wouldn't know a buck's snort from a wet-lunch snort. Christ."

At ten to five—time to leave—a fat, wide-antlered buck appeared out of nowhere and stood before me like an apparition. I was on one leg, leaning over, lifting my day pack off the ground and running its strap up my arm, getting ready to head out. My rifle leaned against a tree. I had a pipe in my mouth. The buck stared. I waited for the beast to turn its head, look the other way. I wondered how long I could hold my off-balance position without moving. I began to tremble and was sure the buck would flag its tail and get the hell out of there. A whitetail deer can see a man blink at forty yards or more. This one stood at forty yards or less. Finally the animal began to turn and I rushed my move. As I brought the rifle up, the stock slammed the pipe out of my mouth, showering ash over my eyeglasses. I couldn't find the deer in the scope. Sighting over the scope, I let off a shot. I needed no companion to say it this time, I said it myself. "Sweet Jeeeeeesus! You clipped bark three feet over his back."

It was getting dark; time for the Official Wizard to emerge from the woods as the Court Buffoon. The others must have heard the shot, and I would have to tell them the story or come up with a better one. To hell with making up stories. Halfway out of the woods, I saw a fat possum swaying in a spindly sapling. All right, if they want a Court Buffoon they'll have a Court Buffoon. I walked onto the road swinging a dead possum by its tail. And I loathe possum meat.

The jinx deepened. I was a company man now and I had to shave every morning, and one morning I spat at my face in the mirror. That night I shouted at my son, and when my wife gently laid her hand on my arm I snarled, "Quit your damn nagging." I would have to leave soon, if only for a little while. I would have to go somewhere, even knowing that the jinx would crawl into my luggage, would be with me until something helped me beat it. Something like reaching the bottom of this depression and not caring anymore. Letting the caring go, the way compressed air sighs and fizzes out of a release valve.

I numbed myself with work while waiting for Wyoming's deer and antelope seasons to open. The night before I left, I worked until well past midnight, then drove home and packed. I locked the gun case and crammed the last items of gear into a duffel bag, slept for a couple of hours, and caught my plane for Cheyenne. I knew the jinx flew with me, and I began to believe it would take some tangible form. I even hoped so, for then, I felt, it could be exorcised. Somewhere below me in the plane, dozing and waiting as I dozed and waited, my jinx must be bulging my duffel or my gun case. I did not know that, in a sense, it had already taken form, that it did not ride in the bag or case because it was a silly little thing I had forgotten to pack—the removable clip that was so nicely constructed to hold a second, third, and fourth shot in my battered old bolt-action rifle.

Unpacking in Cheyenne, I discovered its absence and almost as quickly discovered that a clip of the right model and caliber was not to be found in Wyoming. To obtain a replacement or have the original shipped from home would cost me a day of hunting. That was unthinkable. Strangely, I felt no anger at myself—only amusement and relief. My jinx had metamorphosed, and in its new manifestation had, indeed, assumed a tangible, ridiculous form—a missing clip, not some vague social alienation, no pressure inside the mind, just a simple goddamn handicap. Something easy. Something real, a handicap to be ignored, like the temptation to join the team or quit smoking. Screw the clip. Without it I had a single-shot rifle, I would be making one of those famous one-shot hunts, though involuntarily. Miss the first time and you lose. You get no second chance unless by some astonishing quirk of good fortune. Beautiful. Let's do it.

My partner on the first leg of the hunt—a quest for a good antelope—was a friend named Merritt Benson, and on the first day and night we would be accompanied by his sweetheart, his future bride Margaret. Magee, he called her fondly. I like people like Merritt: lean, young, sandy, serious, apt to be a bit weathered-looking toward the end of the season. Undecayed youth with an adult mustache. He can talk or listen. Earnest youth. It was our first hunt together, but I knew we'd get along. And Magee too: big eyes; the soft angularity of pretty young girls; a good voice, a good laugh. The quiet type, I suppose, but not self-effacing like some of the quiet ones. Resilient enough to like people. Merritt had taught her to shoot and was teaching her to hunt.

The first day out was Magee's, because she had to get back to town by the next evening to teach a Bible class or some such thing. I spent the day exploring and glassing the plains, liking the muted tones, the size of the rolling prairie, the rough irregularity of the terrain that looked so smooth in the hazy distance. I thought of the sea. I liked the sight and smell of the sage, and the numbers of jack-in-the-box jackrabbits, and the single lumbering sage grouse I saw, and the numbers and incredible fleetness of the pronghorn antelope, which made me think no more of the sea but of African plains game.

We were about an hour out of Medicine Bow, at a campsite overlooking a wide, shallow basin of amber and greenish-gray prairie. Sprinkled over the basin like wildflowers—as small as golden sage blossoms seen through the wrong end of a telescope—were loose clusters of russet and white dots, bands of pronghorn antelope against the distant hillocks. A few of them grazed their way closer, and every so often I saw one flash a burst of white, flaring the rosette of its rump patch, an alarm signal twinkling like a heliograph. Almost invariably, that animal and those nearby would then run, sometimes a short way, sometimes beyond the far screening hillocks. They streamed along, not bobbing like mule deer but with their backs nearly level, their bursts of speed effortless, a perfection of nature. I spotted a couple of hunters on the prairie, but could not tell what it was that sent any given band of animals into flight. I had the distinct impression that some of them were running just for the sheer hell of it.

Alert though the animals were, Magee could have rested her rifle over the hood of the slaty-blue pickup truck and killed one at, say, three hundred yards or so. She had learned to shoot, she carried a rifle that could do the job, and pronghorns are easier to approach in a vehicle than on foot—as most plains animals are. But that was not the way of our hunt. She was on foot, as I would be the next day. She would walk and glass and walk some more until she found an animal she wanted, and then she would get within range by slithering on her elbows and belly, rubbing her forearms raw and bruised as she inched forward, using every clump of sage, every rock, every knoll and gully for cover. There is something gratifying about sweating for one's meat.

No such gratification was to be hers that day. Back in camp that evening, she slumped to the ground, bedraggled. No wonder, I thought—it couldn't have been any cinch keeping up with that coltish lope of Merritt's all day. But her eyes shone in a way I'd seen before in others—the glow of a hard day of stalking without blunder or calamity, with all the easy assurance of having left the manufactured world to rejoin the real world and work the senses and muscles and be just another predatory animal, an integral part of the vast organic whole.

We made a cooking fire and lay on the pebbly ground, elbow-propped like Romans at an ancient feast, chewing venison chops and thick bread and salad and washing it down with a sharp, almost meaty Bordeaux. We used no tent, just sleeping bags, and the stars that night were so brilliant, so profuse that their light awakened me sometime after midnight. Behind us, behind a couple of game poles, were pale, spindly aspens on a gentle slope, and beyond them black conifers, blacker than the horizon under the stars. Hunters used the game poles to hang their "goats," as antelope are called out there, and skin them and remove the lower legs and put the final touches to the dressing-out, and slip protective cheesecloth game bags over the carcasses and let them hang there, cooling. The scraps of bone and ragged meat, sinew, and hide were lugged up the slope and tossed on the other side, where nature would quickly begin the recycling process.

Maybe it wasn't the stars that woke me. Maybe it was the coyotes, yelping and howling on the other side of the slope, less than a couple of hundred yards away. The recycling had begun. The howling told of something, I wondered what. Just hunger sated, perhaps, and an impulse to comment on a fine meal. Glee and a full belly. The fellowship of a good full group howl. I wished I had thought to howl when I had mopped up the juice with a final chunk of bread and downed the last swallow of Bordeaux. I clambered out of the sleeping bag, walked off a little way to relieve my suddenly strained bladder, thought about strolling out on the prairie under the stars, and immediately changed my mind as the cold penetrated my long underwear.

"Unsilent night, holy night . . . every night is holy and there is peace on earth where the stars sing, the coyotes sing, the grateful earth rejoices, and the mind hears carols in October or July." At the moment I didn't need the comfort of my atheism, and I fell asleep recalling bits and phrases from a Psalm: *"Sing . . . all the earth . . . Let the heavens rejoice, and let the earth be glad. . . . Let the field be joyful, and all that is therein . . . all the trees of the wood rejoice."*

The next morning Magee killed her antelope, a small buck, so small when she knelt beside its body that the remorse hit her harder than it should have. Watching her, I felt a sudden irrational guilt and wondered if somehow I had jinxed Magee as well as myself. Distant size is hard to judge on the open plains. All she said was, "It was a young one, wasn't it?" In an instant she had come to know about the human hunter's sympathy, empathy in fact, for that which breathed and ate and will be eaten. Then she left, to teach her evening Bible class.

We watched her rumble down a dirt road in her little beetle of a car. We raised a glass of beer in her honor, and went hunting.

We had walked less than a mile when Merritt spied a fine head in a band of about two dozen pronghorns atop a hill, silhouetted against the now graying sky and gazing in our direction as if taunting us, daring us to attempt an approach. After a few seconds they disappeared, slowly, nonchalantly, over the brow of the hill. We followed them up and down hills and rock-strewn ravines until my thighs ached, and always the herd faded back and away, drawing us. The next hill was steep and jagged with eroded gullies and rubble. Merritt's steady, loping walk took him up the hill faster than I could follow and I had to stop for a minute, rest, and get my wind back. I called to him that I would come when I could. He called back that he would top the rise, glass the herd again, and wait. I regretted the beer and my last five cigars as I went after him—not after the antelope anymore, really, but after him, taking my time.

He was sitting, slowly scanning the hills with his binocular. He waved toward the horizon and shrugged. "They were gone when I got up here. Damned if I know where." Yes, I thought, still jinxed, and then had a contradictory, unexpected thought: I wasn't unhappy. I was very happy. I was panting and coughing and my legs hurt and I was happy. Jinxed, hell. Except for the moment when I had feared that Magee might cry, I had felt right ever since the coyotes had howled in the night. It was just possible that the exorcism had begun.

We walked back to the truck. It wasn't as long a hike as I thought it would be. We got in and drove across the prairie, scouting. Merritt had a spotting scope affixed to the left window, and I had my binocular, and we made frequent stops.

In midafternoon we spotted a big band of antelope, actually two clusters feeding together, totaling perhaps three dozen animals. In the smaller cluster was a good buck, its black horns jutting high and wide above its ears. The two groups seemed to be drifting apart, the larger cluster moving over the hills to the right, the smaller cluster heading toward a shallow ravine on the left. Merritt pointed and I nodded. Taking care not to slam the doors, we got out and walked to the ravine, keeping the low hills between us and the herd. If we crouched and moved quietly, we should be able to walk the ravine, come up over its rim, and intercept the pronghorns. Merritt led the way. I was panting as we climbed the side of the ravine where Merritt thought I would have a shot. I was puzzled. I was sure we hadn't walked far enough, we'd still be hundreds of yards from the animals.

I had been watching Merritt hunt, though, and decided to put more trust in his judgment than in mine. As I climbed to him, he pointed ahead and gestured to me to keep low and come on silently. Finally I was almost next to him, my head level with his upper back, and I peered over a skeletal tangle of ancient sage. Forty yards away my buck stood like a statue, almost facing me, its great dark left eye fixed precisely in my direction. I knew it didn't see me. Perhaps it had heard a rustle. Perhaps it was just keeping a lookout.

The roof of my mouth was dry and my breath rasped in my throat. I could feel my chest heaving. My hands, which never shake, were shaking. The short climb had winded me, but it was more than that. I have said I don't get buck fever, meaning I have never been too numbed by excitement to fire at a deer. But I have, many times, felt my wrists weaken when the morning's first geese came in over the decoys, and I knew at those times that I would miss my first shot and then settle down, and I was used to that, I wouldn't mind. Staring at the antelope, that feeling returned. I had a cartridge in the rifle's chamber. At this range there should be no need for a clip to hold a second, third, and fourth in reserve. Still, there was that feeling. I dug another cartridge from the shell holder in my pocket and stuck it between two fingers so that I could chamber a second round quickly. There was my antelope, standing forty yards from me, and I expected to miss. The hunter must control the kill, not let the kill control him. I felt as if the world had stopped, awaiting that pivotal instant that pales all other events, yet I was not in control.

"Can you shoot from the kneel?" Merritt whispered. Despite the breeze in our faces, I was surprised I could hear him and the antelope could not. I nodded, but I did not lower my haunch onto one solidly placed ankle and raise the opposite knee for support in a proper shooting kneel. Unaware of what I was doing, with all experience vanquished by this new quintessential experience, I knelt on both knees as if praying before my quarry in this open cathedral of prairie. I was on my knees, shooting offhand, an idiot's gambit. I missed the antelope at forty yards, the shot going just over the shoulder as the rifle wavered.

In that instant, I became calm. I had surpassed all the blunders of my hunting life, the crucial moment could not be retrieved, there was nothing more to lose, and I was calm again, even confident. The band of antelope ran, but not in a single direction as a herd normally does. They could not tell the direction of the sound, the source of alarm. Some of them scattered. Others, my buck among them, ran rearward and to my left for a short distance and then slowed to a nervous walk, milling about. I had the second chance, the rare second chance. My buck stood still, broadside but shielded by two does. Merritt tapped his left shoulder with his right hand. I knelt and rested my forward arm on his shoulder. It was a rock-solid shooting position. The two does moved. I did not hear my shot. I merely watched my buck collapse, as abruptly as if the animal had been slammed flat by a lightning bolt. Striking the ground, its body sent up a cloud of dust.

In my elation, I chambered another round, fired an offhand shot at a jackrabbit that had sat through this entire spectacle of disruption, and knew I'd missed the rabbit before the trigger was fully pressed. I laughed. Merritt went back for the truck while I began dressing out the buck. It was my first antelope. I lifted its head and examined its thick black horns and its dark buck's snout and cheek patches and the brown and white stripes on the upper neck. "God. How beautiful you are. Were and are." I stroked its coarse coat and then set to work with my knife, hesitantly, in awe of what had been created and destroyed. "Come on, you damn fool," I told myself, "it's no different from dressing a small deer," and my confidence came back with a tactile familiarity as my hands felt the hot paunch and blood.

It always surprises me how hot a newly killed animal is inside. Its machinery and mortality and mine—no difference of any consequence. And then I begin the job and grow comfortable with it, accepting it. Bob Stoutenburgh has killed more deer than I ever will, and evisceration still makes him queasy. I understand, but I raised Belgian hares and hunted cottontails when I was a little boy, and was too curious to merely slit them and spill their entrails on the grass as older people did. I dissected them. They felt nothing and I wondered how like them I might be inside. That impervious curiosity must be what the surgeon feels, and feels good feeling that way.

How odd that I could not look at a "benign" tumor a surgeon took out of my mother. "The size of a grapefruit," my father said, shaking his head and weeping. I didn't believe him. She was too forgiving, too loving to contain a horror. The surgeon, however, is all mechanic and pagan priest, and afterward dines heartily. Why should it be different for me, I thought, taking apart what I will eat? I have a compassion the lion lacks, but I am a predatory animal and content with what I am. I have good canine teeth and once I had a gallbladder, the gallbladder of a meat eater, unlike my poor herbivorous prey. . . . By God, what a fine thick ham that little antelope has!

That evening, Merritt and I ate diced antelope heart simmered with onions in a wine sauce while we watched a wall of cloud and snow blow toward us from the horizon, and then we broke camp.

I left Medicine Bow unjinxed, very unjinxed, and went west almost to the Utah line to hunt mule deer with another friend, Jim Zumbo, a hairy, rough-hewn log of a man with a bushy black moustache and sometimes, on a hunt, an equally bushy beard, and forever loving, gleaming, carnivorous eyes and a toothy grin and a hat that must have been dragged through prickly pear. "Uncle Bob!" he bellowed, and threw his arms around me. I hugged him and planted a wet kiss on his porcupine cheek and asked if he'd been treating Lois right. He laughed and asked me for a cigar and I asked him if he had any dago red or schnapps in his gear. He did. We each took a great swallow of almost syrupy, throat-heating schnapps.

"Here we go," he said. "You ready to find the biggest-racked old Roman-nosed mossy-backed buck in the mountains?"

"Damn right. The Dago and the Sheeny strike again!"

"Can't beat that team," he said, and we clinked our cups together.

"Bobby Marvin with black whiskers."

"Huh?"

"Never mind. Just thinking about an old friend. Haven't seen him for years."

"Hey, listen, don't be killing any puny fork-horns, we've got some big deer in the mountains, *good* antlers, we don't need to settle for anything less than a four-point hat rack on each side."

There were others on the hunt, good people and important to me and others but not to the final part of what I have to tell now. We got into the mountains, and it snowed the first morning. Jim is a hard walker. I once watched him walk up a mountain while way off to my right eight or ten wild horses walked up the same slope. Jim reached the top first. He would slow down for me, of course, but he and I both like to hunt alone sometimes, so on that first morning he went his way and I went mine.

I climbed a great bald dome. At the top I found that a wide portion of it was as level and bare and long as a football field. On the far side was an overhanging ledge just behind some junipers, a nice place to take a stand and not get blanketed with snow. I started toward it, then stopped when I heard a muffled sound, like stones kicked loose and rolling. Over a hump strode two does, and behind them a fat fork-horned young buck. They had no notion that another creature shared their pasture. With the snow and no wind, they couldn't see or scent me. I centered the cross hairs on the buck's shoulder and watched him come closer. *"Don't be killing any puny fork-horns."*

"Who needs to?" I asked myself. "And for Christ's sake, who needs to play God, aiming and rejecting like the governor giving the condemned a last-minute reprieve? To hell with that." I lowered the rifle and just watched the deer coming nearer. The leading doe stopped and looked at me, trying to make out what I could possibly be. I waved and shouted. I don't recall the words. All three deer turned and bounded out of sight the way they had come.

"See any?" Jim asked when we met for lunch out at the road's end.

"Yeah. I passed up a fork-horn."

"You *what?*"

For three days Jim worried that I would go home without deer meat just because I'd taken his advice literally. After breakfast one morning, he chewed one of my cigars in half, and that evening, when I brought in no deer, he finished off the schnapps and started on the dago red. I was beginning to relish this business. If I played it right and didn't overdo it, I could needle him at least twice a day, before and after the hunt. Good banter, nothing serious. And as long as we hunted hard, gave ourselves and our world every chance, I didn't care about scoring.

The weather warmed, each day was prettier than the previous one, and the mountains here were different from the antelope prairies to the east. They were splotched with green—pinyon pine and juniper and such, and low tangles of mountain mahogany and plants I didn't know, and grasses. The land looked greener each day, as if spring had come.

"How're things going back home?" he asked on the third day.

"About the same," I said, "but just now, walking around the hills here, I decided it's time for a change." I hadn't known until I spoke that I had decided anything at all, or even thought about anything.

"What kind of change?"

"I'm gonna quit the job, go back to free-lancing. I guess this is the only team I'm fit to play on."

"I'll be go to hell."

"Yeah. Well, now let's hunt."

I was hunting harder. Evidently I'd also decided I wanted a deer, and the one bullet in the rifle no longer worried me. With the second shot at the antelope I had recaptured some power of concentration that I didn't understand but accepted with gratitude.

I thought of a story I'd once read, an account by John Muir about a very dangerous exploration of a glacier. Accompanied by a small dog, he had set out that morning despite an oncoming storm. The snow came, and Muir discovered that to reach safety he would have to cross a narrow ice bridge over a deep crevasse. He was concerned for his own life and the dog's, but there was no choice. As he chopped toeholds with a small ice ax, he realized he had risen to a new degree of concentration. I couldn't remember Muir's exact words until later, when I looked them up: "At such times one's whole body is eye, and common skill and fortitude are replaced by power beyond our call or knowledge."

I had trouble remembering the words, but I felt their meaning. My being out there, unconsciously sorting things out, had somehow replaced what little skill I possessed with another kind of power. My deer would come. I needed only one bullet in the rifle. When the time came, my whole body would be eye.

But on the fourth day, the last day, I was troubled. The members of the party had voted unanimously to come in early and drive like mad for town to have dinner at a restaurant with the Zumbo family. Here I was in my little wilderness, once again a make-believe wilderness, back to being little Running Deer, with steam heat and restaurants two hours away. Resentment was coming up as sour as bile. Maybe I'd find my deer that morning, maybe I wouldn't. If not, I was supposed to meet Zumbo and these three other clowns out at the road, at a designated spot, at three-for-Christ's-sake-thirty in the afternoon, with an hour and a half of good hunting time left.

High on a pine and juniper ridge at two o'clock, however, my resentment evaporated in the warm sun. I knew again that Zumbo was my friend. No clown, that one. The others were my friends too. How beautiful the woods smelled. It was public land, Bureau of Land Management range, and out where the ridge widened into an open flat, cattle were grazing. Intruders in my natural world, the domestic impinging on the wild, yet the day was too soft for resentment, and I found myself liking all of it, even the odor of their dung.

I was watching for deer, and it was a fine spot for a stand. The junipers were high and luxuriant. I'd picked pocketfuls of the berries to take home for meat seasoning. The ridge was splashed with greens and browns, purplish-gray rusty juniper berries with a chalky patina like that on dark grapes, black loam, gray and orange rocks. My spot overlooked a grassy basin, a bowl rimmed with ridges like mine. The sky was turquoise over and around snow-white cotton-candy cumulus clouds. The basin was gold and green, the ridges dappled with sun and shadow.

When I looked at my watch, it was time to start for the road. Damn! But now the twinge of resentment was mild. I felt that I would still, after all, get my deer on this last day, unlikely though it might seem if likelihood must be measured by logic. I gazed one last time at the green basin and bright sky before turning back into the woods. Again I thought of that story by Muir, of a passage describing a storm. My day was balmy, but the great white cumulus clouds reminded me of snow, and the ridge was a vast cathedral, as the prairie had been, though I was not kneeling now. "What a psalm the storm was singing," Muir wrote, "and how fresh the smell of the washed earth and leaves, and how sweet the small voices . . ."

Here was the church, here only, the church where God was allowed to give the orders and decide, where God was allowed to be God because there was no congregation around to stop such nonsense. Where

God was allowed to be worshipped by people in out-of-style hunting clothes, and prayers were silent utterances of awe and love and gratitude, not bids for handouts. Where God was allowed to be worshipped by Catholics or Hindus or Jews or Presbyterians or Pentecostal Pantheists or even, by God, by atheists like me. Surely, surely, what a psalm the wilderness sings. What a hymn of the unrepentant.

Rejoice, rejoice. Emmanuel shall come to thee, O Israel.

I headed out through the woods, reaching the road before the appointed time, and a couple of hundred yards down the shoulder there was the whole crew, lounging around the truck, with the big chow box open, everyone eating, guns stowed, everyone sipping wine. "Peabrains," I muttered. "Some hunters. I bet they've been here half an hour getting tanked."

Seeing me, they called and waved. I didn't respond. I still had five minutes—and it wouldn't matter a damn anyway if I was an *hour* late. I crossed to the woods on the other side and heard a sound ahead of me and didn't think it was steers. I went forward crouched, very slowly, becoming aware that I was on the wooded rim of another open basin. Trying to move like a cougar, I inched forward and peered over the rim, and all of my body was eye.

Two bucks were just coming off the wooded rim a hundred yards to my left, a big-bodied fork-horn in the lead, followed by a fine four-point buck. They saw me and I saw them in the same instant. The four-pointer wheeled, and I knew as my rifle came up that he would be back in the woods before the stock touched my cheek. The fork-horn, having left the woods first, was farther out in the open—too far to turn tail, his instincts must have told him—and he was halfway down the slope at a dead-out run as my rifle came up and swung ahead of him. The old rifle, sometimes so heavy and awkward, moved like an integral part of my body, my eye, my arms sweeping ahead of the running deer.

Again I did not hear the shot. The recoil made me lose sight of the target, so that the deer vanished as the rifle went off. In other circumstances, I would have looked down the slope, trying to find the deer, to verify whether I had hit it. But I knew. I ran straight down to the boulder and clump of juniper that hid the buck where it had fallen. There it lay, on its side, dead, with its forelegs horizontal and still running, hooves tracing circles in the air. I had to stop that motor-reflex spasm of life after death. I couldn't watch it. I rammed another cartridge into the chamber and delivered a superfluous coup de grace, disrupting the equally superfluous electric charges coursing through a beast's dead nerves.

I haven't shot another running deer. I don't know whether I will. How can limitations—mine, Red's, Charley's, Bobby Marvin's, anyone's—be foretold out there amid the psalm singing and the running deer?

SEASONS OF THE HUNTER
ALFRED A. KNOPF, 1985

Baron Bror von Blixen-Finecke was the stereotype of the professional hunter in Africa. He guided safaris and hunted Africa between 1913 and the late 1930s, at a time when it was okay to use the term "white hunter." Blixen was a superb hunter at a time when the game laws in the bush were either lenient or nonexistent. Here's a tale that describes Blixen and his attitudes toward lions both as the hunted and as unusual pets. It's a unique piece of writing. Blixen had a strange reputation, to say the least. It seems he hunted women with the same vigor with which he hunted game. This ultimately led to his divorce from Baroness Karen von Blixen-Finecke, perhaps better known as Isak Dinesen, author of "Out of Africa." Here's old Africa at its best.

The Lion—His Majesty and King

by BARON BROR VON BLIXEN-FINECKE

OF all the faithful animals I have had during my pretty varied life, there is none that can in any way be compared with Kom. It was somewhere about the spring of 1925 when a native appeared with him and laid him in my arms—the sweetest little creature in the world, soft and pleasant to hold, with four feeble little pegs which could hardly bear him across the floor—a little lion prince, only a few days old. The Negro had found him behind a bush out in the country and had run home for dear life with him, desperately afraid lest the royal mother should come after him and give him a nip from behind.

"I thought the cub would be happy with you, *bwana*," he said simply.

And I venture to say that he was. I lavished as much tenderness and care on him as it was in my power to do—in the dependent position in which, for my sins, I then was. Untoward events had compelled me to sign a labor contract as carter at a sawmill; from early morning to late evening I was out in the wood with my team of oxen, but Kom was always with me. He was quite independent at the age of six weeks, and his intelligence was more developed than that of a puppy of the same age. And how he could play! There was no limit to his powers of invention in thinking of mischievous pranks. Funniest of all was when he came into illegal possession of newspapers and books. In two swift seconds they were transformed into grotesque lumps of paper with which he played ball to his heart's delight—until the unpleasant hour of discovery struck, for there was something else which struck, and that he did not like.

Punishment is an inevitable part of every affectionate upbringing, and naturally Kom experienced it. It was not pleasant; but it had to be. He knew exactly what was allowed and what was not, but temptation was too strong for him when he caught sight of a bundle of newspapers, which made such a nice crackling noise when he tore it into a thousand pieces with his sharp claws. Temperamental like all cats, he could not bear punishment; he crept into a corner, wept like a child for long after, and would have nothing to do with his master—firmly determined to heap coals of fire upon his head. On such occasions it was best to take no notice of him—if I had shown the least sign of regret at having punished him he would have got the upper hand of me. If, on the contrary, I left him alone and let him have his cry out he never bore malice—incredibly sociable creature as he was—and when happy relations were restored between us he was beside himself with joy.

At six months Kom was a fine big lion, but not once during those first six months had the real lion's claws emerged from his pads. He went about among the oxen as a good friend, and they were no more afraid of him than of a fly—they did not even notice his leonine smell. But on one occasion the instinct of a wild beast flared up in Kom. I had been obliged to shoot an ox which had broken its leg, and Kom was present at the execution. The instant the ox fell and the smell of blood came to Kom's nostrils, he was upon the fallen animal with one stately bound and a kingly roar; he began to lap its blood, and it was not advisable for any of the blacks to try to approach him. He defended his booty till he had eaten his fill, and when it was over he slipped back into civilized life as if nothing had happened.

Kom was perfectly at home among the belts and saws in the mill, and the black workmen took no more notice of him than if he had been a gentle big dog. He seemed positively to enjoy himself among the hissing, screaming machinery. But he did not like the sirens. One morning he happened to be between two of them when they blew simultaneously to summon the men to work. Little Kom was terrified. He set off, a good deal faster than the Mombasa-Nairobi train, for the place where he always sought shelter when danger threatened—my bed. My bed was his sanctuary; he slept in it at night and crept under it by day when he felt his security in any way endangered.

Kom loved a ride in a car, and used to stand inside with his paws on the front seat. Once he tried jumping out when the car was at full speed, but he did not try it again. He had caught sight of a fat hen, and the temptation was too strong—at her! But was he killed? Not a bit of it. He crawled up out of a huge cloud of dust, a bit dazed, with his tail between his legs and no hen. If ever anyone was glad to get into a car it was Kom on that occasion.

We remained together for many months after this, but when my contract came to an end we had to part. I puzzled my head as to what I was to do with my friend Kom. I could not, unhappily, take him with me, and it would have been cruel to shut him up in a cage. To hand him over to the blacks was out of the question; they could not manage Kom. Should I restore him to the freedom he had never lost—in other words, let him return to the steppe? That too would have been a merciless act, for a cruel fate would have met him there. The only way out was to let him end his days in a painless manner—and this was done.

Kom taught me a great deal in his short life. All that I know of the lion's mentality I got from him; and it was of inestimable value to me later: I came to know the lion's capricious temper, which can change from good to ill humor like thunder and sunshine; I learned his language and found out whether it was rage, hunger, or love that sounded in his voice; and it is a consoling thought to me that all his days were happy and carefree.

IF I were to give a detailed account of all the lions I have shot or fired at, I fear that I should be too long-winded. I will content myself with relating some episodes which throw more or less light on the lion's mentality and his reactions in certain situations.

My earliest meeting with a lion was during my very first expedition in Africa, when I was out collecting workers for my coffee plantation. We had pitched camp near a water hole—a quiet, peaceful place it seemed, but nevertheless the night was a trifle disturbed. The tropical night symphony was in too full blast. The crickets chirped more furiously than usual—it sounds like a thousand bows at work behind the bridge of a violin; the jackals howled far off, and at times the air resounded with the beating of heavy wings. Suddenly there was a moment's silence. The invisible conductor had silenced the music for a fraction of a second to make the famous solo singer's interjection the more effective. There came the long-drawn, melodious roar of a lion, ending in a staccato "huh-uh-uh."

I listened to the sound with every nerve drawn tight, as when I used to lie in bed at Näsbyholm and listen to the thunder; and I wondered, just as I had done then: would the sound come nearer? Another rumbling sound, duller, angrier than the first, but at the same distance from the tent. What was the royal route tonight? There—for a third time! Right by the tent, if you please! Were we to receive a nocturnal visitor?

I glanced toward the corner where Fara Aden, my Somali boy—still in my service, by the way—had his sleeping place. Fara was awake too; I could see in the faint starlight that he had raised himself on his elbow. I nodded, and with noiseless movements we made ready to go out. While I was making sure that my rifle was in order I heard the lion again; the roaring suggested that he had turned and gone off in another direction.

Outside, it had become silent all at once; the tropical night was holding its breath, waiting for the sun. The stars were paling, the air had grown thinner. The black velvet curtain had been replaced by a dark, steel-gray silk veil which might be swept aside at any moment by the breaking of day.

Fara and I set off toward the line of rocks from which the last roar had come. But we had not gone many steps before the miracle happened. A red flame spurted up behind the rocks to eastward, and against the fiery background there stood out the silhouette of a splendid male lion, striding toward the rocks slowly, with head erect, to seek there a well-earned rest after the night's exertions. He did not honor us poor human reptiles with a look; he carried his admirably proportioned body with majestic strength and dignity—the King of Beasts.

"Piga, bwana, simba!" Fara whispered, and I knew very well that it meant: "Shoot, master, lion!" But I could not. The rifle remained under my arm.

One could not shoot a vision like that to pieces.

WHEN I first came to Africa people used to shoot lions at night from what is called a *boma,* a sort of shelter made of thorny branches, in which the hunter sat well protected against attacks from animals. The only risk to which one was exposed was that of being killed by the stench of the putrefying carcasses which were used to attract the lions. It was a rather unsportsmanlike form of shooting, which fortunately soon fell into disrepute among African hunters. Now all shooting is forbidden between sunset and sunrise, but there was a period between these two stages when a self-respecting hunter could find an opportunity of getting in a shot at a lion at night without using a *boma.* One killed a zebra for bait, sat down by the carcass with one's rifle, and waited.

It is of one of these nights that I write. I had learned from the natives that there was a fine male lion in the neighborhood, and although I had only that one night at my disposal, I decided to make

an attempt. I had rocks behind me, a spring in front, and between
me and it—about five yards away—lay the zebra.

I am not exactly what is called afraid of the dark, but I do not deny
that a certain percentage of my boldness disappears with the daylight.
It was an unusually dark night, with thick clouds, and I had not been
sitting there long before rain began to pour. In five minutes I was
like a drowned rat; cooling streams tickled my spine; there was a
splashing noise as soon as I moved a limb, the night cold began to
penetrate my marrow, and it was as dark as the inside of a black sack.
Cursing my idiotic idea—and all male lions into the bargain—I reckoned that I had at least half a dozen night hours of the same kind
before me.

After two hours of tropical rain, at last something happened. First
I heard the characteristic trampling of lions' paws on the drenched
ground, and, that there might be no misunderstanding, the scratching
sound was followed by a loud, clear roar only a few yards from my
right ear.

I beg your pardon—are there two of you? Yes, four pairs of paws
were moving down to the spring, about ten yards from my feet. The
lion as a rule drinks slowly, but long. I was prepared to have to wait
a good time, but this got on my nerves; did they mean to drain the
spring to the last drop? At last! Now they were licking their lips loudly
and with relish, as they took a few uncertain steps in my direction. I
could clearly hear the air being drawn in through their nostrils when
they snuffed—of course I could not see them. My heart had leaped
to my throat; I was afraid.

But nothing happened. I was not to experience, for the moment
at any rate, what it feels like to have a lion's body across one's neck
and five times four claws plus a few fangs through one's skin.

The strongest part of the third act of the drama was its dialogue.
The two lions moved off a few hundred yards nearer the back of the
stage and began to talk. They roared their replies and made a deaf-
ening noise. I was once daring enough to assert that no music can be
more beautiful than the roaring of a lion in the wilds of Africa. But
I should really have preferred any other kind of music imaginable
just then—and it seemed as if it would never end. They went on roaring at each other for two whole hours; it sounded exactly like a con-
nubial tiff.

Suddenly the conversation stopped. The rain stopped as unexpectedly as it had begun; the pall of clouds was suddenly cleft in two,
and a few stars began to blink drowsily. A dark shadow stole right up
to the dead zebra. Rifle to shoulder, a shot, a flash which lit up the
scene for a hundredth part of a second. But the shot was directly
followed by a roaring the like of which I have never heard, either

before or since. The leonine conversation just before was a mild zephyr in comparison with this thunderclap, which might have foretold an earthquake.

The epilogue of the drama was near, however the play was to end. I dared not lower my rifle to reload the first barrel—and it was a bit of luck for me that I did not. I saw the outline of a lion's head in movement and discharged the second barrel.

Dead silence. I reloaded swiftly and mechanically. The darkness thickened again. I listened. The crickets again raised their fiddlelike voices, the hyena called his mate far away. Had I really fired, or was it a dream? A dream. . . .

The birds' song at gray of dawn woke me. Nervous strain and weariness had claimed their due. I had fallen asleep where I sat, when all around me suddenly became quiet. But now I clearly remembered the events of the night and sprang up to see what had happened.

On my side of the zebra lay a lion with the most beautiful black mane I have ever seen—stone dead. He had received my bullet in his shoulder and died instantaneously. Across him—with hind legs on one side of his body and forelegs on the other, ready to spring—the lioness, his mate, lay stiff and cold. But so true to life was her attitude that if her tongue had not hung far out of her mouth, I should have thought her ready to attack at any moment to avenge her spouse.

She had defied death and peril without an instant's hesitation, though she knew very well that a few lithe bounds in the opposite direction would have saved her.

This wonderful feminine courage recalls to my memory—I make no comparisons, of course—another episode which also happened some years ago. During the war I was acting as a scout on the Tanganyika front, and on one occasion it became necessary to move off in haste. It was impossible to take the whole camp with us at once; I hurried on ahead, while Tanne, my wife, took command of the transport wagon, drawn by sixteen oxen, which was to follow rather more slowly.

On the third evening, just as they were preparing to pitch camp, there was a fearful disturbance among the oxen, which had been left quite alone for a few moments. Tanne hurried up and saw two lions, each of which had jumped on an ox's back. It need not be said that the teamsters had disappeared like phantoms, and my wife faced the two lions alone and unarmed, for, through an oversight, the rifles had been carefully stowed away among the baggage. But she had the heavy stockwhip, and with it she literally whipped the lions away from the oxen.

My wife made light of the incident.

"What else could I do?" she asked. "If I'd had a gun I'd have used it, of course; but the stockwhip isn't to be despised, as you see."

One of the oxen had been so severely mauled by the lion in those few seconds that it died of its wounds, but my wife's care succeeded in saving the life of the other.

It is not only peaceable oxen, however, that the lion attacks in this manner. I remember that once in the Tanga hills, when I was out shooting with a countryman of mine, we were crossing a valley when we suddenly heard a tremendous crashing and bellowing in the forest. Next moment a herd of about fifty buffaloes came thundering out from among the trees. We had to leap aside in order not to be crushed to pulp under the buffaloes' hoofs, and then we discovered the cause of the panic: on the back of the largest buffalo—a regular giant—rode a lion, with his claws round the buffalo's throat and his teeth in its neck. The Swede shot the lion, and in a way I thought this was a pity, for otherwise a rather strange battle between the king of beasts and one of the most dreaded of his vassals would certainly have been fought out on the open ground at the edge of the forest. Do not ask me whom I should have backed as winner. Although the lion had won the first round, it is not at all certain that he would have won the last.

SIMBA, the lion, is a creature of night and the plain, but he has no objection to any rock caves, copses, and undergrowth the plain may afford, where he can rest by day after his night's "work." He has no need to over-exert himself; the herds of gazelles, antelopes, and zebras that roam the endless African plains constitute his ample store of food; he has only to take what he wants. Ravenous as his appetite is, he need never be afraid of having to crawl to his lair hungry in the small hours.

He lives, on the whole, a pleasant family life. He contents himself as a rule with one wife at a time, but sometimes changes his mate. During the mating season His and Her Majesty go in company, and the family usually keep together till the cubs are grown up—thirteen or fourteen months. One often meets groups of four, five, or more animals; but old male lions with bad teeth usually live a solitary life.

It is sad, but not much is left of the old-time romance of the lion. The screen has destroyed it. I need only mention the name Serengeti for the reader to understand what I mean. Imagine an immense plain of eleven thousand square miles, which absolutely swarms with game on a fantastic scale. A large part of the fauna of Africa is represented here. I do not exaggerate if I say that over a million animals of different kinds can be seen from certain viewpoints: and the whole of this vast area has been a sanctuary since the beginning of 1936.

Practically all moving-picture films of African big game are made here. The lions have not merely grown accustomed to movie cameras—rather as my Kom became a household pet at the sawmill—but have come to like both them and the men who manipulate them. It is a case of "cupboard love." Simba has become accustomed to having food thrown to him from the cameramen's cars.

I shall never forget an incident in 1935, when I was traveling through these regions with a party of Americans. We had pitched camp in the morning, and it included a real kitchen, with every modern convenience. About three o'clock in the afternoon the cook came rushing in with his hair standing on end and reported that a lion had come into the kitchen. What was he to do? Should he drive it away?

"Give Simba food and he'll go when he's had enough," I advised. And Simba did. But afterward that lion followed our party as faithfully as a watchdog—and was never more than a hundred yards away from us. One should never be astonished at anything—nowadays! Early one morning I found four lions standing quenching their thirst in the bath in which I was going to have a dip. They went on drinking, slowly and deliberately, without taking the least notice of me.

Yes, that is what Serengeti is like. But Africa is large, and in other places Simba is still true to the classic picture we have formed of him. There he still ravages the herds and makes certain roads and regions unsafe for human beings. It is in these regions that lions are hunted, and lion hunting demands coolness, good trackers, and a sure eye. A wounded lion is, in my opinion, one of the most dangerous animals in the world. Like the great cat he is, he can make himself practically invisible even in short grass. He crouches ready to spring, and the attack comes with almost incredible swiftness. He kills, too, in the cat's way; he strikes his victim to the ground with one heavy blow of his paw, and then stops for a moment and looks round, as though considering the next step. There have been cases in which a revolver, drawn at the last second with lightning rapidity, has saved the hunter's life.

One of my neighbors, Colonel Gray, was the chief actor in one of the most marvelous escapes of which I have ever heard. He had sworn a feud against Simba for the simple reason that the lions could not be induced to leave his cattle in peace. Time after time the old man—Gray was sixty-five—postponed the execution of his resolve, but one morning, when he found that the four-legged robbers had killed his best heifer, he felt that the cup was full to overflowing. The colonel built himself a platform in a tree near one of the cattlefolds and began his watch an hour after nightfall.

Hour after hour passed without any of the robber band showing themselves. But just when the colonel had half decided to give it up, he caught sight of three creeping shadows moving in the direction of the fold. Criminals! He fired at all three of them, but in the darkness he was not sure of the result and resolved to await the dawn, which could not be far off.

In the first dim light of day he clambered down to the ground and found that he had killed two of the lions on the spot, while the third— from all indications badly wounded—had withdrawn to some brushwood. As the trail of blood showed plainly the route the beast had taken, the colonel decided to follow it up.

He did not need to search long; the lion was waiting for him and attacked him. Gray fired as the beast sprang, but did not hit it exactly where he meant to; the animal leaped on him, and so began a hand-to-hand fight which recalls Samson's Biblical contest with the lion. Two seconds later the colonel found himself disarmed; the lion tore the rifle out of his hand and flung it aside. Then it dug its teeth into the colonel's right hand and positively led its prey off toward the neighboring brushwood to make an end of him. The colonel, worn out by loss of blood and his exertions—as he himself told me next day—had no choice but reluctantly to go with the lion to the death which awaited him. But they had taken only a few steps when he felt the grip on his right hand weaken—and the lion fell to the ground dead. The last bullet had finally done its work.

Luckily Arusha hospital was only a few miles away, but as telephone and ambulance are still unknown luxuries in the depths of Africa, the colonel—despite the shock to his nerves, the loss of blood, and the horrible pain in his hand—had himself to drive his Ford to the hospital, an achievement that bears eloquent testimony to the coolness and presence of mind of this man of sixty-five. After a bare month's detention he was discharged from hospital, and in memory of the event he adorned one of his walls with the rifle, in the butt of which the lion's broken teeth had lodged. He also framed the story of Samson's duel with the lion and hung it up under the trophy.

AFRICAN HUNTER by Baron Bror von Blixen-Finecke. Translated from Swedish by F.H. Lyon. Peter Capstick, Series Editor. St. Martin's Press, Inc., New York. Copyright 1986 by Peter Hathaway Capstick.

It's hard to say what special quality makes an outdoor story a classic. Whatever it is, this story has it. Joan Tyler Fairbanks is a new author to me, but I know I'll never forget her name or her story. "Nat's Dog," Joan's first story, appeared in Sports Afield *in 1985, and after reading it, I knew it belonged in this book. It's a story about a special woman and an exceptional dog, and how they both handle a certain problem. If you can read this without shedding a few tears or getting a big lump in your throat, I can only assume that you missed out on the best part of life. I mean love, of course.*

Nat's Dog

by JOAN TYLER FAIRBANKS

ALL winter, spring, and summer Nat's dog had waited for him to come home. For hours each day she had sat in front of the picture window in the living room hoping for the sound of his truck tires on the gravel drive, the banging of the old Chevy door, May's voice calling brightly, "Nat, that you?"

She had seen the seasons change from her spot by the window. The first snowflakes falling gently, then faster and faster until they covered the ground with a paper-thin white icing. The big nor'easter that began the day after Christmas and continued fierce and howling for forty eight hours, leaving the house all but buried and May stranded for two more days until the plows got through.

Then winter had gentled into spring and the rains came and the world beyond the window was brown and muddy. When May would let her out in the morning she would pad carefully around the puddles, but still her snow-white paws were chocolate colored and slick, and May would carefully wipe them with an old towel so as to keep the carpets clean. This too passed, and one morning the rain stopped, the sun broke through, the sky was azure, and the air was sweet with summer again. And Nat's dog waited by the window, and still Nat did not come home.

Where he had gone and why he did not return remained a mystery
to her, for she was, after all, only a dog, and dogs do not understand
the meaning of tears, and of neighbors bringing casseroles and pies,
and of Nat's old friends coming and holding May close and whispering,
"I'm so sorry." A dog could not know that when Pete, the oldest son,
had burst in the door that cold November day, his face ashen, his
voice broken, and cried, "Mom, it's Pop!" that Nat Walker would never
come home again.

She had greeted each one of his old friends hopefully. Perhaps he
was with Joe, or Steve, or Mike, as he had been so many times before
when he had left, only to return, sometimes days later, his rifle tucked
under his arm, his red plaid hunting jacket smelling of the woods and
fields. Then all would be right again in her world. May would make
coffee and put out a plate of doughnuts, and the dog would sit under
the table while Nat's friends slipped her pieces of the sweet cakes until
Nat would say, laughing, "Whoa, now. That's enough, old girl. You'll
be fatter than those partridge you keep telling me are out there."
Then she would come out from beneath the table and lie by Nat's
side and smell the familiar woodsy smells emanating from his clothes
until it grew late and all the stories of the hunt were told and told
again.

One day her heart leapt when she heard Nat's truck coming up the
drive, and she raced to the door, barking joyfully. At last he had come.
Where he had been for so long did not matter. He was here now, and
she forgave him. But it was not Nat, only Mike, his oldest friend and
hunting companion who had come to talk with May.

"Glad I bought the old truck," Mike said as he approached the
doorway. "It's good for bumping down dirt roads. How are you doing,
May?"

"Okay," she answered. "I get through each day somehow. The nights
are the hardest."

"It doesn't mean much, I know," Mike said gently, "but he died
doing the thing he liked best. I guess pulling that deer was just too
much for him. The old fool just wouldn't wait until we got there to
help."

"It was the way he would have wanted it," May agreed. "But it doesn't
make it any easier for the boys and me."

"I don't like to think of you all alone out here," Mike said, "the boys
living so far away and all. If you need anything, just give Marion or
me a call, will you?"

May had nodded her head slowly.

"Thanks, Mike. Actually, I was thinking of going south next winter.
Staying with my sister. But I don't know about the dog."

"Maybe you could give her away," Mike suggested. "I'd take her myself, but she never would hunt for anyone but him. I've got three as it is, anyway. Not to mention the fact that Marion would shoot me."

May had smiled, remembering. Even when she herself had gone out with them, the dog never would give the bird over to anyone but Nat.

"No," May had said slowly. "I wouldn't expect you to take her. Likely as not I'll just keep her. She's getting older. She probably couldn't adjust."

When spring came Nat's dog had been sure he would come home. Spring meant fishing, and Nat loved to fish. They would leave very early in the old truck, slipping quietly out of the house into the misty dawn while May slept. Nat would drive to his secret spot and stop the Chevy. "You stay," he would say to his dog. "I'll be back soon." And she would wait patiently until she saw him coming out of the brush, his old fishing basket dangling at his side and full of trout. But spring passed, and he did not come to fish.

She expected him in summer. Summer had always meant long, lazy afternoons and golden twilight evenings bass fishing at the lake. On Friday nights in the summer he would come in from work and call out, "Who wants to go to camp?" and she always knew the words and would race madly around the house, her stubby tail wagging until it ached. May would have everything ready and Nat would load it in the back of the pickup and off they would go, the three of them, to Nat's camp. But summer passed, and still he did not come. But she never doubted.

It was in the autumn that she knew he would, though, for autumn was their time. The best time. The time when he would take down his Winchester 12-gauge and carefully clean it, and she would sit by his side watching him, shivering with excitement.

"Tomorrow's the day," he would say. "Going to get birds, are you?"

She knew the phrase "going to get birds." She would whine and dance around on her snow-white feet, and he would laugh and ruffle her head gently. The next day, when the October dew had lifted from the grass and the weakening sun had warmed the brambles and thickets, he would call to her, "Time to get birds!" and off they would go into the woods behind the house, just the two of them usually. They would hunt until the shadows grew long and the sun sank behind the hills in the field.

So now it was October, and she was sure he would come home. She waited by the window hour after hour, day after day, watching, listening, never giving up hope.

May sat in the living room chair day after day and watched the dog grow thinner and thinner. The dog seldom ate anymore, and then only enough to keep herself alive. May had tried tempting her with bits of beef and chicken, but she only licked them once or twice and then left them in her dish.

"I know how she feels," May thought as she forced herself to eat and sleep and go about her life, trying to put it back together. She didn't cry. She had not cried. Not once, even when she knew that thirty-eight years of being Nat Walker's wife had ended abruptly on a cold, gray November afternoon. Sometimes she was mad at him for leaving her, but she could not cry. She wondered if people thought that was strange. Probably they figured she cried herself to sleep at night. Most likely they said to each other, "Poor May. Look how brave she is."

So now it was October, almost a year. October was the time she equated most with Nat Walker because it was on a crisp, fresh October evening forty years before, when she was eighteen, that she had met him at the Windsor Fair Dance. He was handsome and full of laughter and fun, but he was a Walker, and the Walkers were known for being independent and even a little wild at times. She had resisted and tried not to fall in love with him, but the following October she became his wife.

On their first anniversary he had presented her with a Remington 16-gauge. It was not quite what she had expected, but she knew why he had done it and she acted pleased anyway. Sometimes, in the first years, she even went out with him on those sharp, clean fall days when the birds were fat and plentiful in the woods behind their house. Then Pete was born and then Mark and then Tim. She stayed home with the children and was secretly just as glad. Still, every year he would carefully clean her gun and hang it beneath his on the rack. "In case you decide to go out," he'd say, and once in a while she would. He was proud that she was a fair shot and boasted of it to his friends. He did not tell them she was a good mother, or that she made great blueberry pies, or that she could sew him a flannel shirt that was equal to anything L.L. Bean sold. No, he told them she was a fair shot. And she understood and knew he loved her.

It was one of those sunny Indian summer afternoons when the air is heavy with the musky smell of fallen leaves and there is an urgency in the calling of birds flying overhead that May Walker sat in her living room and stared first at the thin, mournful dog sitting by the window and then at the old Remington hanging on the rack. She remembered how he had given it to her, and she remembered when he had come in that cold winter day, almost nine years before, with a small bundle wrapped in his sweater and tucked under his arm.

"What's that?" she had asked.

"Present for you," he had said, and handed her the sweater. It had wiggled, and a small head had popped out from a sleeve.

"Oh, Nat," she had said. "I thought we agreed! No more dogs after Snook went."

"It's one of Bill Lee's bitch's pups," he had told her. "Bill gave her to me. How could I refuse? I didn't want to hurt his feelings. Besides, this is a Brittany. She won't get as big as Snook."

The puppy licked her hand. Nat grinned and the dog stayed.

May got up from the chair and took her gun down from the rack. She ran her hands over the fine walnut stock and thought how Nat's hands had been the last to touch it.

The dog pricked up her ears and watched. For a moment her heart soared. Guns meant birds, and birds meant Nat. But it was not Nat holding the gun. She laid her head on her paws and sighed. May stared at the dog and at the gun and then out the window, where a breeze was swirling the orange and red maple leaves.

"Come on," she said. "Let's get birds."

The dog leapt to her feet. She knew those words. She forgot her misery—the instinct was just too powerful and the years of training too well done. She danced around happily as May donned her jacket and tucked some shells into the pocket. May loaded the gun and opened the door. Together they went out to hunt partridge.

The first leaves were crackly beneath their feet, but as they entered the woods there was a sweet dampness in the air, and they walked almost silently on the leaf-padded ground. The dog ranged ahead at just the distance Nat had taught her. Her nose caught each passing breeze as she moved carefully back and forth across the path. Suddenly she found what she was looking for. She tested the air one more time and snapped to a point.

May came up quietly and motioned her into the brush. She leapt forward, and there was a whir of wings as a bird whistled into the sky. May lifted the gun and shot, and the bird fell heavily. The dog waited until May motioned her after it. She bounded joyfully into the brush at the signal.

It did not take her long to find the bird. Gently she picked it up, and began carrying it back. Her eyes were bright, and her heart was beating with anticipation. Now Nat would come. He would be there to take the bird. His hands would stroke her head and his voice would say, "Good old girl." She broke from the brush and looked for him.

May stood with her hand outstretched.

"Give," she said. The dog looked around, confused. Where was he? He had always been there to take the bird. She sat down to wait.

"Give," May said again.

The dog sat unmoving and stared at May stubbornly.

"Damn you, give!" May cried. "Don't you understand? He's gone. He's not coming back. It's just us now. Do you hear me? Give!"

The dog looked at the woman whose hands had fed her all her life and brushed her and treated her when she had cut herself on barbed wire or low brambles. She looked for Nat again. He was not there. "Give" echoed in her mind, and the years of training told. Slowly she got up and approached May. Gently she laid the partridge in May's outstretched hand. She looked into the woman's face and waited.

"Good girl," May sobbed. "Oh, good old girl!" And she threw her arms around Nat's dog. The dog rested her head on May's shoulder and gently licked her ear.

"Oh, Natty, Natty," May sobbed over and over again.

After a while the crying stopped, and she wiped her eyes with her jacket sleeve. She drew a deep breath and pushed her hair from her face. She got up slowly and picked up the Remington Nat had given her thirty-eight Octobers before.

"We'll both love him till the day *we* die, old girl," she said. "But we'll get by. We'll go on."

The dog slowly wagged her stubby tail. Somehow she understood. He was not coming back. His gentle hands would never touch her again. She would never hear his voice or see his face. But they would go on. She understood as best a dog can.

May reached down and stroked the dog absentmindedly. The tears had finally come. The terrible ache was gone. There was a loneliness in its place that she knew she would feel forever, but the pain was gone.

"Come," she said. Together, she and Nat's dog went on into the cool October woods to get birds.

SPORTS AFIELD
DECEMBER 1985

We have a genuine outdoor hero here. His name is Bill Jones, and in a way, he's the envy of all of us bound by the restraints of jobs, families, and the dozens of other obligations that keep us from doing what we love best. Go ahead, cheer Bill Jones on. And I dare you to follow in his tracks. I know this isn't a hunting story, but it's Gordon MacQuarrie's best, and that gives it a place in these pages.

Nervous Breakdown

by GORDON MacQUARRIE

FOR one thing, there was that confoundedly efficient Miss Benson. Always at him, she was. "Good morning, Mr. Jones. . . . Mr. Smith to see you, Mr. Jones. . . . Will you sign these, Mr. Jones? . . . Goodnight, Mr. Jones."

What was he thinking of, anyway? Gertrude Benson was the finest secretary in New York. Snap out of it, Bill Jones. You're certainly going balmy in the head!

He dropped the fishing camp folder in the wastebasket and turned to his desk. Too old, he thought. Should have done it twenty years ago. But twenty years ago the kids were hardly more than babies, and there was Mom and a job.

Now that the kids were grown, Mom was coddling him more than ever. Yes, coddling him! Dear Mom, always thinking of someone other than herself. Mom could see no sense in a browse bed—"Will! At your age, sleeping on the ground!"

He picked up the memorandum which Miss Benson had left. Mr. Blake of National Metals at 9:30; Mr. Peddy of Empire Sales at 10; senior committee meeting at 11:00. His gaze strayed to the wastebasket.

The folder said: "Off the beaten track . . . the last frontier . . . our guides really take you back in there . . ."

Fifty-five years old, with a belly and a half million dollars. He looked out the window, off across the tops of the tall buildings. Thirty-five years of it, from clerk to a vice-presidency. Mom and the kids were very proud of him. They thought it screamingly funny when he took off a week or two and went fishing.

A pigeon, city vagabond of the species, yet somehow wild and free among skyscraper chasms, landed on the window sill. Miss Benson, who forgot nothing, had spread the daily ration of grain. The bird pecked. His thoughts dreamed away. . . .

He could tell Mom he was taking a guide so that she would not worry. There was country up there, country for a man to see. Not with a guide—not this time. This was something he had to do for himself. Last summer Hanson, the guide on the fringes of this country, had told him it was solid wilderness north to the Arctic Circle. He remembered Hansons' grin as he explained: "During the depression, when guiding fell off, I spent a season up in there. Got lost a-purpose. Never had such a good time in my life!"

No, he would not be afraid. He had not been afraid as a boy in Pennsylvania when he had camped out on his own trap line. He might break a leg. Sure! He might get bumped by a truck in town, too.

Miss Benson found him staring out the window. Brisk, efficient Miss Benson, whose words were as crisp as her tailored clothes. He hated Miss Benson. He wanted to say, "Damn it, Gerty, why don't you leave me alone?"

"Mr. Jones of National Metals to see you, sir."

He wanted to answer, "Tell him to go to the devil." He must have telegraphed the thought to Miss Benson, for she frowned. "I'm tired, Miss Benson," he said. "Mr. Pitcairn knows about this order. I suggest—"

"Yes, sir. I'll see Mr. Pitcairn right away. I hope everything is all right." There was real anxiety in her voice.

He smiled at her and suddenly did not hate her at all. It was ridiculous to hate Miss Benson. A brick, she was. Good as a man—yes, better than a man.

"Am I cracking up?" he wondered. It was something he could not quite put his finger on. He wasn't interested in his work the way he had been. The consuming passion to try the impossible was gone. For months he had found himself making an effort to do things. It wasn't like him. Was that why Mom hovered around him? She did hover!

His phone tinkled distantly in the big room. It was Banks, the president. Good old Banks—solid, sensible, old Banks.

"Miss Benson mentioned you weren't feeling well. I don't want to intrude. I'm rather awkward about such things. I'm wondering—"

"Mr. Banks, I have got to get out of here." His own words surprised him. He hadn't meant to say it quite that way.

"I'll be right in," Banks said.

He came, cool and steady as always. He came smiling and walked across the heavy rug. "Fellow," he said, "you don't look good to me." It was like Banks to speak his mind.

"Banks—" He could go no further. He was choked up.

Banks put a firm hand on his shoulder. "Spit it out. We've always worked that way."

For five minutes he talked. He talked rapidly, and at times his eyes shone. When he had finished, Banks laughed.

"Fine!" he said. "I'd rather you'd take a guide, but do it your way. I respect your way, as I always have."

He fidgeted. "Banks, is this a nervous breakdown?"

"Some call it that."

"Mom will want to get a doctor."

"I think you've written your own prescription."

"I—"

"Nuts!" said J. Forsythe Banks, leader of industry. "Don't let me see you around here in the next month. Git!"

Mom had been difficult, he thought as the train carried him north out of Duluth. But she had felt better about it when he lied cheerfully and said he was taking a cook as well as a guide.

The conductor came through and eyed him. "Lookin' up timber?"

"Yes. Be sure and wake me at six. I want to see the country."

His eyes were open long before the porter came to jerk at the green curtain of his berth. In the September dawn there flashed by an endless land of prim stunted spruce, pink-gray boulders and lakes that seemed to be waiting for someone to come and use them. He put away the business suit and climbed into store new wool. He had to rip the price tag off the checked flannel shirt.

He transferred personal items to the rough clothing that felt so good, then folded his pin-striped double-breasted suit and handed it to the porter to be shipped back to the hotel in Duluth.

"Yes suh, 'deed, suh. We is about two hours from Nine Mile watertank."

He ate a huge breakfast, for he would not want to stop at noon to boil the kettle.

At the watertank, where the train stopped, he hurried forward to the baggage car and helped with the unloading of the canoe and gear. The train pulled out. His dunnage beside the watertank made a formidable pile. A hundred yards away lay the edge of Wabigoon Lake.

Long before he had toted all the stuff to the rocky lake shore he was
weary. He fastened the tiny motor to the bracket of the fifteen-foot
canoe and set forth. The outfitter in town had insisted on the small
canoe. "It's a sixty-pounder. A two-man job would break your back
on the portages."

He had to stop and trim the load so that the bow dropped. After
that his speed increased. From an aluminum fishing rod tube he took
out a roll-up map of Ontario. Wabigoon looked pretty big the way he
was going, north.

He felt free, yet he was anxious. Could he do all the things as well
as Hanson had done them? He went over the outfit item by item. The
fellow in the store knew his business. He had told this clerk that he
had wanted to go with canoe and paddle. The man had insisted on
the tiny motor and ten gallons of fuel.

"If you run out of fuel and have to come home light, throw away
everything you don't need, including the motor," he had said.

Yes, the outfitter knew his business. He was traveling six miles an
hour in a light chop. Almost one hundred sixty pounds of equipment,
fuel and man in a craft that weighed sixty pounds. By noon the wind
had picked up, but a boyhood sense for water had returned. He caught
the knack of running on the lee side of the islands. In the open reaches
he learned to jockey the waves by quartering into them and away from
them.

In the late afternoon, more than forty miles from the put-in, he
chose a spruce-grown island for the night. It had a windswept point
where the late-season mosquitoes would not be present. The island
looked like some ancient seafaring craft, with spruce trees for masts
and sails. He cut the motor and swung in. Just before the nose of the
canoe touched land the sharp edge of a rock slashed a six-inch gash
in the canvas. He would have to be more careful in landing hereafter.

It took an hour to build a fire, heat the tiny can of marine glue,
and "iron on" a canvas patch with heated rocks. He scorched a finger
doing it. A blister ballooned up.

He longed for a deep, soft chair to sink into, like one at the club
or his easy chair at home. And a highball and the evening paper. And
an evening meal on a white tablecloth. He unpacked gear and dived
into the woods with an ax for browse.

It was near dark when the silk tent was pitched and the air mattress
spread over the browse. The wind went down, and his breezy point
attracted its quota of mosquitoes. The sunset was tremendous behind
spires of spruce. But he did not enjoy it. He lay down awhile before
starting to prepare supper. It had been like that for a long time. He
wanted to lie down and look at a job before beginning it. In other
days he had just pitched in.

He was hungry. How did guides like Hanson manage things so deftly on the ground? He struggled with the fire, which got too hot and then too cold. He burned his other hand. The loons of Wabigoon struck up their song, and he became definitely lonely and uncertain of himself. Just how smart was he in going away by himself without a guide.

By trial and error he adjusted the reflector baker so that the biscuits got done, though some were doughy and some burned. The dried soup which he spilled into the stew pan swelled enormously and overflowed into the fire. The tea was more like tannin, steeped too long. He must remember to do that last.

The supper did not taste good. The soup got cold and the tea stayed hot. Washing dishes was a chore. There was no sand on the rocky island with which to scour the dishes. He noted as he washed in the lake that his hands were already creviced with dirt.

Well, he would sleep, anyway. He drew tight the mosquito netting in the tent door and flopped down. He did not sleep. Three mosquitoes had to be hunted down. The browse under his hip was too high and had to be readjusted. When this was done, he was nervously wide-awake. He tossed in the sleeping bag. It was after midnight when he dozed off.

A few hours later the flapping of the tent awakened him. The wind was shaking it. There was a bright glow through the green tent. He leaped up. The wind had fanned the embers of his cooking fire, and sparks were flying. Without pausing to put on boots, he grabbed a folding bucket and dashed to the lake. He stubbed his toe and swore. It took a half dozen pailfuls to extinguish the fire, and by then the wind had torn out the stakes on one side of the tent.

In the dark he replaced the stakes, as deep as he could in the thin soil, and anchored them with rocks. He tightened the ridge rope by lifting the shear poles front and back. The rain caught him as he finished. It came horizontally from the west, cold and stabbing—a fall rain. Inside the tent, he lit the aluminum lantern's single fat candle and lay on his back. He fell asleep from sheer exhaustion.

In the morning he felt as though he had not slept at all. The long water hop of the previous day had brought the reflected sun up beneath his hat brim. His face was painfully burned. The oatmeal he cooked was good, but the taste of powdered milk on it was unfamiliar. Mom, right now, was in the breakfast nook, having the kind of breakfast he wanted. If he were there, she would wheel the car up and honk and he would get in and they would drive away and the traffic cops would wave cheerfully.

As it was, he faced a run with the canoe and then a two-mile portage. He dreaded it. If only Hanson were here to take over!

The portage was worse than he had anticipated. It had been a wet September. There was one low spot of a hundred yards where he waded to his knees, feeling the trail with his boots. The gear was in two packsacks. Then there was the canoe, the motor and the two tins of fuel, each weighing thirty pounds.

As long as he lived he would not forget that portage! Hanson had said that this portage was what kept a lot of trippers from going back in there. Even the good guides did not like it. The sweat ran into his eyes. He drank quarts of water at either end of the punishing trail. Pack straps cut his shoulders. He could not complete the job in the day. He left the canoe and motor until next day and hurried camp in the rain. Just in time, too. A needle-fine rain of the lasting kind came down. He gulped hot soup and eased himself into the sleeping bag.

He slept. He slept like a log. In the morning, still groggy, he put on a rain jacket and limped back for the canoe and motor.

The lake before him had no name on the map. It was just a number put there by a surveyor, Lake One. There were others, named and numbered, stretching beyond to the north. He rigged a casting rod and took a four-pound walleyed pike with the third cast. He was using a pork rind lure, but he felt he might have done as well with a clothes-pin bearing hooks.

In the rain he dressed the fish and baked it in the reflector oven with rashers of bacon. He brewed his coffee carefully and saw to it that the biscuits browned evenly. It all tasted good. He ate it, watching a moose on the far shore of the lake. When he had finished, a Canada jay came to his plate and dined. The bird was unafraid and greedy.

The skies cleared in the early afternoon, and he set off. He portaged out of Lake One to another, Lake Three on the map. The portage was a mere hundred yard haul-over, up a hogback, down the other side. Without waiting to set up camp he cast the pork rind from the shore. A ten-pound northern took it. He got in the canoe and fished the shore. The water was alive with northern pike and walleyed pike. It was a carnival of fishing. He saved one for supper.

There was a white frost in the night. He felt it coming before bedtime so he folded back the canoe tent to make a lean-to and built a roaring fire before it. By the firelight he ate, picking the firm pike flesh from his plate with his fingers and wondering what Mom would say if she could have seen him. Owls were abroad, and beaver were working not far away. He tidied up camp and lay in the sleeping bag. The last thing he remembered was the strong whistle of wings. Ducks on the move . . . He fell asleep.

For a week he stayed at this place. Mornings he killed a duck or two, reaching for them with a .410 as they came low across a pass.

There were mornings when he might have killed a hundred. All he wanted was enough to eat. Each morning it seemed colder and the white frost heavier. The birch leaves had been yellowish when he began the trip. Now there were gone. The wild cherry leaves were brown and drying. Sumac groves were carmine. The song birds were gone except for an occasional flicker. He was busy, and the days passed quicker than he cared to see them pass.

It was while he walked around this lake to retrieve a wave-borne mallard that he realized he was not tired! It was a long walk of three miles to where the wind and waves carried the mallard. He thought it would be better for him to walk it than to take the canoe. He picked up the bird.

Ten days of wilderness had made his trousers gape at the waist. One day he permitted himself the luxury of a shave. To his surprise, his face was not left raw and razor-chopped. The skin had toughened. It had had a chance to heal itself from incessant, hurried scrapings.

His appetite amazed him. He found he was no longer dragging himself to camp tasks. He went at them eagerly and did them efficiently. There was always something to do—too much, in fact. The days were too short. They zipped by. He broke out his camera and renewed an old hobby. He built a table and chair for the camp. He fed the trusting whisky jacks and stalked the shoreline moose, and counted it a red-letter day when he got close enough to one to touch it with a paddle. He was no longer lonely. There was life and activity all about him.

He pushed north from this camp for a steady week, through many lakes, over endless portages. Almost every night the aurora borealis spread over the heavens. Every morning his boots were stiff with frost. A porcupine gnawed his sweat-saturated paddle, and he spent half a day chopping down a spruce and fashioning another with ax and knife. He was inordinately proud of that paddle. Just as he was proud of the neat patching he put on the tent where campfire sparks burned through its walls.

The routine of making camp was so perfected that he could slide the canoe ashore, set up camp, and be eating a meal in a half hour. He found out that the way to eat bacon and fish in a one-man camp was right out of the frying pan. It saved doing dishes.

He planned and prepared delicious meals and ate them ravenously. Planked fish, bean-hole beans, hot cornmeal muffins. One day he triumphed with his last can of peaches dedicated to a shortcake. In town it would have been enough for four. He licked up the last crumbs and wished he had another can of sliced peaches.

Thin ice in the portage trail hollow sent him south. He studied the map and penciled out a great arc of travel that would fetch him back by another route. The Nine Mile watertower was his goal. He was not sure of the date. He had either lost a day or gained a day somewhere. It didn't matter.

It was on a lake named Papoose that he lost the motor. He had neglected to make fast the safety rope to the bracket, and the thrifty eggbeater went down. A weighted fish line showed seventy feet of water, so he did not bother to drag for it. Many miles of paddling and portaging lay before him. He grinned. This is what he had come for: to see how much of him was left. He grinned with anticipation.

First he unscrewed the outboard bracket, threw it away, and heaved overboard the remaining four gallons of fuel. Then he paddled ashore and went over his outfit carefully. Every item was scanned for weight and utility. When he had finished, everything went into one packsack. On the next portage he went across in one trip with canoe and pack.

For five days he paddled and portaged, eating twice a day, morning and evening. It was hard work, but it was good work. His hands had hardened and his back had stiffened before the loss of the motor. They became harder and stiffer. His palms were calloused. In the evenings when he went ashore he welcomed the wilderness with a weary zest. Every place seemed like home, for he was self-sufficient. He got lost for a day and a half by missing a portage trail, but took a short cut back to the penciled route via a new and shorter portage. He wondered what Mom would say when she found him so lean.

"Will! At your age sleeping on the ground!" He laughed. He knew what he would do when he saw Mom. He would sweep her off the floor, and she would protest. "Will, you fool! Let me down!" It had been fifteen years since he had picked up Mom like that. If Mom grew anxious and tried to hover over him again, he would have to spank her, even if one of her grandchildren was present.

On a long, narrow water, which the map said was Burnt-over Lake, he started supper one night. A seaplane circled, spotted his tent and landed. It taxied in, and the pilot came ashore. He was a commercial flyer, looking for a lost camper. He explained the man's name was William Jones, and that Jones was two days overdue at Nine Mile watertank. Railway officials had reported that he had not appeared.

"You can stop looking. How bout supper?"

"But you're not lost," said the flyer, who had studied the shipshape camp and the hard brown man.

"Nope, just tardy. Lost my outboard, and I'm paddling in."

"I'll fly you in tonight in a half hour."

"That's what you think."

"A Mr. Banks has asked us to find you."

"Good old Banks."

The flyer sat down to a meal of fresh caught walleyed pike, baking powder biscuits with maple syrup, and hot green tea. He was a nice chap. He took off while there was still a little daylight. In forty-five minutes he was on the phone.

"But are you sure he is all right?" Banks demanded.

"I've lived in this country most of my life. If I needed a guide, I'd hire that bird."

"Does he feel all right?"

"Well, he carried a fifty-pound down log to the fire with one hand."

"Did he say when he would reach Nine Mile?"

"Yes, sir. He said he would get there when he was damn good and ready."

There was a pause and a sigh at the other end of the line. Then Banks said, "That's him, all right."

Reprinted by permission of THE MILWAUKEE JOURNAL, Milwaukee, Wisconsin.

Other than bears, there're not many animals that can really harm man in the North American woods. There are a couple, however, and the cougar is one of them. Cougars are tough critters. They have one bad trait: they never seem to pick on anyone their own size. When one of these mountain cats decides to pick on a human, it more often than not will single out a child. I suspect a lion thinks a child is a small animal, and a small animal is easier to kill and devour than a big one that may put a good fight. This is the story about an eight-year-old boy and a very unusual mountain lion in Big Bend National Park. Perhaps you read about it in the newspaper. Here's the complete story with all its terrifying details.

Killer Cougar of the Chisos

by LARRY MUELLER

PERHAPS the cougar was already stalking the Brown family from behind trailside cover. Mrs. Brown, Kim, had been crying. She had stepped on a column of army ants. One had crawled up her pants leg, biting as it climbed. Her response to the stinging pain, and the frustration of being unable to get at and remove the ant quickly, could have been interpreted by the mountain lion as sounds of an animal in distress. Whatever his reason, the cat had chosen to lie in wait just beyond a sharp bend in the trail where anything coming around it would be too close to escape.

Mr. Brown, Chris, really hadn't wanted to go on this hike. They had just arrived at Big Bend National Park, and he wanted to unpack. But David Vaught, his eight-year-old stepson of less than a year, was excited and anxious. This mountainous area was different Texas than he knew in his Garland home near Dallas.

Rattlesnakes are always a possibility in the rocky southwest, so Chris led the hike while every now and again David yelled, "Snake!" to test his mother's fright reactions. It worked the first few times, but then Kim encountered the real problem of ants. Chris stopped to help her, but David and his four-year-old brother, Justin, walked ahead. In fact, Justin also got ahead of David, and David figured he was next in command to watch for snakes. So he pushed Justin behind shortly before he turned the bend where the trail darkened as it entered a more heavily wooded area.

"Mountain lion!" David yelled. He stared in disbelief, transfixed for an instant by the twitching tail and laid-back ears. Then the cat snarled, baring its fangs. David turned to run.

Nobody believed David's yell. Cougars are shy, secretive creatures, rarely even seen from a distance. Besides, David had repeatedly yelled "Snakes!" But Chris glanced up and felt an instinctive foreboding about the darkened bend in the trail.

The next thing Chris saw was David three steps into a run and the lion right behind. David glanced over his left shoulder, and the cat leaped, his mouth opened to almost 180 degrees like a striking snake. The cougar dug hind claws into David's thigh and front claws deep into both shoulders as he clamped his jaws on the boy's head. Just as quickly the lion relaxed its grip on all but the head. Plugs of flesh pulled out with the twisting claws as the lion's weight and momentum carried it over David's body in an action intended to break the victim's neck. They slammed to the ground.

David lay limp as his mother screamed in terror that her son was dead. The snarling mountain lion chewed rapidly on David's head. Chris ran yelling at the cat, trying to frighten it off. It glanced up defiantly, snarled, then continued its attempt to sink fangs through David's skull. Running at the lion, Chris kicked, slipped on the slope, missed, and fell alongside the cat. He grabbed at the cougar. Guilt swept over him because his efforts weren't succeeding, and the cougar was still chewing. He couldn't seem to get hold of the tight skin over the lion's bulging muscles. But it did make the animal pause a moment in his chewing and turn to look at Chris. When the cat turned back to David, Chris grabbed its neck by both hands and pulled.

The lion screamed at being yanked off of its prey. Or maybe it screamed in anger because it thought Chris was trying to steal its prey. Chris doesn't remember the scream. Blood pumping against his eardrums muffled the sounds of battle. Kim remembered. The scream sounded much like one of her own. She was sure her son was dead, and now the lion was on top of her husband. Chris was on his back, stiff arms trying to hold the cougar's fangs away from his face. Back and forth the cat jerked, trying to force past those arms. Hind claws scratched for a grip in Chris' pants and legs. Fangs were inches from Brown's face. Finally, with adrenalin pumped strength, Chris threw the cat six feet down the slope.

Instantly, the lion jumped back. Still on the ground, Chris met the charge with all the muscle he could force into a kick. The surprised cougar retreated a step or two. Chris jumped to his feet and grabbed a stick from the ground. It was a frail stick, but Chris brandished it with authority as he reached back thousands of years and brought forth a primitive screaming roar of his own. The cat hesitated. Kim heard it scream once more. Then it turned and ran into the bushes.

David regained consciousness in time to hear Kim's anguished cries. "It killed David! David is dying! David!" Her screams were being heard all the way back to park headquarters.

Chris rushed to the boy. A big patch of scalp was missing, apparently eaten by the lion. Most of the remaining scalp was torn loose. Fang marks scratched the skull, but hadn't penetrated it. A fang or claw had punctured the boy's left cheek. Blood covered David's eyes, and indeed Chris feared the eyes were gone. He grabbed his son and ran fifty yards back on the trail where he stopped to wrap his own shirt around David's head to stop the bleeding.

"Am I dead, Dad?" the eight-year-old asked.

"Of course not," Chris answered. "You're talking, aren't you?"

"But I can't see!"

"It's just blood over your eyes."

"But Mom said . . . don't let me die, Dad."

"That's just your Mom. You know how excited she gets. You're just bleeding a little. You've had a cut before. It quits bleeding, and then you're all right again. It'll be that way now. Say a little prayer with me, and everything is going to be fine."

They prayed a moment, then Chris picked up his son and ran. It would have been closer to return to park headquarters by finishing the trail in the direction they had been hiking, but they thought the lion had gone in that direction. Everyone wanted to run pell-mell for camp, but Chris kept them together, afraid the cougar might follow. Indeed, Kim kept saying she heard something moving in the bushes. But Chris continued to deny that, trying to keep everyone, especially David, calm. All the way back, Chris kept David talking so the boy wouldn't slip into shock and never return. Amazingly, David never cried through the whole ordeal. Chris' ankles would be swollen for three days from that thirty five minute race against death over large, loose rock in the trail, but he got his family safely back to park headquarters.

Park rangers administrated first aid and summoned an ambulance from Alpine, but everyone's troubles were far from over. General practitioner/psychologist Dr. Joanna Sanchez did what she could for the wounds and performed a near miracle on David's mental attitude. (He still has nightmares, as do all members of the family, but he exhibits no irrational fears.) However, nobody at Big Bend Memorial

Hospital was qualified to initiate surgery on the scalp. In his serious condition, it was essential to quickly move him to a bigger facility back at Dallas.

"We tried to get a local pilot to fly us," Kim recalled later, "but he wanted in the neighborhood of three or four thousand dollars—cash and up front—before he'd take off. We didn't have it. The sherriff at Alpine said don't worry about it. He'd drive the ambulance those six hundred miles and get us there almost as fast. Despite having to stop three times for gas, he got us there in seven hours!"

Back at the Chisos (meaning ghost or enchanted) Mountains, in the big bend of the Rio Grande River, troubles were growing. A mountain lion that had lost its fear of humans, and probably would attack again, was running free in the nearly million acre park. The attack had occurred about 6 P.M. Anxious to solve the problem before dark, armed rangers fanned out to dispatch the animal. Not surprisingly, the only man who believes he saw the animal was an unarmed concessioner. In the meantime, the scent trail was diminishing.

Texas Ranger Clayton McKinney heard about the attack on his radio, and at 7:30 P.M. called his nephew, state predator hunter and trapper Bill McKinney to see if he had been notified. Stationed adjacent to Big Bend National Park on the roughly hundred thousand acre Black Gap Wildlife Management Area, McKinney had used his hounds to help in the park's telemetry (radio-collared) lion studies. He also had been on call in case of emergency need for his dogs. McKinney tried to telephone park management, but the phone was busy.

Bill McKinney loaded his hounds, confident that if he got there quickly it would be a short chase. When he reached the park by phone, however, he learned that both Supervisor and Chief Ranger were away. An assistant would pass along Bill's offer of help.

It was 10:30 P.M. when the decision reached McKinney to bring his hounds. By then it was well after dark, and the track was four and a half hours old. It would take at least another hour to reach the attack site. Chance of a short chase had become slim, and a long chase after dark in the steep, rough Chisos Mountains would not only be dangerous to men and dogs, it would multiply the risk of mistakes that might permit the lion to escape. It was mutually agreed upon to begin the hunt before daylight the next morning.

Bill asked Doug Waid to join him. Bill was working with Waid on the lion study, and knew the biologist to be tough, wiry, and of great help on the chase. The pair were in the park before 5 A.M., anxious to begin while it was still cool and moist and before the sun might burn out the track. Instead, they were asked by the rangers present to wait for their troubleshooter who rescues people off of bluffs, etc.

Other rangers showed up, milling around, making small talk, waiting. McKinney grew nervous. Scent trails do not last forever, and the scent may have been disturbed by searchers the night before. Also, Bill's hounds were not accustomed to crowds; he feared it might distract them from making their best efforts. Further, if the lion wasn't caught . . . he tried not to think of another attack, maybe even on his own four-year-old boy. He lives within easy lion range of the park.

Finally, at 6 A.M., Bill was permitted to free Missy, one of his two best lion dogs, on the now twelve-hour-old track at the attack site. Missy showed immediate interest. She made one circle just downhill from the park's foot trail, and raced around the hillside parallel to the foot trail in the same direction the Browns ran after the attack.

(Apparently, Kim Brown had been correct. The lion had not lost interest in its attempted kill. Or perhaps it followed simply because the Browns were running. Predator response is triggered by anything that flees. At any rate, the cougar's trail ran parallel with the Brown's for roughly 150 yards.)

Finally, the cat track turned ninety degrees from the foot trail and headed across Laguna Meadow toward a gray rock foothill in front of Ward Mountain.

Bill McKinney felt a wave of hope, if not relief. The cat's trail was still strong enough for the hounds to follow, at least for the moment. Three more hounds were released as McKinney and Waid ran through the underbrush toward Missy. The oldest hound, Toby, heard yelling, thought he was being called, and ran back to the crowd where somebody tried to catch him. He was spooked out of the race permanently, as were those men who tried to follow the hounds by staying on the foot trail. All extra hands, including the two-way radio carrier, fell out of the chase by the time it started up the steep, east, sliderock face of the more than 7,000-foot Ward Mountain.

Bill and Doug were on their own and climbing as fast as their breath allowed, often sliding two steps down on the loose rock for every one up, but determined to make progress. Feeling he should be halfway up, Bill looked back and saw they barely had a good start. "Doug," he yelled, "get up here with me!"

Doug put on a burst of speed, scrambling up red-faced and out of breath. "Where are they?"

"Out of hearing," Bill answered.

"I thought you yelled the hounds were treed."

"No," Bill said, "I want you close to me. If these football knees give out, can you take my revolver and go on to kill that cat? You'll have to get in close—right in with the hounds."

"I can do it," Waid assured, even though he isn't a hunter. "Let's go!"

About halfway up McKinney stopped again, this time realizing the chase could have gone out of hearing either over the top or by turning to the right through a gap called "The Window." Right here the average houndsman would have had a fifty-fifty chance of choosing the wrong direction, getting separated from his hounds for perhaps days, and never ever knowing where the killer cat went. Bill unpacked his Taconics receiver (essentially the same equipment used to track wildlife) and assembled the directional antenna. It's a pain to carry eight pounds of extra equipment, but there's no better way to locate out-of-hearing hounds. No signal came through the gap. That meant the chase went over the mountain.

After two hours of slipping and sliding, often on hands and feet, Bill and Doug topped out in a small saddle between peaks. The hounds could have gone three ways, but the radio signals said turn left. Walking along the narrow hogback in that direction, the men eventually heard their dogs—just before the steady roar of an airplane engine blanketed all other sounds.

"Damn it!" Doug said. "That plane is supposed to be monitoring telemetry-equipped lions, not us."

It seems the radio-collared lions in the basin had left at the first sound of dogs, and someone, not realizing they were doing more harm than good, had asked the pilot to keep the media informed about the hunters' progress. Eventually, the plane left, and by 11 A.M. the men were able to catch up with the hounds where the lion had killed and eaten a skunk.

The morning had remained overcast, helping hold the scent from completely evaporating, but strong contrast between skunk and the old lion trail wasn't helping. Also, the hounds had climbed fast and were too hot to work effectively. As any good houndsman in the Southwest knows, especially if he hunts desert country, overheating diminishes scenting ability. Again, it's a pain to carry, but the men had brought along enough water to pour in Bill's hat to wet the hounds' noses and mouths occasionally.

Somewhat refreshed and their nasal passages moistened, the hounds trailed into a deep, hard to negotiate canyon on the back side of the mountain. Once more the hounds overheated and found trailing difficult. The canteen was empty.

Twice the men found water in the canyon, led the dogs off of the track to drink, then led them back to resume trailing. They also filled the canteen each time to keep the dogs noses moist inbetween. Three times the hounds couldn't follow where the lion jumped up twelve- to twenty-foot bluffs. Each time Doug climbed halfway up and wedged himself in. Bill passed him the hounds, then Doug threw them up to the top. Doggedly, determinedly, the men helped the hounds through this rugged rocky canyon.

Finally, the lion's trail came back out to the top of Ward Mountain. It was easier walking, and the hunters hoped for faster trailing. Instead, the overcast had cleared about 2 P.M., and a warm August wind had swept away the track.

"Water won't help here," Bill growled. He was near desperation. The hounds were tired, the track was blown out, the day was two-thirds gone, and he'd feel to blame if the killer lion went free.

"We've got to make up time," Bill told Doug. "My guess is it headed across to the thicker trees around the pour-offs." The two led all three hounds across the half-mile shortcut, trying not to think about the consequences if they put the dogs onto a new trail made by a different cougar.

Walking instead of trailing did refresh the hounds somewhat. In minutes, Missy gave voice. Right track or wrong, she was on a lion again. Sam and Rowdy packed in.

The track seemed improved. The bigger, thicker trees and greater amount of ground vegetation held more moisture and protected the scent from wind and sun. The hounds moved rapidly until they reached the "pour-offs," rock faces fifteen to twenty feet high where rain pours off as it races down a crease in the mountainside. Sometimes the cougar jumped down or across in places where the hounds had to be lowered by rope.

That was no trouble. Or it wasn't until the plane returned. Twice more it circled overhead, once for at least thirty minutes. Difficulty hearing the hounds over the engine caused additional delays before the men could find the dogs and lower them down the pour-offs.

Finally, the cat track left the mountain, dropped back down to Laguna Meadow, and headed toward the foot trail less than a quarter mile from where David Brown had been attacked. About sixty yards from the foot trail, Missy gave a surprised "Whoo-whoo-whoo" and began barking up a pinion pine tree. After twelve hours and seven or eight miles of cold trailing, a lion was suddenly treed without even a short jump chase.

Bill cautioned Doug as they approached. Lions sometimes jump out at the sound of human voices.

"What do you think Doug?" Bill whispered. "Is it the right cat?"

"Has to be. Kill it!"

McKinney drew his revolver and made a safe lung shot rather than risk wounding the lion and starting another chase with exhausted dogs. The cougar jumped out, ran two hundred yards, and climbed again where McKinney finished him with a head shot.

The cat was a male estimated to be sixteen to twenty-four months old, about eighty-five pounds in weight, and was dark red as described by both Chris Brown and the concessionaire. However, positive proof that this was the offending cat would come from prompt analysis by the Midland narcotics lab. David's hair was found in the lower intestinal tract. The State Public Health lab in El Paso tested the head and reported negative on rabies.

This mountain lion would not attack again, but one question would remain unanswered. Why did he do it? The cat was not in poor condition. It did not have a faceful of porcupine quills. It was not compelled by any physical disability to seek easy prey. In fact, this cougar wasn't especially hungry. Its intestinal contents indicated it had fed on deer before it ate part of David's scalp. The lion had returned to a three-day-old deer kill; that's where the hounds caught up and winded him.

Perhaps this cougar, raised near people in the park, had no fear of humans. Perhaps it was a released pet that had grown too bold. Or maybe it was just an ordinary cat responding instinctively to fleeing prey.

The more important question, of course, is will it happen again? Some large predators have lost their respect for humans. And some humans, educated by cute cartoons, have lost their healthy respect for large predators. With both in parks, either can cause conflict.

The unfinished story is young David. After several operations, he fully recovered from his ordeal. The Dallas Cowboy Cheerleaders heard about his high medical bills and gave a benefit for David in 1984. The night before, he said, "I'm already embarrassed!"

"About what?" he was asked.

"Getting up on the stage."

"Anybody who can handle a lion attack without crying," he was told, "should have no fear of a stage."

"There was only *one* lion," David shot back. "There'll be a *bunch* of people out there."

OUTDOOR LIFE
APRIL 1985

Kenneth Douglas Stuart Anderson (1910–1974) lived most of his life in Bangalore, India. He was an avid hunter of man-killing tigers and panthers. This story is about a very special demonic leopard—or panther, as they are known in India—that Anderson called the Spotted Devil of Gummalapur. This cat roamed 250 square miles and killed forty-two humans. The panther seemed almost untouchable, but then Anderson took up his hunt of a lifetime.

The Spotted Devil of Gummalapur

by KENNETH DOUGLAS STUART ANDERSON

THE leopard is common to practically all tropical jungles, and unlike the tiger, indigenous to the forests of India; for whereas it has been established that the tiger is a comparatively recent newcomer from regions in the colder north, records and remains have shown that the leopard—or panther, as it is better known in India—has lived in the peninsula from the earliest times.

Because of its smaller size and decidedly lesser strength, together with its innate fear of mankind, the panther is often treated with some derision, sometimes coupled with truly astonishing carelessness, two factors that have resulted in the maulings and occasional deaths of otherwise intrepid but cautious tiger hunters. Even when attacking a human being the panther rarely kills, but confines itself to a series of quick bites and quicker raking scratches with its small but sharp claws; on the other hand, few persons live to tell that they have been attacked by a tiger.

This general rule has one fearful exception, however, and that is the panther that has turned man-eater. Although examples of such animals are comparatively rare, when they do occur they depict the panther as an engine of destruction quite equal to his far larger cousin, the tiger. Because of his smaller size he can conceal himself in places

163

impossible to a tiger, his need for water is far less, and in veritable demoniac cunning and daring, coupled with the uncanny sense of self-preservation and stealthy disappearance when danger threatens, he has no equal.

Such an animal was the man-eating leopard of Gummalapur. This leopard had established a record of some forty-two human killings and a reputation for veritable cunning that almost exceeded human intelligence. Some fearful stories of diabolical craftiness had been attributed to him, but certain it was that the panther was held in awe throughout an area of some 250 square miles over which it held undisputable sway.

Before sundown the door of each hut in every one of the villages within this area was fastened shut, some being reinforced by piles of boxes or large stones kept for the purpose. Not until the sun was well up in the heavens next morning did the timid inhabitants venture to expose themselves. This state of affairs rapidly told on the sanitary condition of the houses, the majority of which were not equipped with latrines of any sort, the adjacent waste land being used for the purpose.

Finding that its human meals were increasingly difficult to obtain, the panther became correspondingly bolder, and in two instances burrowed its way in through the thatched walls of the smaller huts, dragging its screaming victim out the same way, while the whole village lay awake, trembling behind closed doors, listening to the shrieks of the victim as he was carried away. In one case the panther, frustrated from burrowing its way in through the walls, which had been boarded up with rough planks, resorted to the novel method of entering through the thatched roof. In this instance it found itself unable to carry its prey back through the hole it had made, so in a paroxysm of fury had killed all four inhabitants of the hut—a man, his wife and two children—before clawing its way back to the darkness outside and to safety.

Only during the day did the villagers enjoy any respite. Even then they moved about in large, armed groups, but so far no instance had occurred of the leopard attacking in daylight, although it had been very frequently seen at dawn within the precincts of a village.

Such was the position when I arrived at Gummalapur, in response to an invitation from Jepson, the District Magistrate, to rid his area of this scourge. Preliminary conversation with some of the inhabitants revealed that they appeared dejected beyond hope, and with true eastern fatalism had decided to resign themselves to the fact that this shaitan, from whom they believed deliverance to be impossible, had come to stay, till each one of them had been devoured or had fled the district as the only alternative.

It was soon apparent that I would get little or no cooperation from the villagers, many of whom openly stated that if they dared to assist me the shaitan would come to hear of it and would hasten their end. Indeed, they spoke in whispers as if afraid that loud talking would be overheard by the panther, who would single them out for revenge.

That night, I sat in a chair in the midst of the village, with my back to the only house that possessed a twelve-foot wall, having taken the precaution to cover the roof with a deep layer of thorns and brambles, in case I should be attacked from behind by the leopard leaping down on me. It was a moonless night, but the clear sky promised to provide sufficient illumination from its myriad stars to enable me to see the panther should it approach.

The evening, at six o'clock, found the inhabitants behind locked doors, while I sat alone on my chair, with my rifle across my lap, loaded and cocked, a flask of hot tea nearby, a blanket, a water bottle, some biscuits, a torch at hand, and of course my pipe, tobacco and matches as my only consolation during the long vigil till daylight returned.

With the going down of the sun a period of acute anxiety began, for the stars were as yet not brilliant enough to light the scene even dimly. Moreover, immediately to westward of the village lay two abrupt hills which hastened the dusky uncertainty that might otherwise have been lessened by some reflection from the recently set sun.

I gripped my rifle and stared around me, my eyes darting in all directions and from end to end of the deserted village street. At that moment I would have welcomed the jungle, where by their cries of alarm I could rely on the animals and birds to warn me of the approach of the panther. Here all was deathly silent, and the whole village might have been entirely deserted, for not a sound escaped from the many inhabitants whom I knew lay listening behind closed doors, and listening for the scream that would herald my death and another victim for the panther.

Time passed, and one by one the stars became visible, till by 7:15 P.M. they shed a sufficiently diffused glow to enable me to see along the whole village street, although somewhat indistinctly. My confidence returned, and I began to think of some way to draw the leopard toward me, should he be in the vicinity. I forced myself to cough loudly at intervals and then began to talk to myself, hoping that my voice would be heard by the panther and bring him to me quickly.

I do not know if any of my readers have ever tried talking to themselves loudly for any reason, whether to attract a man-eating leopard or not. I suppose there must be a few, for I realize what reputation the man who talks to himself acquires. I am sure I acquired that reputation with the villagers, who from behind their closed doors listened to me that night as I talked to myself. But believe me, it is no easy task to talk loudly to yourself for hours on end, while watching intently for the stealthy approach of a killer.

By 9 P.M. I got tired of it, and considered taking a walk around the streets of the village. After some deliberation I did this, still talking to myself as I moved cautiously up one lane and down the next, frequently glancing back over my shoulder. I soon realized, however, that I was exposing myself to extreme danger, as the panther might pounce on me from any corner, from behind any pile of garbage, or from the rooftops of any of the huts. Ceasing my talking abruptly, I returned to my chair, thankful to get back alive.

Time dragged by very slowly and monotonously, the hours seeming to pass on leaden wheels. Midnight came and I found myself feeling cold, due to a sharp breeze that had set in from the direction of the adjacent forest, which began beyond the two hillocks. I drew the blanket closely around me, while consuming tobacco far in excess of what was good for me. By 2 A.M. I found I was growing sleepy. Hot tea and some biscuits, followed by icy water from the bottle dashed into my face, and a quick raising and lowering of my body from the chair half a dozen times, revived me a little, and I fell to talking to myself again, as a means of keeping awake thereafter.

At 3:30 A.M. came an event which caused me untold discomfort for the next two hours. With the sharp wind banks of heavy cloud were carried along, and these soon covered the heavens and obscured the stars, making the darkness intense, and it would have been quite impossible to see the panther a yard away. I had undoubtedly placed myself in an awkward position, and entirely at the mercy of the beast should it choose to attack me now. I fell to flashing my torch every half minute from end to end of the street, a proceeding which was very necessary if I hoped to remain alive with the panther anywhere near, although I felt I was ruining my chances of shooting the beast, as the bright torchbeams would probably scare it away. Still, there was the possibility that it might not be frightened by the light, and that I might be able to see it and bring off a lucky shot, a circumstance that did not materialize, as morning found me still shining the torch after a night-long and futile vigil.

I snatched a few hours' sleep and at noon fell to questioning the villagers again. Having found me still alive that morning—quite obviously contrary to their expectations—and possibly crediting me with the power to communicate with spirits because they had heard me walking around their village talking, they were considerably more communicative and gave me a few more particulars about the beast. Apparently the leopard wandered about its domain a great deal, killing erratically and at places widely distant from one another, and as I had already found out, never in succession at the same village. As no human had been killed at Gummalapur within the past three weeks, it seemed that there was much to be said in favor of staying where I was, rather than moving around, in a haphazard fashion, hoping to come up with the panther. Another factor against wandering about was that this beast was rarely visible in the daytime, and there was therefore practically no chance of my meeting it, as might have been the case with a man-eating tiger. It was reported that the animal had been wounded in its right forefoot, since it had the habit of placing the pad sideward, a fact which I was later able to confirm when I actually came across the tracks of the animal.

After lunch, I conceived a fresh plan for that night, which would certainly save me from the great personal discomforts I had experienced the night before. This was to leave a door of one of the huts ajar, and to rig up inside it a very lifelike dummy of a human being; meanwhile, I would remain in a corner of the same hut behind a barricade of boxes. This would provide an opportunity to slay the beast as he became visible in the partially-opened doorway, or even as he attacked the dummy, while I myself would be comparatively safe and warm behind my barricade.

I explained the plan to the villagers, who, to my surprise, entered into it with some enthusiasm. A hut was placed at my disposal immediately next to that through the roof of which the leopard had once entered and killed the four inmates. A very lifelike dummy was rigged up, made of straw, an old pillow, a jacket, and a saree. This was placed within the doorway of the hut in a sitting position, the door itself being kept half open. I sat myself behind a low parapet of boxes, placed diagonally across the opposite end of the small hut, the floor of which measured about twelve feet by ten feet. At this short range, I was confident of accounting for the panther as soon as it made itself visible in the doorway. Furthermore, should it attempt to enter by the roof, or through the thatched walls, I would have ample time to deal with it. To make matters even more realistic, I instructed the inhabitants of both the adjacent huts, especially the women folk, to endeavor to talk in low tones as far into the night as was possible, in order to attract the killer to that vicinity.

An objection was immediately raised, that the leopard might be led to enter one of their huts, instead of attacking the dummy in the doorway of the hut in which I was sitting. This fear was only overcome by promising to come to their aid should they hear the animal attempting an entry. The signal was to be a normal call for help, with which experience had shown the panther to be perfectly familiar, and of which he took no notice. This plan also assured me that the inhabitants would themselves keep awake and continue their low conversation in snatches, in accordance with my instructions.

Everything was in position by 6 P.M., at which time all doors in the village were secured, except that of the hut where I sat. The usual uncertain dusk was followed by bright starlight that threw the open doorway and the crouched figure of the draped dummy into clear relief. Now and again I could hear the low hum of conversation from the two neighboring huts.

The hours dragged by in dreadful monotony. Suddenly the silence was disturbed by a rustle in the thatched roof which brought me to full alertness. But it was only a rat, which scampered across and then dropped with a thud to the floor nearby, from where it ran along the tops of the boxes before me, becoming clearly visible as it passed across the comparatively light patch of the open doorway. As the early hours of the morning approached, I noticed that the conversation from my neighbors died down and finally ceased, showing that they had fallen asleep, regardless of man-eating panther, or anything else that might threaten them.

I kept awake, occasionally smoking my pipe, or sipping hot tea from the flask, but nothing happened beyond the noises made by the tireless rats, which chased each other about and around the room, and even across me, till daylight finally dawned, and I lay back to fall asleep after another tiring vigil.

The following night, for want of a better plan, and feeling that sooner or later the man-eater would appear, I decided to repeat the performance with the dummy, and I met with an adventure which will remain indelibly impressed on my memory till my dying day.

I was in position again by six o'clock, and the first plan of the night was but a repetition of the night before. The usual noise of scurrying rats, broken now and again by the low-voiced speakers in the neighboring huts, were the only sounds to mar the stillness of the night. Shortly after 1 A.M. a sharp wind sprang up, and I could hear the breeze rustling through the thatched roof. This rapidly increased in strength, till it was blowing quite a gale. The rectangular patch of light from the partly open doorway practically disappeared as the sky became overcast with storm clouds, and soon the steady rhythmic patter of raindrops, which increased to a regular downpour, made me feel that the leopard, who like all his family are not over-fond of water, would not venture out on this stormy night, and that I would draw a blank once more.

By now the murmuring voices from the neighboring huts had ceased or become inaudible, drowned in the swish of the rain. I strained my eyes to see the scarcely perceptible doorway, while the crouched figure of the dummy could not be seen at all, and while I looked I evidently fell asleep, tired out by my vigil of the two previous nights.

How long I slept I cannot tell, but it must have been for some considerable time. I awoke abruptly with a start, and a feeling that all was not well. The ordinary person in awaking takes some time to collect his faculties, but my jungle training and long years spent in dangerous places enabled me to remember where I was and in what circumstances, as soon as I awoke.

The rain had ceased and the sky had cleared a little, for the oblong patch of open doorway was more visible now, with the crouched figure of the dummy seated as its base. Then, as I watched, a strange thing happened. The dummy seemed to move, and as I looked more intently it suddenly disappeared to the accompaniment of a snarling growl. I realized that the panther had come, seen the crouched figure of the dummy in the doorway, which it had mistaken for a human being, and then proceeded to stalk it, creeping in at the opening on its belly, and so low to the ground that its form had not been outlined in the faint light as I had hoped. The growl I had heard was at the panther's realization that the thing it had attacked was not human after all.

Switching on my torch and springing to my feet, I hurdled the barricade of boxes and sprang to the open doorway, to dash outside and almost trip over the dummy which lay across my path. I shone the beam of torchlight in both directions, but nothing could be seen. Hoping that the panther might still be lurking nearby and shining my torchbeam into every corner, I walked slowly down the village street, cautiously negotiated the bend at its end, and walked back up the next street, in fear and trembling of a sudden attack. But although the light lit up every corner, every rooftop and every likely hiding place in the street, there was no sign of my enemy anywhere. Then only did I realize the true significance of the reputation this animal had acquired of possessing diabolical cunning. Just as my own sixth sense had wakened me from sleep at a time of danger, a similar sixth sense had warned the leopard that here was no ordinary human being, but one that was bent upon its destruction. Perhaps it was the bright beam of torchlight that had unnerved it at the last moment; but, whatever the cause, the man-eater had silently, completely and effectively disappeared, for although I searched for it through all the streets of Gummalapur that night, it had vanished as mysteriously as it had come.

Disappointment, and annoyance with myself at having fallen asleep, were overcome with a grim determination to get even with this beast at any cost.

Next morning the tracks of the leopard were clearly visible at the spot it had entered the village and crossed a muddy drain, where for the first time I saw the pugmarks of the slayer and the peculiar indentation of its right forefoot, the paw of which was not visible as a pugmark, but remained a blur, due to this animal's habit of placing it on edge. Thus it was clear to me that the panther had at some time received an injury to its foot, which had turned it into a man-eater. Later I was able to view the injured foot for myself, and I was probably wrong in my deductions as to the cause of its man-eating propensities; for I came to learn that the animal had acquired the habit of eating the corpses that the people of that area, after a cholera epidemic within the last year, had by custom carried into the forest and left to the vultures. These easily procured meals had given the panther a taste for human flesh, and the injury to its foot, which made normal hunting and swift movement difficult, had been the concluding factor in turning it into that worst of all menaces to an Indian village—a man-eating panther.

I also realized that, granting the panther was equipped with an almost-human power of deduction, it would not appear in Gummalapur again for a long time after the fright I had given it the night before in following it with my torch light. It was therefore obvious that I would have to change my scene of operations, and so, after considerable thought, I decided to move on to the village of Devarabetta, diagonally across an intervening range of forest hills, and some eighteen miles away, where the panther had already secured five victims, though it had not been visited for a month.

Therefore, I set out before 11 A.M. that very day, after an early lunch. The going was difficult, as the path led across two hills. Along the valley that lay between them ran a small jungle stream, and beside it I noted the fresh pugs of a big male tiger that had followed the watercourse for some two hundred yards before crossing to the other side. It had evidently passed early that morning, as was apparent from the minute trickles of moisture that had seeped into the pugmarks through the river sand, but had not had time to evaporate in the morning sun. Holding steadfastly to the job in hand, however, I did not follow the tiger and arrived at Devarabetta just after 5 P.M.

The inhabitants were preparing to shut themselves into their huts when I appeared, and scarcely had the time nor inclination to talk to me. However, I gathered that they agreed that a visit from the man-eater was likely any day, for a full month had elapsed since his last visit and he had never been known to stay away for so long.

Time being short, I hastily looked around for the hut with the highest wall, before which I seated myself as on my first night at Gummalapur, having hastily arranged some dried thorny bushes across its roof as protection against attack from my rear and above. These thorns had been brought from the hedge of a field bordering the village itself, and I had had to escort the men who carried them with my rifle, so afraid they were of the man-eater's early appearance.

Devarabetta was a far smaller village than Gummalapur, and situated much closer to the forest, a fact which I welcomed for the reason that I would be able to obtain information as to the movements of carnivora by the warning notes that the beasts and birds of the jungle would utter, provided I was within hearing.

The night fell with surprising rapidity, though this time a thin sickle of new moon was showing in the sky. The occasional call of a roosting jungle cock, and the plaintive call of peafowl answering one another from the nearby forest, told me that all was still well. And then it was night, the faint starlight rendering hardly visible, and as if in a dream, the tortuously winding and filthy lane that formed the main street of Devarabetta. At 8:30 P.M. a sambar hind belled from the forest, following her original short note with a series of warning cries in steady succession. Undoubtedly a beast of prey was afoot and had been seen by the watchful deer, who was telling the other junglefolk to look out for their lives. Was it the panther or one of the larger carnivora? Time alone would tell, but at least I had been warned.

The hind ceased her belling, and some fifteen minutes later, from the direction in which she had first sounded her alarm, I heard the low moan of a tiger, to be repeated twice in succession, before all became silent again. It was not a mating call that I had heard, but the call of the King of the Jungle in his normal search for food, reminding the inhabitants of the forest that their master was on the move in search of prey, and that one of them must die that night to appease his voracious appetite.

Time passed, and then down the lane I caught sight of some movement. Raising my cocked rifle, I covered the object, which slowly approached me, walking in the middle of the street. Was this the panther after all, and would it walk this openly, and in the middle of the lane, without any attempt at concealment? It was now about thirty yards away and still it came on boldly, without any attempt to take cover or to creep along the edges of objects in the usual manner of a leopard when stalking its prey. Moreover, it seemed a frail and slender animal, as I could see it fairly clearly now. Twenty yards and I pressed the button of my torch, which this night I had clamped to my rifle.

As the powerful beam threw across the intervening space it lighted a village cur, commonly known to us in India as a 'pariah' dog. Starving and lonely, it had sought out human company; it stared blankly into the bright beam of light, feebly wagging a skinny tail in unmistakable signs of friendliness.

Welcoming a companion, if only a lonely cur, I switched off the light and called it to my side by a series of flicks of thumb and finger. It approached cringingly, still wagging its ridiculous tail. I fed it some biscuits and a sandwich, and in the dull light of the starlit sky its eyes looked back at me in dumb gratitude for the little food I had given it, perhaps the first to enter its stomach for the past two days. Then it curled up at my feet and fell asleep.

Time passed and midnight came. A great horned owl hooted dismally from the edge of the forest, its prolonged mysterious cry of *"Whooo-whooo"* seeming to sound a death knell, or a precursor to that haunting part of the night when the souls of those not at rest return to the scenes of their earthly activities, to live over and over again the deeds that bind them to the earth.

One o'clock, two, and then three o'clock passed in dragging monotony, while I strained my tired and aching eyes and ears for movement or sound. Fortunately it had remained a cloudless night and visibility was comparatively good by the radiance of the myriad stars that spangled the heavens in glorious array, a sight that cannot be seen in any of our dusty towns or cities.

And then, abruptly, the alarmed cry of a plover, or "Did-you-do-it" bird, as it is known in India, sounded from the nearby muddy tank on the immediate outskirts of the village. *"Did-you-do-it, Did-you-do-it, Did-you-do-it, Did-you-do-it,"* it called in rapid regularity. No doubt the bird was excited and had been disturbed, or it had seen something. The cur at my feet stirred, raised its head, then sank down again, as if without a care in the world.

The minutes passed, and then suddenly the dog became fully awake. Its ears, that had been drooping in dejection, were standing on end, it trembled violently against my legs, while a low prolonged growl came from its throat. I noticed that it was looking down the lane that led into the village from the vicinity of the tank.

I stared intently in that direction. For a long time I could see nothing, and then it seemed that a shadow moved at a corner of a building some distance away and on the same side of the lane. I focused my eyes on this spot, and after a few seconds again noticed a furtive movement, but this time a little closer.

Placing my left thumb on the switch that would actuate the torch, I waited in the breathless silence. A few minutes passed, five or ten at the most, and then I saw an elongated body spring swiftly and noiselessly on to the roof of a hut some twenty yards away. As it happened, all the huts adjoined each other at this spot, and I guessed the panther had decided to walk along the roofs of these adjoining huts and spring upon me from the rear, rather than continue stalking me in full view.

I got to my feet quickly and placed my back against the wall. In this position the eave of the roof above my head passed over me and on to the road where I had been sitting, for about eighteen inches. The rifle I kept ready, finger on trigger, with my left thumb on the torch switch, pressed to my side and pointing upward.

A few seconds later I heard a faint rustling as the leopard endeavored to negotiate the thorns that I had taken the precaution of placing on the roof. He evidently failed in this, for there was silence again. Now I had no means of knowing where he was.

The next fifteen minutes passed in terrible anxiety, with me glancing in all directions in the attempt to locate the leopard before he sprang, while thanking Providence that the night remained clear. And then the cur, that had been restless and whining at my feet, shot out into the middle of the street, faced the corner of the hut against that I was sheltering and began to bark lustily.

This warning saved my life, for within five seconds the panther charged around the corner and sprang at me. I had just time to press the torch switch and fire from my hip, full into the blazing eyes that showed above the wide-opened, snarling mouth. The .405 bullet struck squarely, but the impetus of the charge carried the animal on to me. I jumped nimbly to one side, and as the panther crashed against the wall of the hut, emptied two more rounds from the magazine into the evil, spotted body.

It collapsed and was still, except for the spasmodic jerking of the still-opened jaws and long, extended tail. And then my friend the cur, staunch in faithfulness to his newfound master, rushed in and fixed his feeble teeth in the throat of the dead monster.

And so passed the "Spotted Devil of Gummalapur," a panther of whose malignant craftiness I had never heard the like before and hope never to have to meet again.

When skinning the animal the next morning, I found that the injury to the right paw had not been caused, as I had surmised, by a previous bullet wound, but by two porcupine quills that had penetrated between the toes within an inch of each other and then broken off short. This must have happened quite a while before, as a gristly formation between the bones inside the foot had covered the quills. No doubt it had hurt the animal to place his paw on the ground in the normal way, and he had acquired the habit of walking on its edge.

I took the cur home, washed and fed it, and named it "Nipper." Nipper has been with me many years since then, and never have I had reason to regret giving him the few biscuits and sandwich that won his staunch little heart, and caused him to repay that small debt within a couple of hours, by saving my life.

NINE MAN-EATERS AND ONE ROGUE
GEORGE ALLEN & UNWIN LTD. LONDON, ENGLAND 1954

Back in the 1930s, Eric Collier took his wife, Lillian, and their son, Veasy, and moved into the primitive wilderness of British Columbia. He built his cabin, and his family lived off the land by hunting, fishing, and trapping. Collier wrote a book about his family and their experiences. It's titled Three Against the Wilderness, *and was published by E. P. Dutton & Co., Inc. in 1959. If you can locate a copy, get it and read it. You won't be sorry. Why did I pick a chapter from this book? Because of one comment Collier made about his run-ins with Wolf. Collier says, "Whenever I took a mink, muskrat, or otter from a trap, I was killing. The wilderness insisted that I kill, or else pack up and leave it and never come back. No man can hope to survive long in a wilderness without killing. That's how it was with Wolf."*

The Wolf and I
by ERIC COLLIER

THERE was black rage born in my heart, an oath on my lips, the day I stalked broodily around one of our finest beaver colonies and marked the telltale evidence of the havoc that Wolf's penchant for murder had wrecked upon the beavers. There was the offal of one's guts here, a few bedraggled scraps of fur there. There was the half-eaten carcass of an old buck beaver alongside a recently felled cottonwood tree, and that was ample indication to me that Wolf was almost full of belly before ever he sank teeth into that one.

But it was the killing of the old mother beaver that fanned my rage into wild and terrible flame. There she lay, belly to the sun, not more than a dozen steps from the lodge, bloated and stinking, dark underfur speckled white with blowfly eggs. She was an old beaver, true, but right in her very prime where motherhood is concerned. She was an old sow beaver who could be reckoned upon to give birth to four or five sturdy kits each June for many a year to come. But now she was dead, killed by a single crunch of Wolf's rapacious jaws. Yet not an ounce of her flesh had Wolf eaten. Here before me was the wilderness in its sourest mood; a mother beaver killed for no useful purpose whatsoever, at least none that I could think of.

It was mid-June 1932, and the aspens and willows were properly

leafed out. Water lilies and similar aquatic plants pushed their stems
to the surface of the water, and a raft of newly hatched geese had
been perched on the beaver house when first it came into my view.
It was mid-June and young wilderness life was everywhere, and rotten
though the underbelly of the old sow was, I knew that her udder had
been full of milk when Wolf snuffed out her life. I stepped on to the
lodge, reluctantly, and stood there a few moments, listening for what
I knew I must hear. Then suddenly I heard it, the faint whimper
from deep within the lodge that told me of the kits, dying the lingering,
bitter death of starvation.

That's when I lifted my face to the sky and vowed, "I'll get you if
it takes until the crack of doom to do it!" But it was a threat easily
spoken, not quite so easily fulfilled.

Despite all the damage he did us in the four years of our feuding,
never at any time was I able to consider him entirely as an enemy.
There was a bond linking us together that the whole bloody score of
his crimes could not altogether sever: we were both a part of the wilderness, both reliant upon the wilderness for our daily bread. Whenever I took a mink, muskrat, or otter from a trap I was killing. The
wilderness insisted that I kill; or else pack up and leave it and never
come back. No man can hope to survive long in a wilderness without
killing.

That's how it was with Wolf. He could no more deny himself the
pleasure (or the need) of killing than a bull moose can deny the fever
of the mating season. His sanguinary lust for destruction was his by
right of heritage, born in him and nurtured in him at the dugs of the
shaggy furred bitch that whelped him.

His huge footprint in mud or snow where he ranged will-'o-the-
wisp over our trap line often stared me in the face during those four
years that I hunted him, yet only once did I catch sight of him in the
living flesh. That was in mid-December when I was trapping for mink
and otter in a warm spring of water that boiled up unfrozen among
the spruce trees girding a muskrat marsh. Such springs are not un-
common on any northern trap line and their water stays open even
at a chill forty below. I had ridden a horse down to the edge of the
marsh but then tied it to a tree and crossed the ice on foot. My heavy
gun was in its scabbard on the saddle, a single-shot .22 slung over my
shoulder in case there should be a live mink or otter in the traps.

A gray form suddenly took shape among the bulrushes, so large
that at first I thought it was a deer. But as it turned to run I knew
that at long last Wolf and I had met, with only 120 yards of ice between
us. For a half dozen seconds the killer wolf stood broadside to me, a
capital shot for any rifle powerful enough to drop him. But the .22
on my shoulder might as well have been a slingshot for all the good

it was. Then his head turned and he broke into swift flight, an elusive flash of gray in the blinding winter sunlight, and melted from sight beneath the vague shadows of the spruces.

I angled over to the bulrushes to see what had he been up to now. The answer glared at me from the ice. The roofs of four muskrats houses were leveled to the ice, which to my reckoning meant that four muskrats had died limp and bleeding in Wolf's jaws.

The total sum of the losses he occasioned us in the four years that I hunted him is beyond reasonable tally. Some of his crimes were minor affairs—for a wolf—but they hurt just the same.

Such as the time he happened onto my sets in the spruce timber and without so much as a by your leave devoured two prime mink that were dead in the traps. Mink pelts at the time were in very active demand, worth fifty dollars apiece. He stole one hundred dollars from us then at a couple of licks of his jaws, and to show there was no ill feeling on his part about it, cocked his leg and urinated on the empty traps to boot.

Oh, he was sharp, as sharp as the keenest razor ever honed. If I carefully concealed three No. 4½ wolf traps under the dry spruce needles and tied the head of a deer above them for bait, what did he do? He circled the whole package, cocked his leg against a bush and moved on to kill a deer of his own. Yet if a lynx or a mink were caught in the traps he'd walk in, scornful of the scent of steel, and stow the furbearers away in his own cavernous gut. According to Indian folklore, all cultus (bad) Indians returned to earth after they'd died in the form of a timber wolf. If that is really so, the reincarnated Indian who had taken on the form of our wolf must have been a very cultus one indeed. Clever one too.

Wherever the phantom killer journeyed, you could be sure that at least a half dozen coyotes would be padding along at a safe but respectful distance in his backtracks. Opportunists that they were, coyotes are ever willing to let a wolf do the actual killing while they bring up the rear to feed at the leftovers when the wolf moves on. There was no lack of leftovers while Wolf ranged our trap line.

I was running a line of traps up the shoreline of Meldrum Lake. The lake ice, eight inches thick, was clear as a sheet of glass. I could look down out of the saddle and see shoals of fat squawfish beneath the horse's hoofs as if there were no ice at all. But the caulks in my horse's shoes were new caulks so there was little danger of the horse's skidding and spilling me on the ice.

A sliver of land jutted out into the lake and there an inch or two of snow covered the frozen ground. I left the ice to short-cut over the peninsula, and as soon as my horse was on snow I knew there had been murder committed somewhere close by. The coyote tracks on the peninsula told me that. Just before hitting ice again, I cut a track that dwarfed those of the coyote's as a cougar's would a house cat's. I knew who had made those tracks as soon as I saw them. "He's at it again," I bleakly informed the horse. "Wonder where?"

It was a question answered as soon as I rode onto ice again.

I'd seen the two deer, a doe and a fawn, sunning themselves on the spine of a ridge above the lake a couple of days earlier. All that was left of them now was a crimson smudge on the ice and a tuft or two of hair. Force of habit impelled me to drop seven or eight strychnine baits on the frozen blood, and scrape deer hair over them with a stick so that magpies or blue jays wouldn't find them and haul them away to the top of some nearby tree. Since Wolf began raiding our trap line I always carried a few poison baits in my travels, spurred by the hope that someday he'd blunder and gobble one or two down.

Then I neck-reined away from the ice and circled up in the timber. I located the fir tree beneath which the doe and fawn had bedded. Their tracks in the snow led in wild leaps to the lake, Wolf's loping prints moving in behind. The deer had no hope of survival when they began skidding crazily on the ice.

Two days later I was again tending the Meldrum Lake traps with but slender hope that Wolf might have returned to the scene of the kill and picked up one of the baits. As I hove in sight of *x* marks the spot, I saw two coyotes forty yards from the kill, stiff in death. Just where timber and ice met was a third coyote that had also fallen victim to one of the baits. But Wolf hadn't been back. He was perhaps forty or fifty miles away by now for distance mattered little to him in a few inches of snow. He traveled here and traveled there, moving all the time, as if the guilt of his many crimes would not allow him to rest.

As time went on I lost all count of the coyotes that perished in traps, snares, or from poison bait set expressly for Wolf. But not for a moment did I swerve from my vow to bring him to justice.

The fourth winter of my hunt was a "heller" as we call such winters back here. I've lived through a half dozen such winters and each left its claw mark on me somewhere. As usual, he'd been ranging our trap line all fall. I was only a hundred or so yards behind him the day he chased a two-year-old cow moose out of a litter of windfalls and pulled her down on the edge of a two hundred acre beaver pond. I arrived on the scene in time to find her guts beginning to ooze through the gash he'd ripped in her flanks. But of course he heard me coming and was a half mile away maybe when I got there.

Between Christmas and New Year's Day a muddy overcast shoved in from the north. About midnight I was awakened by the banshee howling of wind. I got up and right then and there knew we were in for a "heller." I could feel the bitterness of the wind seeping in through the house logs. I loaded the heater stove with wood, and crawled back into bed, thinking about all the traps that were set and wondering when I'd get to visit them again.

In the morning, as I headed for the barn, I faced a north wind that almost cut me in two. Slanting in with the wind was a pitiless lash of snow. When snow falls in wet feathery flakes I know that the storm will soon blow over. It's the harsh granulated fall carried by screeching arctic winds that gives me cause for concern. You never know when it will quit or what its depth will be when it does.

For three days there was scarce a let-up to the blizzard. Perhaps there was a lull of sorts around lamp-lighting time, but after supper we could again hear the snow spitting against the kitchen window.

Lillian's flower garden was fenced by mesh wire, five feet high, and I sat broodily watching the snow inch steadily up the wire. When only a little of the fence showed above snow level I decided I'd better jar myself loose, saddle up the horse and go pull some traps set in the overflow of the beaver dams to the west.

Despite the sheepskin coat, fur chaps, moosehide mittens with woolen ones inside, I came near to freezing solid as I went from dam to dam. It was only twenty-three below when I pulled away from the house, but the drive of the wind and snow chilled the marrow in my bones. I bucked the storm for eight cruel hours, pulled my traps and was rewarded with a couple of mink and an otter. In all that bitter travel I never cut the track of a single animal, never set eyes upon a bird. It was like riding through a kingdom of the dead.

Only a few inches of the wire fence was in sight when the snow ceased falling. The overcast broke and by night a swollen, bitter moon bathed the forest in frigid light. The air became deathly still, not a single branch moving beneath its weight of snow, and a silent, searing cold stalked remorselessly across the wilderness. Water buckets in the kitchen froze overnight, and cans of milk and jars of fruit were frozen up too. The sting of the cold made me retch and cough as I went about the outside chores. Frost covered the horses when I opened the barn door in the morning and at any moment of the night we could hear the monotonous crunch of snow outside as moose moved to and fro, trying to keep warm by the simple process of forever keeping moving. Our thermometer ceases registering at fifty below. For six mornings in a row the mercury was cuddled despondently at the bottom of the glass, unable to go any lower. Was it sixty below or sixty-five? That's a question I'll never be able to answer but there were moments when I'd have sworn it was eighty.

January was almost spent when the chinook finally came. A warm wind spewed in from the Pacific, driving back the mass of polar air that had crucified the wilderness for so long. For thirty hours the mild air pushed in from the ocean, licking at the snow, moistening it, yet barely lessening its depth. Then as suddenly as it had arisen, the wind died, stars pricked the heavens, and the snow started to freeze.

"The snow will hold a twenty-five-pound coyote by morning," I uneasily remarked to Lillian. "And by the following morning, a full-grown wolf." I might have added that it would give beneath the hoofs of a moose or deer but that would have been superfluous; Lillian knew all about that.

That evening, when filling the water buckets at the water hole in the ice, I suddenly tensed, listening. What I heard welled up faintly from out of the east, mournful and eerie. It wasn't exactly an oath and it wasn't exactly a prayer; it was just the dismal, spine-chilling anthem of a timber wolf hunkered back on its haunches, howling at the moon. And I shook my head; death was again unleashed upon the land.

Was it *our* Wolf? That I couldn't say but I had every intention of soon finding out. The cry came from downcreek, in the neighborhood of our trapping cabin, I judged. By the time the water buckets were filled I knew just what we had to do and returned to the cabin and conveyed my thoughts to Lillian and Veasy.

"Timber wolf on the loose somewhere around the cabin downcreek," I said. "Reckon we'll pack up and move down there for a few days of look-see."

At the slight lift of Lillian's eyebrows, I went on, "There'll be blood on the crust come morning, maybe deer, maybe moose, but one or the other for sure. Maybe—" I shrugged and shifted course. "Might just as well be down there as up here."

"Just when are we going to move down?" Lillian asked with a frown.

"Day after tomorrow. I'll bust a track through in the morning." I knew the sheer impossibility of ever getting through to the cabin with a loaded sleigh unless I first broke out a track with the loose horses.

"That's not giving me much time to get things ready," she complained.

No, it wasn't. "If we don't get down there right away," I explained, "the son of a gun might be clear out of the country when we do." For time, tide, and timber wolves wait for no man.

"I'll have to bake bread, make up some pies, and do a lot of other cooking," groused Lillian. "Drat the timber wolves anyway. Why don't they behave themselves."

"They are behaving themselves," Veasy slipped in. "They're doing what comes naturally."

Veasy was a realist. At fourteen years of age he could run a line of traps as competently as men with a lifetime of experience at the job. Seldom did a buck deer get away from him once he latched onto its

tracks. Of course, Veasy had a little Indian blood in his veins and
sometimes that blood asserted itself. He could find his way out of the
deep woods in the middle of the night if need be, and without trail
or star to steer him. To Veasy, trapping was a means of making money,
hunting a means of getting meat. Both were just a part of the daily
chores, like packing water or splitting wood. Another job to be done,
and the sooner done the better.

His mind was miles ahead of his years. At an age when other children
were still reading comics, Veasy was reading Karl Marx (though not
agreeing with all that he read). And instead of giving his mind to
whodunnits, he gave it to Lewis's *Theory of Economic Growth.*

By the time he was fifteen Veasy had killed three timber wolves
and collected a forty dollar government bounty on their scalps. A coyote that came within the sights of his gun was dead when he touched
off the trigger. But he got no enjoyment out of killing either. At a
very early age the granite realism of his wilderness upbringing taught
him that every muskrat killed by an owl, or beaver by a coyote was a
financial loss to us. Yet he knew that all predators were born to fulfill
a purpose, and that when taking the life of another creature they
were merely "doing what comes naturally."

The trap line cabin was only four or five miles away. The road we
had cut to it followed the downward course of the creek, and when
the ice of the beaver ponds was safe we traveled it where possible.

Five miles! I could snowshoe there in an hour and a half given the
right kind of snow, yet it was to take me all of three days to get there
with a loaded sleigh. I struck out at sunup in the morning, riding my
saddle horse and driving the harnessed team ahead of me. They wer-
en't hitched to anything, just breaking out the track. The front legs
of the horses were bandaged in canvas wraps much as the traps were
bandaged when we live trapped the beavers. If they hadn't been, the
crust would have slashed their skin and drawn blood within a half
mile of leaving the house.

Travel was woefully slow, for the full depth of the snow hit the
horses at the point of their shoulders. Coyote tracks criss-crossed the
road every few yards, and about a mile out from home I cut the track
of a single deer. On the windward side of the deep furrow he'd left
behind in the snow were the claw marks of three or four loping coyotes.
I thought—"They'll haul up to the critter before it's gone a mile." By
now there'd be a crimson splash or two on the snow here, a few scraps
of hide there, and maybe a thin scattering of offal. But no more. The
deer had no chance at all.

It took four hours to get through to the cabin, and the horses were
gray with frosted sweat when I hitched them to a cottonwood tree

close to the building. The wrappings on their legs were slashed to ribbons but that didn't matter now that the track was broken out.

I took a half dozen pack rats out of the traps that had been left set for them, cursed those that hadn't been caught but had left their droppings all over the table. I started a fire in the sheet iron cookstove, and fried a half dozen rashers of bacon. The bacon was hanging on a wire from the ridge logs where pack rats couldn't get at it. The cold had given me an appetite and after mopping up the grease with soda biscuits the world seemed a whole lot brighter, and I was ready for the trip back.

Before I could haul a load down though—hay and oats for the horses, bedding and provisions for ourselves—I first had to plow out the track with the front runners of the sleigh. This took most all of a second day so it was close to light-the-lamp time of the third day when we reined a tired team alongside the cabin door and began tossing out gear.

Late the previous October I'd killed a bull moose about a mile and a half from the cabin. After quartering the bull out and loading the meat on packhorses, I'd liberally sprinkled poison bait around the innards and other offal in certain expectation that either a wolf or a coyote would happen along for a meal. And that is what had lured me to the cabin now: the slender chance that perhaps acute hunger had brought Wolf to the leftovers, and that when pawing in the snow he'd make a mistake and swallow one of the baits.

The weather sided with me that night. Half an inch of powdery snow fell that would allow me to follow clear-cut sign on the crust. I knew I could make far better tracking time on snowshoes than on horseback, so I softened up the snowshoe harness with coyote grease, pocketed the venison sandwiches Lillian had packaged for me, and struck off through the woods, rifle cradled in my arm, hope warming my heart. The crust under my webs was as solid as set cement, and I clipped along at a good three miles an hour.

I braked up a little as I neared the site of the kill, for now I was cutting coyote tracks, lots of them. There was little left of the guts. Coyotes had dug down in the snow and got most of them. I didn't take time out to circle for dead coyotes. About a hundred yards from the old kill was a bare knoll with a single massive fir tree growing square on the top. I knew that wolves have a penchant for lying in such spots, where they can see all that is going on around them. So I moved over to the knoll.

I was almost on top of it when I stopped the soft swish of my snowshoes. I was looking down on a track that had not been made by any coyote.

"Wolf!" I said slowly. For by now I knew his track when I saw it as well as I knew that of my own saddle horse. I was looking at the pad marks of the wolf that had been cheating me out of my beavers, the wolf that had killed countless scores of moose and deer, that had robbed our traps of their catch whenever he came across them. He'd bellied at the foot of the tree long enough for the heat of his body to melt the crusted snow. He knew exactly where the moose guts were, but he hadn't come closer than a hundred yards of them. Oh, he was crafty, ever suspicious of any meat he hadn't just killed himself.

I circled the knoll and picked up his tracks leading away to the north. He traveled the length of a pothole meadow, wove through a stand of spruce as thick as the fur on a lynx. He climbed a drear, timberless hogback, dropped down the other side, and suddenly swung sharp east into scattered pine timber. Here he stopped abruptly and crouched down in the snow.

Fifty yards ahead of me a single deer had furrowed through the snow. Thin lines of blood on either side of its trail were visible from where I stood. "The crust," I told myself. "It's slicing the deer's legs."

Wolf had trotted up to the deer's trail and nosed the blood. Then he broke into a lope, keeping on the windward side of the sign. The one-sided contest had commenced.

Beneath a huge pine I was able to read the deer's tracks clearly. They had been made by either a very large buck or an equally large doe. Wolf's tracks lengthened, and a half mile farther on I came to where the deer was jumped. Wolf's stride let out a little. The deer bounded off through the crust in lunges twenty feet apart. Wolf's stride let out still more. The deer tracks began to weave crazily, here and there the doomed animal had staggered. Now Wolf was loping with every ounce of speed he could summon.

He caught up to the deer as it broke out of the timber, and started across a clearing. There it piled up in a ten-foot snowdrift. It may have died from fright and exertion even before Wolf's teeth ripped through its liver. Anyway, I hoped so.

Wolf had eaten the heart and the liver, strewn guts over the snow, and chewed off most of one hindquarter. That was all he ate, so by that I knew that this wasn't his only kill since the snow crusted. A really hungry timber wolf will eat a deer at a meal.

I judged that the deer had been killed around daybreak, so Wolf had at least a four hour start on me and might now be a dozen or more miles away. But the whole afternoon was ahead of me, so I ate my sandwiches, sucked at a mouthful of snow, and inspected my snowshoe webbing. Then I slipped forward on the tracks.

Wolf had bedded down under a tree for maybe an hour, then struck east again at a steady trot.

"He'll come out at the Big Lakes if he holds in that direction." I calculated aloud. The Big Lakes, six miles long, marked the eastern boundary of our trap line.

As I neared the lakes I saw considerable moose sign. The lake shore was heavily fringed with willow and here the moose were yarded up. Though some of the tracks were quite fresh, Wolf paid them no attention as he moved steadily eastward.

Almost within sight of the ice I came out on a narrow avenue that I had cut through the thick spruce as a trail for saddle horses and pack animals when scattering traps out along the lake shore. Coyotes, foxes, and an occasional wolf traveled this easy path through the spruce so I had a few snares set out on it now that had been there since late fall. They were beneath the heavy overhang of leaning trees, where a deep fall of snow wouldn't put them out of action.

Wolf's tracks shortened as he came in sight of the snow-covered ice. I noted where he had bellied down in the snow a moment, before getting up and moving on. At the edge of the ice he stopped again and I wondered, "What's on his mind now?" Then as my eyes swept the ice I exploded, "You damned murderer!"

Tufts of dark hair were scattered over the ice ahead, and the snow was spangled with blood, as if a half dozen moose and as many wolves had battled there at the same time. But at closer range I saw that a single calf moose and the one wolf had made all the sign.

Wolf had played with and tortured the calf as a cat plays with a mouse. On a full stomach too. I wouldn't have begrudged Wolf even that calf if his belly was truly empty. But he had already gorged himself at the carcass of the deer.

The tufts of hair and blood in the snow told their own sordid tale of what had happened next. The calf moose was about to cross the ice when Wolf darted out between it and the shore. The killer drove the calf still farther out on the ice, then headed it off as a cow pony heads a steer. And every now and then, whenever the fancy struck him, Wolf closed in on the calf's flanks, leaping up at it with slashing fangs that drew blood with every leap. Wolf could have finished the job quickly there on the ice, but he preferred to prolong the calf's agony and his own sport.

Following the tracks on the lake I saw where Wolf had bellied down in the snow and allowed the calf to lurch ashore. I studied the belly mark in the snow a moment. I could picture Wolf lying there, an unholy grin on his face. And I thought, "You know the calf can't get far. You'll let him get into the timber, then you'll haul up on him, and enjoy another round of bloodletting."

I followed the calf's tracks into the timber. There Wolf's sign cut in again, in long lopes. Up through dense willow and thinning poplar the tracks took me, and spruce loomed ahead. I could see the blazed trees that denoted my trapping trail, along which snares were set.

I moved onto the trail, glanced along it, and suddenly rooted down in my tracks. My eyes bulged, and my heart beat slightly faster. "The snare!" The cry that leaped from my lips was one of surprise, and pent-up excitement. "Ye gods, he hit the snare." Then the huge gray body dangling at the end of the snare seemed to move. "He's alive!" I muttered aloud. And quickly I bolted a cartridge into my rifle and snapped the gun into my shoulder. Then slowly and foolishly lowered it. "He's dead as salt salmon," I told myself. It was the gentle movement of the tree to which the spring pole was fastened that swung his body to and fro as if indeed there were life in him yet.

Then I saw the calf, down in the snow thirty feet beyond the snare. I forgot for the moment about Wolf and slid past his dangling body to look at the mangled calf. It would never come to its feet again even though a beat or two of life was yet left in it. So I put the muzzle of the gun behind its ears and gently squeezed the trigger. It was better thus.

Again I turned to Wolf. I judged his weight at one hundred and ten pounds. Certainly he was the largest dead wolf I'd ever seen. I squatted slowly back on my snowshoes, grappling with the question of how and why he had blundered. In cold blood Wolf would never have thrust his head into that snare, camouflaged though it might be. Wolf had smelt the steel of too many snares for that. Perhaps it was the old, old story of a pitcher going to the well just once too often. Momentarily blinded to all else but his desire to haul up to the calf, Wolf had thrust his head into the snare without having time to scent its whereabouts. His first frantic lunge had released the trigger that held the tip of the twenty-five-foot pole to which the snare was fastened. As the pole raised, Wolf was lifted into the air and though he struggled to escape the clutch of the thing that was choking away his life, the snare, like Wolf himself, knew nothing at all of pity. All that it caught it killed.

Thus Wolf died. A murderer all his life, he died a murderer's death. With wind sobbing mournfully through the treetops, and moon's first crescent staring sardonically down, seeing much, saying nothing.

From THREE AGAINST THE WILDERNESS by Eric Collier. Copyright 1959 by Eric Collier. Reprinted by permission of the publisher, E. P. Dutton & Co., Inc., a division of New American Library.

In "Hard Choice," Jim tells us about the awesome task that faced him when his father died and he had to choose one of his guns and the memories that came along with it. It's a story you're not likely to forget and one that will one day face most of us. Let's hope that all our shotguns and deer rifles become more than just wood and steel to those who follow us.

Hard Choice

by JIM BERLIN

A week or so after the Old Man died, the moment came for my brother and me to split up his guns.

There were only four, but when we laid them side by side on his bed like fallen soldiers after a battle, it seemed an awesome task. For these were much more than guns. Each one, when hefted, became an instant bearer of tales both short and tall, a magic ticket back through time to the days when Dad was young and the future forever.

I decided to choose only one of the four, my excuse being a plane trip ahead and too much baggage already. In fact, it was emotional baggage that concerned me. One gun was all the weight I could bear.

The single-shot 12 was quickly eliminated. It had been Jack's to use during the first years in the field, and I knew how he felt.

"The single is yours," I said.

"Thanks," he said. "Why don't you take the double?"

He was talking about the 10-gauge with Damascus barrels, a collector's item handed down from our grandfather and stored in a series of closets ever since. The Old Man had considered it unsafe to fire, and none of us ever had.

"I've got a daughter; you've got sons," I said. "Give it to one of your boys someday."

That left two guns on our father's bed, the two that meant the most to me—his Remington 16-gauge and the lever-action .38/55 Marlin, put together with caring hands back in 1893. These were not closet guns. The Old Man had kept their barrels warm and working for the past forty years.

I picked up the pump, pressed the slide release, and racked it open. What a fine, familiar sound. And what a fine, familiar sight. . . .

The Old Man is struggling into a brown hunting coat, and I am next to him, belly-button-high, thrilling to the rattle of shotgun shells in his pockets. Now he chambers a round, turns the pump over, and slips one Super X after another into the tubular magazine. There is a soft click as each one catches.

Duke, the black-and-white springer spaniel, is more excited than both of us. He is already working the ditch next to our '49 Ford, plowing a furrow through October leaves with one of the finest noses in all dogdom.

"Duke!" Dad shouts. "C'mere, boy. Don't be getting ahead."

The Old Man hands me two shells and says to keep them ready in case they're needed in a hurry. I am the ammo carrier, a responsibility too heavy to be trusted to pockets. I will clutch the two shells in my hand the entire hunt.

We enter the ditch, clamber up the other side, and begin slowly walking a fenceline that separates a stubble field from several acres of corn. Duke is no more than thirty feet ahead, ranging back and forth, inhaling and analyzing, searching the myriad of scents for that one smell that means the world to him.

Suddenly, the Old Man picks up the pace, closing quickly on the dog.

"Duke is hot," he says. "Duke is hot."

I have to trot now to keep up. The springer is quivering from stem to stern, zeroing in on a heavy clump of brush near a fence post.

Dad stops, tenses, motions for me to stay behind him. "Hunt 'em up, Duke! Hunt 'em up, boy!"

Duke hunts 'em up. The eight-year-old springer plunges into the brush like a pup and sets off an explosion of browns and brilliant red. Two hen pheasants streak toward the corn on the right, but Dad and the dog are not distracted. It's the rooster they're after, beautiful against the blue, breaking left and ten yards out before the Old Man shoulders the gun.

The ringneck is cackling, Duke is leaping and barking, I'm shouting—and then the pump puts an end to all the confusion. The bird folds, and faithful old Duke, Duke with a mouth as soft as his heart, is off and running. And as I watch him go . . .

The bright, crisp colors of autumn fade and dim, and it is ten years later, just after dawn on a dreary November morning. I am one of two dozen or more hunters uniformly spaced and crouched along a ribbon of railroad track that borders the edge of a private duck-hunting marsh. I wondered then, and still do, how ordinary flesh-and-blood men could own something so wonderful as their very own marsh. Yet, because the ducks had no allegiance to wealth and moved freely in and out of the area each morning and night, we were content to hunt the public ground that surrounded it.

There were unspoken but strictly followed rules that governed the regulars who gathered along that half mile of track from October to December. On a first-come basis, each hunter stationed himself at one of the power poles set at intervals of perhaps forty yards. It was in the worst of taste to "split the poles" (plunk down between two correctly stationed hunters), and only a newcomer would make the attempt.

It was also terribly bad form to fire at ducks that appeared to be closer to the next fellow's pole than to your own. Often, the result was that a duck fortunate enough to split the poles as it passed in or out of the marsh was not fired upon at all.

They were fine rules to live by, rules from another era, from a time that no longer exists.

But the pump gun brought it all back, and on that particular dreary November morning the shooting had been good. Now it was past eight, the mist had lifted from the marsh, and only an occasional teal tried a low-level, darting escape across the tracks. Up and down the line, men and boys were standing, stretching, comparing notes, preparing to leave.

It began at the far end of the tracks, a single shot, muffled by distance, quickly followed by two more. A dozen hunters glanced casually to the right, wondering if another teal had made it through.

But then somebody with an autoloader kicked out a string of three—closer now. As far as I could see, hunters began crouching next to their poles.

I picked him out, a single, good size, flying straight and high down the railroad tracks, running the gauntlet, giving every mother's son a crack at his side. And everybody was missing.

On he came, gaining speed and altitude with each string of shot that whistled past his tail. The reports marched closer; the ducks grew larger, right on course, never wavering, nary a feather touched.

I began tracking him when he passed the next pole, matching his speed with the brass bead, now pulling ahead. How far? Three feet, no, go to four, squeeze, boom!—and on he went, undaunted, laughing at us all.

It had a funny sound, that pump gun of my Old Man's. A shallow metallic ring, like a blacksmith striking an anvil with the lightest of hammers. I can hear it even now, echoing down through the years.

Twang!

He was the last man in line, the only hunter there with a chance to preserve the honor of the railroad tracks.

Twang!

That duck hit the wall. It dropped like a stone. A stone, I tell you.

And the Old Man played it out like a pro. With nary a glance down the line, with the pump cradled ever so casually in the crook of his arm, he shuffled to the center of the steel tracks, picked up the duck, slipped it deftly into the game pocket of his coat, and lumbered back down the embankment to his pole.

I wished to God for a bullhorn at that moment. I would have mounted the tracks and aimed it to my right, aimed it at the gauntlet, and shouted out what they already knew:

"Did you see that, fellas, huh? That was my Old Man that just did that fancy piece of shootin'. That's right, my Old Man! The best damn wingshot on this whole damn railroad track!"

Twang! I can hear it even now, echoing down through the years . . .

"Do you want the pump?" Jack asked. "No problem if you do."

I could not reply. Instead, I laid the Remington gently to rest, picked up the old Marlin .38/55, and—before anything else—levered back the slide and checked the chamber. I knew, of course, there hadn't been a round in that chamber for at least three years, but the Old Man said to always check. I always do.

Despite its ninety-plus years, it remained a beautiful piece of work. The bluing had bowed out a generation back, but there was still a proud luster to the stock and a delicate balance that belied its forty-four inches from muzzle to buttplate.

A beautiful piece of work. And yet, as I shouldered it and lined up the sights, I experienced a familiar mixture of guilt and disappointment. It happened every time with that rifle, all because of that solitary incident on my birthday, twenty-four years earlier.

Twenty-four years. From frantic adolescence to the quieter but no less desperate resolves of impending middle age. And still the .38/55 reared up to haunt me.

As I said, it happened on my birthday, which was well within the odds because I was born on November 15, the traditional opening day of the Michigan deer season. (To my Dad's enduring credit, that was the one opening day he elected to miss. Instead, he fastened his metal deer tag to my bassinet and said to Mom, "This year, I'll just have to settle for a shorthorn.")

Fourteen years later, he and the state declared me old enough for big game, and we headed for his favorite hunting spot, several square miles of swamp and heavy timber near the tiny town of Luther.

My mother, an Irish Catholic, claimed that he hunted the Luther area just to bug her about his opposing theological roots, but I don't think the Old Man was that devious. It was simply a matter of going where he'd take his biggest bucks, the biggest of which was mounted on the front porch of our house.

On the front porch, mind you, smack in the middle of a fairly large city. The Old Man did not have a reputation for humility.

But he was well known for his generosity. On this, my first crack at a whitetail, I was assigned his .38/55 while he settled for slugs in the Remington pump. (That grand gesture went largely unappreciated until 1979, when a friend casually asked to borrow my .270 with the Leupold scope for a weekend hunt. The deal fell through when I said he could borrow the rifle but, in exchange, he would have to finance my daughter's college education.)

Yet even back in '56, I was thrilled knowing I'd be taking to the woods with a bona fide brush-buster like the .38/55. In fact, I had tremendous success with the Marlin well before the deer season began. I would close my bedroom door, ease the empty rifle from its cloth case and, in no time, monster bucks would slink from hiding and begin cavorting across the walls. I dropped them all with a single running shot to the neck, usually as they were in midbound over a log.

The hunter who has yet to hunt never misses. And I had yet to hunt.

We pulled into Luther at 4 A.M. on opening day and stopped at one of those diners that blossoms with business during deer season and limps along the rest of the year. There were only two waitresses in the whole place, and they were slapping flapjacks and bacon and eggs on the tables as fast as the short-order cook could scoop them from the griddle.

I was surrounded by a sea of hunters, all dressed in red, all awash with the excitement of another opening day. Stories of past hunts and future heroics filled the diner, blending with the smells of steaming coffee and maple syrup. And the Old Man, at my insistence, had a couple of stories of his own.

"The best shot I ever made? Well, Jamie boy, I've made a lot of terrific shots over the years, you know that. Always been a natural when it comes to shooting, just one of these gifts like playing the piano or painting a picture." (I already told you he wasn't humble.)

"Yeah, Pa, but what was the best you ever made?"

"Did I ever tell you about the time I got three ducks on the wing with just one shell?"

"Lots of times, Pa. I mean, what was the best shot you ever made on deer?"

"Well, it happened about fifteen years ago, right where we'll be hunting today. It was about eleven in the morning, and there wasn't anything moving, so I just kind of decided to take a little snooze. I don't know how long I slept, but something woke me up. Maybe a twig snapping, maybe just the hunter's instinct I was born with."

"What did you see, Pa, what did you see?"

He finished a mouthful of pancakes and washed it down with a slug of coffee before replying.

"What did I see? Well, I saw that same deer head that's hanging on our front porch, that's what I saw. Except it was attached to the rest of the deer and he was standing not fifteen feet to my right, looking me straight in the eye."

"Wow!"

"My feelings exactly. But right away I started figuring all the angles. I said to myself, 'The second I make a move, this buck is going to be hightailing it for parts unknown. If I'm going to get him, I'll have to get him quick.' "

"Wow!"

"Right. So I did the only thing I could do. I wheeled that .38/55 up with just one hand, just like it was a pistol, and let fly."

"And you got him, Pa?"

"Smack through the shoulder, Jamie boy. Dropped him right where he stood."

"Man oh man! Is that what you were aiming at, Dad—his shoulder?"

"Well, let's just say I was hoping for the best."

Did I believe that story he told at 4:15 A.M. in the Luther diner on November 15, 1956? Absolutely.

Do I still believe it today? Hey, if it was a good enough story to believe then, it's a good enough story to believe now. The Old Man was a showman, and he knew the time-honored value of brightening a yarn by adding a splash of color here and there, but he drew the line this side of lying.

Yes, I still believe it today. And because I do, what happened later that same morning still touches me like a dark cloud each time I shoulder the Marlin .38/55.

We arrived at the Luther swamp just before daybreak and started up a fire trail that seemed to go forever. It was thick timber on either side, dark and threatening, scattered with the same logs the monster bucks had so often jumped over on my bedroom wall.

Seeing those familiar logs filled me with a confidence only a greenhorn can experience. I would bag a trophy buck this day, and the Old Man would be filled with pride. Funny, I looked forward to that pride and his approval more than to the actual taking of a deer.

The morning light was growing, and the edges of the fire trail became less defined until they seemed to disappear. The Old Man stopped. We were on the apron of a large area of open timber surrounded by swamp.

He spoke quietly, pointing as he did. "Head that way about a hundred yards or so and you'll find three deer trails crossing one another. Pick yourself a good tree to set against, keep still, and keep your eyes open."

"Pa?"

"What?"

"Is that where you got the big one?"

"Well, somewhere in that area, yeah. I guess it was."

I started off in the direction he'd pointed, watching where I put my feet, stopping to look and listen, doing my darndest to appear the hunter. The .38/55 was cradled in the crook of my left arm, nonchalantly, just the way the Old Man did it. He had always been disparaging of those who carried their pieces in the field like they were on combat patrol.

"When a bird flushes," he said, "or a deer comes busting out of the brush, you need a couple of seconds to sort things out. You have to think before you shoot. The gun will get to your shoulder soon enough."

After a minute or so, I turned to see whether the Old Man was watching, but he was already gone. I guess by leaving he was letting me into his world.

I found the intersecting deer trails almost immediately and wasted no time picking out a thick tree for a backrest. I remember the morning being cold but not uncomfortable, and the sky so overcast that it seemed when dawn finally came and established itself, it refused to move on. The entire day would be one of subdued light, stark and gray all over, replaying itself in my mind in years to come like a black-and-white newsreel from the 1940s.

I was afraid to move during the first two hours against that tree. Like a virgin suitor on his first foray into the world of courtship, I sat stiff and wide-eyed in the woods, convinced that total immobility was the only defense against error.

But if I wasn't moving, neither was anything else. Caution eventually gave way to boredom, and then to imagination. I began shouldering the .38/55 and sighting in on tree stumps, pine cones, and sparrows, all bearing antlers of trophy size.

"Blam!" I would whisper. "Blam, blam!" I was dropping bucks all across my field of vision.

At about 10 A.M. the game grew old, and I decided to move a hundred yards to the northeast, closer to the surrounding swamp. I found another tree, placed my back to it, and slid down to a sitting position. Not being very careful, not being very quiet.

There are two incidents in my life that I can recount in precise sequence and detail. If you had been at my side immediately after the conclusion of either, the story I would have told you then would be exactly the same as the one I would tell you a decade later. Nothing added, nothing taken away.

The second incident occurred when I was a rookie Phoenix cop in foot pursuit of a robbery suspect. The very words I shouted, the feel of the gun belt bouncing on my waist, my excitement instantly transformed to horrified disbelief as he stopped, turned, pointed the revolver, and fired—I have it all on a slow-motion videotape in my mind.

The first incident occurred just seconds after I placed my fourteen-year-old back against that tree in the Luther swamp and slid to a sitting position.

A twig snapped. I barely heard it, but the sound was too distinct to ignore.

I looked to the left, expecting to see a squirrel perhaps, or more likely nothing at all. It had been a morning of nothing at all. But this time, well, let me replay the tape for you. . . .

I looked to the left, and all my deer-hunting fantasies—before and since—came together in an instant. Took on real bone, and flesh, and antlers. Oh my God, the antlers. A rocking chair. It was the first thing I saw and yet, as stunning as they were, it was the entire deer that shocked and stopped every moving part in my body.

If speed and grace are principal ingredients in a deer's survival, this buck seemed to have given it all away. Its neck was no neck at all but a hulking platform that dropped straight down from just behind the tip of the chin, then bulged out almost immediately to form a chest as proud and massive as any ever produced by an old swamp buck.

He was dark and smart and on full alert, picking his steps, glancing from side to side, ears at full cock like he'd been shot at too many times to ever forget, even for a moment.

He was the buck that editors of outdoor magazines put on their cover every October (drawings, not photographs). He was the buck that lurks in the private dreams of young boys and old men, the chance of a lifetime, the prod that pushes us all into the field year after year until everything goes to hell and our hunting days are over.

I can't tell you how much I wanted that buck. I won't even try. But I can tell you this: I didn't panic. I didn't go to pieces. I just plain screwed up. I got impatient.

I looked for an opening in his path and spotted one maybe twenty feet ahead. If he kept walking in the same direction, the .38/55 and I would have a clear shot in about ten seconds.

The moment the buck looked away, I raised the Marlin as slowly as possible and lined it up on the clearing. It was time to get the rifle cocked, and I knew how to do it correctly. The Old Man had carefully schooled me in the necessity of keeping pressure on the trigger while simultaneously easing back the hammer. That kept it from clicking. Kept everything silent.

I knew . . . and yet I decided it just wasn't all that important. The important thing was to shoot this buck the second it stepped into the clearing. Youth.

I thumbed back the hammer. It clicked. It clicked louder than any sound I've ever heard in the woods.

It was important. The old swamp buck reacted as if I'd just fired a cannon. He whirled and raced toward the swamp, whirled so fast and moved so quickly that he was twenty feet on his way before I had sense enough to swing the rifle from the clearing and throw a shot at his bounding back.

I knew I had missed. I knew I deserved to miss.

The Old Man must have been hunting pretty close because he showed up about three minutes later.

I told him what had happened. I told him what a giant buck it was. I told him about clicking the hammer.

"Maybe you hit him," he said. "Let's see if we can find some sign."

We looked. We found what I knew we would. Nothing.

"Hey, don't feel bad," the Old Man said. "Every guy misses a buck now and then. That's part of what makes hunting so much fun."

So much fun . . .

"You want the .38/55?" my brother asked.

The deserts, woodlands, and mountains of the world are teeming with four-footed phantoms, sentenced to hunt and browse in the shadows of human memory for decades beyond their allotted spans. Bear and buck, cougar and ram—each a golden opportunity gone awry, the perceived chance of a lifetime brushed aside by circumstance and error.

Each time an old hunter breathes his last, somewhere a phantom beast also lies down to die. They blink out together, these two, the hunter—and the one that got away.

"You want the .38/55?" he asked.

I have it beside me now. The Marlin .38/55, Model 1893. And you know what? Come this November, I think I'll leave my .270 with the Leupold scope at home when I take to the woods for deer. I think I'll just carry the old Marlin.

And maybe, just maybe, I'll run into the brother of that buck that lurks in the private dreams of young boys and old men.

What do you say, Old Man? Are you up for one more hunt?

OUTDOOR LIFE
JANUARY 1986

I think Leon Waddell, the hunter in this story, is like most hunters who have learned to love the wildlife. It's difficult to explain to a nonhunter how a hunter can love the wildlife yet pursue it and take its life. I know that whenever I kill a bird or animal, I always experience a moment of sadness, but it is always followed by the realization that I am also taking part in a challenge that is pure instinct in me. I feel good about it. So it is with Leon Waddell, a deer hunter who assumes a natural role when he is confronted with a deer under unusual circumstances. As hunters, we understand Leon and what he must do.

A Natural Notion

by DAVID SEYBOLD

LEON Waddell drove into the yard and unloaded the deer from the back of the pickup. His wife did not go out to meet him, but he didn't expect her to. If it had been November or December she would have rushed out the door and made a fuss over him, acting like a mother whose son emerges from the big game banged up but also the hero. She would have told him, among other things, that he was getting too old (he was fifty-three and in better shape than a man half his years) to be chasing deer through the woods. Then she would walk around the back of the pickup and inspect the deer and announce it was the best and most handsome one yet. She would smile and say they would have the heart that night and part of the liver in the morning. And while she carried on he would stand quiet and shy and full of pleasure. He would look at something else (he could never look directly at her when she was making a fuss over him) and think how she had said the same things every deer season (every deer season he killed a deer, that is) for as long as he could remember. Then he would say that he guessed he had got lucky again and that any fool could have shot that deer. They would say these things to each other while standing next to the pickup and deer. It would be cold and their breath would show white and thin as it drifted upward in pale mists and disappeared among the branches of leafless maples. Then he would look at her and see that she was hugging herself to keep warm. He would tell her it was too cold to be outside with nothing more than a sweater on. But he knew she would stay out there with him and not give an inch to the cold. He would say that it was unlikely the deer would skin and butcher itself and that if they were going to have a meal off the animal he had better get to work. And then she would turn for the house and he would carry the deer into the barn.

But it was May and not November or December. And it was six months after the New Hampshire deer season had closed. And it seemed so . . . so unnatural to see him bring a deer home when it was warm and not cold, when the only snow on the ground was deep in the woods, when trees were in new leaf, when there were more robins than evening grosbeaks. No, she would not go out to meet him. She would stay inside and pretend not to have seen any of it.

It came to her that perhaps he had broken the law. Such a farfetched possibility had never before occurred to her. Her husband was a man who believed in laws. Oh, he may not have always believed in the men who wrote and enforced laws, but he did believe in them. Yes, he did. And she recalled how he had explained the importance of laws to Stuart's boy. He had told the boy that laws were to people what motor oil was to an engine. He had said that laws lubricate society. They make things run a lot smoother. Without laws we'd seize up tighter than a frog's rear end, just like an engine that has run too long without oil. What you have to keep in mind, he had told the boy with a wink, is that some laws are good and some are bad. And that there's always someone changing them. Even when they don't need to.

She saw him limp and knew that the deer had not come easily, that he had had to work hard to get it. Then she saw how small the deer was and she sighed. Her husband never shot small deer. He wouldn't even shoot a doe unless it was the last day of the season and every buck in the county had eluded him. The poor thing, she thought, so small and frail. I hope it didn't suffer. And then she put the kettle on.

He had seen her watching him from the kitchen window. She'll stay put, he thought, and worry and wonder until I let on. That was the way of her whenever something out of the ordinary happened. Something would not be the way it was supposed to be and she would put herself behind the crowd. Oh, she'll be in a tizzy, all right. She'll have that kettle boiling up a storm in no time at all. Well, I can't say as I blame her much. No sir, I can't . . . me with a deer out of season and all. I expect she'll have to wait to hear about it, though. If I don't get the hide off this little fellow right now the meat will spoil and then there'll be no sense to any of it.

He hoisted the deer by its hind legs from a beam. Most deer he had hung from the beam were heavy and required muscle, and they were long and cleared the barn floor by only a foot or so. But this one was so light that he never even strained to hoist it, and it was so small that a child could have stood under it.

He had thought that skinning the deer would be fast work. But the deer's lightness worked against the process and it wouldn't hang still while he fisted the hide down toward the head. Most deer had hung heavy and solid from the beam, like a boxer's body bag, but this one swayed with every downward pull, like a carpet on a line that's being swatted with a broom.

When he finished the skinning he wondered if he should let the deer hang for a few days, to let the meat age. He could cover it with cheesecloth or black pepper to keep the flies off and it would probably work fine. But he decided against it and broke out the butchering knives and the saw. Better to be done with it now, he thought. And he wondered if maybe he wasn't a little afraid of being caught with an illegal deer in his barn. After all, he had broken the law. He wondered what they would do to him. Would he be fined or jailed or both? Maybe they would take his hunting and fishing license away. Well, he didn't give a damn what *they* did. The lot of 'em have their heads so far up their rear ends they have to pull down their zippers to brush their teeth, he said to himself, and then worked the boning knife against the sharpening steel. He knew damn well why he wasn't going to let the deer hang, and it had nothing to do with any laws or the breaking of them.

It was pleasant work, he had to admit. The barn was cool and the air and sunlight coming in through the wide barn door carried the scent of the warming earth. Swallows swooped in and out, gathering material for their nests, which they were building under the barn's eaves and among the rafters overhead.

He stopped working then and lit his pipe. He was not in so much of a hurry anymore. And he knew it was because he was working in the barn, which always had a way of calming him. It was the place he went to whenever he couldn't fish or hunt and he wanted to be alone.

I think I'll take a walk tonight, he said to himself. And he thought about the walk he had taken the night before. He had told Nancy he needed some tobacco and that a walk to the store would do him some good. "Well, I should think it would," she had said. "You've been sitting in a truck all winter long. You need some exercise. Yes you do." Which was true. He was the town's Road Agent and his winters were spent working erratic hours driving a snowplow or sander. He wanted to see the stars again, to see the winter constellations passing into the western sky and the approach of spring's constellations from the east. His father and grandfather had taught him about the stars when he was young, and he remembered how he had announced to them that when he grew up he was going to be an astronomer. But that was long ago, back when he was still in school and working for the town only during summer vacations. Well, he could still watch the stars, and he could still take pleasure in his ability to tell of changes in the seasons by observing them as well as a farmer could who knows the land and its subtle ways.

He looked through the small window over the butchering bench and out to the pasture and pine forest that surrounded it. Signs of spring were there, too. Patches of green rye were showing around the edges of pasture granite and fence posts. He had walked through the pasture two days before, when it was raining, and the ground was turning soft. He had walked through the pasture and into the pine forest and listened as the rain fell through the limbs of spruce and hemlock and made the whole forest hiss. The brook that ran from under the pines and out into the southwest corner of the pasture was running full and he thought that maybe this year he would dam it up and make a small pond. Clayton Rowe, who put his cows in the pasture every spring and summer, had offered to help any number of times. The brook would dry up in July or August and Clayton would have to lug water from the barn to the pasture. A pond would help Clayton and the cows and keep the well water that much higher. Well, maybe I'll see my way clear to do it this year, he said to himself. And then he remembered he had to tell Clayton that a section of the barbed-wire fence had been taken down by the limbs of a hemlock that fell during an ice storm last January.

He finished butchering and wrapped up what little meat the deer had yielded and put it in the chest freezer, which was kept in a stall. He cleaned the knives and saw and stored them and made sure the lid on the trash can was tightly on. He had put the deer's head and other unwanted parts in a plastic bag and then put the bag in a trash can, to be taken to the dump on Sunday. Raccoons and skunks lived under the barn and they would try their hardest to get the lid off and make a meal of the remains.

Done and done, he said to himself. And he felt pretty good. The anger and hurt that only a few hours before had been sharp and deep had dulled. He felt tired and strangely satisfied, as if he had made right some terrible wrong.

Now, though, he had to deal with Nancy. And won't she be in a tizzy, though, he thought. Yes she will. And he walked from the barn to the house knowing he would not tell her the truth about the deer.

He had learned a long time ago that when it came to animals and Nancy it was better to lie than to let on that an animal—any animal—

had suffered. And it was the damnedest thing for him to understand. She was so strong in the face of adversity and so understanding of suffering and she could see herself (and a lot of other people too) through any amount of hardship, as long as the adversity and suffering and hardship involved people and not animals. ("Why, folks have family and friends to help them through their troubles, but animals . . . why, the poor little creatures are all alone." And he would say, "Except for you," and she would get mad and walk away.) Oh, she thought hunting was all right, even worthwhile, though she never referred to it as a "sport." Hunting, in her mind, was no different than farming or gardening. It was practical, a natural thing for country folk to do. That her husband enjoyed hunting did not mean he inflicted pain or suffering on the animals he hunted. In fact, she was certain he didn't. (But how, he always wondered, could she think every animal he killed had died instantly, without pain or suffering?) Why, his hunting only made him a better provider. "Why else did the Almighty put deer and partridge and ducks and the like here?" she would say. But dogs and cats and the young of any animal were innocent (dogs running deer and cats killing birds did so only because their owners neglected them and they were bored) and she couldn't bear to hear or see their suffering. When Ransom Sargent's collie got hit by a car and died she took it as a death in the family. It was truly the damnedest thing for him to understand. And at times her carrying on would make him uncomfortable, for it was impossible not to be reminded of bad shots, shots that only wounded, and of animals that got away and died and . . . and suffered. And these were also times when he went to the barn.

He walked into the house and heard her in the front room. She was, by the sound of it, rearranging the china in the corner cupboard. Busywork, he thought. He had heard the sound many times before and knew that she had rearranged and dusted the pieces so many times that by now they were probably back in their original places.

"Any calls?" he said.

"No. Stuart stopped by to borrow your bait trap. He'll be back later on . . . said he was going bass fishing over to Otter Pond."

He washed his hands in the kitchen sink and heard her walk into the room. On the counter was a pie plate filled with chunks of young rhubarb. They were pink and covered with sugar and bread crumbs. He closed his eyes and imagined the smell of the finished pie. They had not had a fresh pie since Thanksgiving. And he realized he had not eaten since breakfast. He grabbed an apple from the fruit basket and took a bite.

"First pie of the season is about the best," he said between bites of the apple.

He turned to look at her and saw her face set in dour seriousness. She wouldn't look at him, not directly anyway, and he caught only a glimpse of her hazel eyes. Handsome she is when she's pleased, blessed she is when she's peeved, he thought.

He ought to tell me, she thought. He knows I know. Yes he does. He'll wait, though, until he's good and ready. Yes he will. And she cut thin slices of butter and placed them on top of the pie.

"Guess this weather will bring things out in proper fashion," he said. "That rain and this sun will put things in a growing mood. Yes they will."

He was watching her slice the butter and waiting for her to say something. Well, I guess she isn't going to say anything agreeable, he thought. I might just as well try to get her to say something disagreeable.

"I see the Sargents put their tomato plants out. We might just as well do the same. Weather like this will tend to them better outside than we can inside."

She covered the pie with a damp cloth and said, "Sargents always put their plants out too early . . . have as long as we've known them. We'll have a frost or two yet, we always do. There'll be a full moon next Saturday night and a killing frost with it. Always is. Yes there is. We'd be right to wait until the first to put them out."

She was right, of course. Not until the first of June did they plant anything but early peas in their garden. But she did speak up, he thought. Yes she did.

She went to put the pie in the icebox and he opened the door for her.

"Got a deer today," he said.

She backed up from the icebox and went to the sink.

"Oh," she said in an even voice. "How'd you come to get a deer this time of year?" My, but you do take your time, Leon Waddell, she thought. Yes you do.

"Road kill," he said matter-of-factly. "Found him up on the East Washington Road. Little thing, no more than fifty pounds soaking wet."

He looked at her and saw she had been looking at him. Her eyes were soft and doelike, motherly, as he had expected. But her expression was still stern and serious and he was surprised. It seemed to suggest he wasn't telling her the whole truth, that there was something more. There was, of course, but he wasn't going to tell her. There's something else on her mind, he thought. Yes there is.

"Was it dead when you found it?" she said. "Was the doe around? My, but how the poor little thing must have suffered." She put the kettle on and went to the cupboard for her tea.

"Dead as dead can be when I arrived," he lied. "I imagine it didn't know what hit it . . . car must have been speeding right along."

"Sometimes the doe will stay right with her young. Did you see her? Oh, the poor thing," she said, refusing to give up thinking the worst had happened. And he could tell she was truly worried and upset by the way she worked her hands in the folds of the apron.

"Didn't see her," he lied again. "Why, I'd bet she had twins and when she saw and heard the one get smacked like that that she took off with the other."

The kettle sang and she poured her tea. He made a cup of instant coffee and walked into the front room. He thought it was over and that she'd worry herself for a time but that by supper she'd be somewhat calm. He sat down by the window and drank his coffee. She followed him into the room and took her chair by the front window.

"What did the warden say?" she said. "Did he say you could have it?"

"I didn't tell the warden or anyone else," he said. There was a new warden in their area and he had not been at all impressed with him. He was young and lazy and he considered him a "roadside warden," which meant he never left his cruiser for more than a few minutes at a time.

"Then you broke the law," she said sternly. "If you don't report that deer to the warden, won't they arrest you?"

"I don't give a damn what *they* do. As for that warden, all he'd do is write it up in his book and take the deer to the dump. That's what he does. He takes road kills to the dump and leaves them for the rats and anything else that happens along."

So that's what it is, he thought. I've broken the law and she's afraid I'm going to jail.

"Ain't anyone going to jail," he said. "Let them try and I'll tell them what's right and what's wrong. Yes I will. Why, all he'd have to do is dress out the deer and take it to a state home or to someone he knows who's in need of some fresh meat. Lord knows, there's a lot of folks who'd welcome some venison. Kiernan used to do it all the time. Yes he did. He knew it was the proper thing to do. Yes he did. But this new one . . . why, he's too damn lazy. Hell, he even admitted to Jim Lamson that road kills are a waste of his time. His gut should be empty sometime. Yes it should be. Why, if Kiernan were alive today he'd have him across a stone wall counting chipmunk droppings faster than you can blink your eyes. Yes he would!"

By God, but what I wouldn't give to have Kiernan back in uniform, he thought. Here it is 1981 and there are fewer deer in the woods than ever before, and the game wardens these days are all educated and lazy and throwing away any animal that might mean they'll have to get their hands dirty. Yes sir, it's something, all right. Makes you wonder if all that education they get takes away all notion of what's right and what's wrong. Yes it does.

She let him have his say and when he was done they were silent. He sat and stared out the window and she fidgeted with the folds of her apron. Her husband was not given to such emotional outbursts. He was a quiet man who preferred listening and thinking to speaking.

"Kiernan isn't here anymore," she said in a voice that was only slightly above a whisper. "He's dead and so are a great many of his kind. Even so, right or wrong, the law's the law . . . the same now as it ever was. You can't just go off and take what isn't yours. No you can't."

She had never seen him this way. He was different and she didn't understand him. (Had she really talked to him that way, as if he were Stuart's boy?) She looked at him and saw his face was tense and that his eyes were set in a seriousness she had seen only once before— when he had found the Clarke boy drowned in the Blackwater River and told Kiernan that he knew the parents and that he'd tell them. There's something knotted up inside him, she thought. Yes there is.

"Well, I'm not going to call a man to come and get a deer that he's going to throw on a heap of trash. No I'm not!"

He had not expected this to happen. He had not expected her to argue with him, to talk to him as if he were ten years old. Why, he wondered, can't she see that me keeping that deer is my right . . . or anyone else's who has a notion of what's right and what's wrong?

She had had enough of listening and talking and not understanding. She felt empty and hurt and confused. And very tired. In thirty-one years of marriage they had never acted this way to each other. She wished they were in bed and that they were looking up into the darkness and talking to each other in voices that somehow always made sense.

"Well," she said in a tired voice, "at least the poor thing didn't suffer. That's one right thing."

At that he stood up and said he had to call the garage and tell Clark to lock up and that he'd see him in the morning. Then he told her he was going out to the barn and rebuild some of the tomato cages.

He was not a big man, not quite six feet and only about one hundred and seventy pounds. He had a way about him, though, that when he walked he appeared much larger than he really was. But as she watched him walk across the yard to the barn, she thought he looked small, even smaller than he actually was. She saw him limp and wondered what had happened to make his leg act up like that. He's tired, she thought. He's tired and upset. He needs a rest. So do I. Yes we do.

He went to where he kept the tomato cages and sorted out the ones that needed repair. He put them next to the workbench and then went through a pile of scrap hardwood until he found some old maple stakes that would make good legs for the cages.

While he worked he thought about what he had said to Nancy. He had been wrong to talk to her that way. It was not like him. And it was not like her to talk to him like she had. But he was the cause, the reason why she had. Maybe it was the deer, the truth about the deer which he would not tell, maybe it was her arguing about the law, maybe it was a combination of both. He really didn't know. Well, at least she'll never know the truth about the deer, he thought. That's one good thing. And then he pictured the deer as he had found it.

At first, he wasn't sure what it was. It could be a dog, though he doubted a dog would be so far from houses unless it was running with a pack. Or it could be a coyote feeding on a small road kill, which would be understandable.

He approached the animal very slowly, letting the pickup idle along the shoulder of the road. When he got to within a hundred feet he saw it was a deer, a very small one. He stopped the pickup and wondered what a deer was doing on the side of the road flopping around like a fish out of water.

"Now isn't that the damnedest thing," he said. "Yes it is." He saw that the deer was trying to run into the woods on legs that were only half there.

He didn't know what to do, which surprised him. All he could do was stare at the deer in disbelief and feel sick to his stomach.

"Road kill without the kill," he whispered. And he wondered: who in hell would hit a deer and not stop? It didn't make sense. It really didn't. So he sat there and stared at the deer's pathetic attempt to escape into the woods.

He got out of the pickup and walked up to the deer. He looked in its eyes and saw they were glassy and frightened and he turned away. The deer stared at him and tried even harder to escape, but its effort was futile and sad and it moved like a turtle on its back. He saw that the deer's legs were broken at the shoulders and that below the lower joints they were shattered. Its chest had been crushed and he wondered why the deer was still alive.

He looked for tire marks and saw that the deer had been run over and dragged for about twenty feet. There was a smooth swath in the dirt road where the deer had been dragged. It was as if the car had been towing a heavy sack.

He wondered what he should do. He didn't have a rifle with him and couldn't put the deer out of its misery. If he went home for his rifle, the deer would probably have died by the time he got back. He could take the deer home in the back of the pickup, but the ride back over the rutted and potholed road would only make the deer suffer more.

Without thinking he got down on his knees and stroked the deer's side, which was streaked with mud and with both dried and fresh blood. When the deer inhaled, it wheezed and shuddered under his hand, and when it exhaled, a trickle of blood and mucus ran out of its mouth and nostrils and stretched to the dirt. He put his hand under the deer's head and raised it to ease the deer's breathing. Then he sat down and worked the deer's upper body onto his lap. A sharp bone, possibly a rib, dug into his knee and he could feel the old chainsaw wound start to ache. He tried to move without disturbing the deer but couldn't. It'll stiffen, he thought.

He sat there with the deer across his lap and it no longer tried to escape. He held its head up with one hand and stroked its side with the other. He heard a crashing sound and looked up and saw the flash of a white tail disappear through the thick pine.

"This is the best I can do," he said to the deer. "I don't know what else to do. Someone hit you and they didn't stop. Maybe they didn't care or maybe they were just scared and kept going. Out of sight, out of mind . . . that sort of thing. They should have stopped, though."

No one used the East Washington Road during winter or early spring. There were only a few houses along it and they were summer camps and not winterized. The owners came up only from the middle of June to early October. Foliage seekers, joy-riders (kids and lovers), and hunters used the road, but only until either the hunting seasons closed or snow made the road impassable. He drove the road every spring to inspect culverts and check for washouts. Owners of the camps always called him every spring to see if the road was open and if their camps were still standing. No one in recent days, however, had called about his camp or the road.

When half an hour passed without anyone driving by, he knew whoever had hit the deer would not be back. Probably not even from around here, he thought. Flatlanders or newcomers.

He stroked the deer and listened to its erratic breathing. He knew it wouldn't live much longer, and that he'd better figure out what he was going to do with it.

"Well, now, little fellow, I don't figure the Good Lord created you to be killed by people driving cars who don't give a damn what happens to you. But that is the case here."

He shifted his position ever so slightly and realized his bad leg was numb. He thought about the newcomers and how in general they didn't understand country life. Oh, they were nice folks, for the most part. But it bothered him to see them buying land and then posting it to keep hunters, and everyone else, away. If they were working the land, raising crops or cattle, anything but just letting it sit there, he might understand. Most, however, weren't doing a damn thing but paying taxes and saying it was theirs. They're changing the way we live, he thought.

As quietly as a trout slips from sunlight into shade the deer died. There were no last great paroxysms, no last gasps for life. He simply felt the deer go limp, and he knew it was dead. And he sat there and hated the newcomers and their Volvos and Jeep Wagoneers. He hated the new warden and the people who taught the warden his trade.

It came to him that he hated these people and things just like he hated crows that destroy crops and the eggs of nesting birds. There was no way to stop them, either. Not really. You would try something, but they would figure a way to beat it. They would get together in large numbers and take whatever they wanted until they completely destroyed the very thing they wanted. Then they'd move on and do it all over again somewhere else.

"Know what killed you?" he said to the deer. "The times. The times are changing and you and your kind don't figure into what they're changing to. Somehow I always figured I'd see my way through. Now I don't know anymore. I could be wrong. I just don't know."

He decided against calling the warden. And it came to him that although the deer wasn't legally his, it also wasn't anyone else's. He could leave it right there and the coyotes and fisher cats and whatever could have a good meal off it. But then again, so could he and Nancy.

He picked up the deer ("Why, it's no heavier than a large dog," he said) and put it in the back of the pickup and headed for home. He drove down Main Street, past the Texaco station and Town Hall. He saw Jay Gurnsey going into the bank and waved to him. He knows, he thought. He's been up against changing times longer than me. Then he pulled over and motioned to Jay to come over. He watched to see his friend's expression when he got close enough to see the deer.

"Well now, look at what you have. Looks like a little skipper . . . a pretty beat-up one, at that. How'd you come by him?"

He told his friend the story and watched as his face went from anger to sadness to understanding. Yes he does, he thought.

"Well, he'll eat as well now as one in fall. Say, did you see the doe? I wonder if she had twins? Maybe she did. Maybe we should think about hunting up there next fall." And he smiled.

"Well, I think we'd be right to try. Yes I do." Then he drove down the hill to his home, figuring he'd spend some time in the barn.

SEASONS OF THE HUNTER
ALFRED A. KNOPF, 1985

Nearly all turkey hunters, without exception, are nuts. They have embraced this comparatively new game bird and made it a major influence in their lives. How many other hunters have you heard practice their game calls in offices, bars, parties, or wherever they may gather? Not many, I bet. These turkey hunters also attribute great feats of intelligence to the turkey, which may or may not be justified. And when a turkey gets away from them, it becomes a very special turkey and one that must be challenged. It even gets a name: Ghost Gobbler of Oak Ridge, or something like that. These hunters now become slightly irrational (or nuts) as they take up this special challenge. And my old friend Charlie Elliott, one of the finest turkey hunters in America, is no different from the rest of us. He regularly goes ape over a gobbler. Here's his tale of "The Cohutta Gobbler," a bird that gave him his greatest turkey hunt.

The Cohutta Gobbler

by CHARLIE ELLIOTT

FROM the time of man's creation until he steps beyond the shadows, his life is not so much a matter of years, or seasons, or days as it is of moments. A vast majority of these are so vapid and humdrum that the mind makes no attempt to file them away in its incredible storehouse. Many others remain as memories or facts available to our mental computers. A few of the latter stand out bright and vivid and, in spite of the years, never lose one sparkle of their original brilliance or beauty.

One of those highlights in my life had to do with a wild turkey-gobbler. I have avoided saying *the* highlight for fear of domestic or other repercussions, but my moment of grandeur with that magnificent bird stands close to the top of the list. There's not a sound or movement or spot of color in that high drama that I've forgotten, or will ever forget.

When I first met the Cohutta gobbler, I had no faint suspicion that he and I were embarking on such a splendid outdoor adventure. The woods were dressed in pastel shades of greens and golds and splotched with chalky clumps of dogwood, making them seem almost unreal. This was spring gobbling season in the mountains, and I was hunting alone in the Cohutta Range on the Georgia-Tennessee line.

205

For me, this is one of the most stimulating hunt seasons of the year. The forest floor is bright with flowers, tree buds are bursting with new life, and the vitality of the woods and its creatures make it seem on the verge of erupting into some unbelievable fantasy of sound and color.

At dawn I'd walked out the backbone of an isolated ridge and paused to listen for resonant notes that might indicate a big buck turkey on its roost or on the prowl. For an hour I stood there with my back against an oak tree, while the dawn woods came to life and the sun touched a distant mountain with burnished copper.

About flying-down time, when there's light enough for a turkey to distinguish the bushes from the bobcats, I yelped the cedar box in my hand, making notes like those of an amorous hen. This sound will sometimes set a silent old tom's genes to percolating and motivate him to reply with a lusty gobble to tell his intended that he's in the mood to solve her problem—and his.

When, after fifteen minutes, my yelps brought no response, I strolled another quarter mile along the ridgetop to try again.

There I first heard him, somewhere beyond the wild jumble of ridges and valleys sprawled out below me. His notes, high-pitched and vibrant, denoted an old gobbler. From long experience I knew that the closer I could get without spooking him, the better my chances would be to put him in the bag. So I struck out in a beeline across the ragged series of ridges, navigating the rough valleys and pausing on each ridge to call and get an answer.

On the fourth ridge I sensed that he was somewhere near. When I clucked my yelper and didn't get an answer, I considered that the bird and I were at close range. I stood motionless, straining my ears, and after a few minutes heard some creature working in the dry leaves that blanketed the shallow cove just beyond the hilltop. The crest of the summit was thinly clad in laurel, and the ground around the thickets was reasonably bare of leaves. In a half-crouch to keep my head below the narrow backbone of the ridge, I circled to a point directly above where I could hear the parched leaves rattling.

After listening for a moment, I concluded definitely that the sound was made by turkeys scratching for sustenance in the brown carpet, though they hadn't made a note of any kind to verify their presence. I stood perfectly still, trying to determine what my next move should be.

I have little doubt that I'd have concocted some scheme to get a look at those birds over my gunsights, if a gray squirrel hadn't chosen that exact moment to make a trip through the scrubby timber. When I heard him rattle the bark on a tree above me, I instinctively glanced up. The squirrel was so close I could have touched him with the tip of my gun barrel. I had my camouflage clothing on but had neglected to smear my face that morning with bowhunter's paint, preferring instead to use a gauze mask when the time came to sit in a blind and call up a gobbler.

When the squirrel saw my white face and identified me, he seemed to go berserk. He made a flying arc to the next tree, another long leap, and then in his third jump he either misjudged distance or broke a limb in his headlong flight. I got a glimpse of him in midair, then heard him hit the leaves on the slope below.

If those startled turkeys had taken to the sky, I could have killed one. They were scratching within forty feet of where I stood. When I heard them running in the leaves, I charged through the laurel, hoping for a shot. But by the time I spotted the birds, they were sprinting up the far slope, out of shotgun range. One was the tallest gobbler I'd ever seen in the woods. He simply dwarfed the two jakes with him.

The season was running out, but I spent my last eight days on the trail of that big turkey. I still feel that if all those slopes were piled on top of one another, I must have climbed a hundred miles high. Joel Biggs, a local wildlife officer, told me that turkeys often range as far as four or five miles, and I must have looked in every cove and on top of every ridge in those twenty square miles.

I hunted through the open seasons in Georgia and Tennessee and on the Ocoee Wildlife Management Area. On five different occasions I could have put a young gobbler in the bag, but I passed up each one. One had a raspy voice I thought belonged to my old bird. He gave me a few hair-raising moments. Yet when he walked around the end of a log, fifty feet away, I saw that his beard was no longer than my index finger.

I was stricken with big turkey fever. That huge gobbler had my tag on him and I wanted him more than any big game trophy I'd ever brought home—and that included sheep, bears, elk, and caribou.

Before the hunt was over that spring, I met one other mountain man who was on the trail of this same bird. Gobbler hunters have a special feeling of camaraderie. If they happen to meet on a high ridge or isolated woodland trail, it's like two Daniel Boones bumping into one another. They exchange cordialities either by sign language or in whispers, briefly swap plans so they won't conflict in choice of territory, and trade bits of information on fresh scratchings or other sign. They might even take a few minutes off to compare the tones of their turkey calls. Then, for the remainder of the day, each man will listen for the sound of the other's gun—hoping all the while he won't hear it.

This grizzled mountaineer I met came down the trail as softly as a forest cat. After the usual ritual of greetings, he showed me his call and I yelped my box for him. The old fellow listened with a slightly cocked ear to the notes, then nodded.

"Gobblers around here shore oughta like that Southern accent," he commented. Since he seemed a very affable and gracious fellow, I took his words with a grain of saltpeter.

During the three seasons that I devoted my full attention to this long-bearded old patriarch of the forest, I learned all over again that killing a large wild gobbler presents perhaps the greatest challenge in hunting. It doesn't take the courage needed to coldly face a charging grizzly or the stamina necessary to climb for a mountain goat or trophy ram. But nothing else requires more in woodsmanship, patience, and ingenuity.

As I said, I stayed on the trail of the Cohutta gobbler for three seasons. I filed my license in my home state of Georgia and took birds in Alabama, Mississippi, Oklahoma, and New Mexico, and could have added Tennessee to the list with a lesser gobbler, had there not been only this one I was truly interested in.

To make the cheese more binding, as they say in Crackerese, I learned that my old gobbler had already acquired a reputation in both the Cohutta Mountains and around Ocoee. Several of the local sportsmen had an eye on him, and more than a few had devoted most of their spring gunning to the bird. So I approached each April season with the growing apprehension that one of those mountain men might get to the gobbler before I had another chance at it.

I saw the bird a number of times. It seemed to lead a charmed life. Only once could I have blown the whistle on him. He walked across the road in front of my car. He was only a few yards away when I stopped, jumped from behind the steering wheel, and threw a shell into the chamber of my gun. The huge gobbler walked unhurriedly and almost majestically up the slope, as though he knew just as well as I that I wouldn't shoot. To bushwhack that old patriarch would have been as heinous a crime as ambushing my best friend.

Once I called him to within seventy-five yards of my blind. For thirty minutes he stayed in one spot, strutting and gobbling. Then he vanished as suddenly and completely as if he had been erased. It made me wonder if I'd seen him at all and should seek psychiatric help.

On another occasion I ran into him at least a couple of miles from where we'd first met. He was on the Georgia side of the line, on the last day of the Georgia open season. I was traveling a long "lead" (which is the local term for a main ridge) just after daylight. When I paused on the brow of a slope to call, he answered. At least, I was almost certain I recognized his voice.

I made a breathless detour of more than a mile to the ridge above him. But before I could get into position, half a dozen crows spotted the tom. Ganging up on and harassing a lone wild turkey is a favorite crow pastime, and from their language I knew they were really working this one over.

I crept downhill as close as I dared to get to the melee and set up my stand for business. For more than an hour we maneuvered around on that point of the ridge. Finally the crows, or an unknown intruder, or something I said on my wingbone call or cedar box spooked him. Or maybe he just got tired of playing games. He turned away and crossed a shallow cove to the thick laurel on the next ridge. The crows apparently lost him in the laurel, but when he hit the open ridgetop they found him again. Finally the whole sideshow continued out of hearing over the crest.

The foreboding that someone else would get to that gobbler before me grew acute when, on the third season of our acquaintance, I had to miss the first three open days. My only consolation was that spring came later than usual that year and those first legal days were rainy and cold, which might somewhat dampen the ardor between toms and hens, normally in full blossom by then. As for the dedicated gobbler hunters, I knew they'd be in the woods even if we were in the middle of a second ice age.

On the morning of the fourth day, I was on the mountain half an hour before daylight. The brown carpet of leaves was white with frost, and a cold blanket of air lay across the hills.

I wasn't exactly pleased with the way my plans had been disrupted on this particular morning. Phil Stone (an old hunting partner) and I had decided to hunt together through the gobbling hours, then separate and scout out a tremendous territory for signs. My wife Kayte refused to stay in camp alone and insisted on coming with us.

Three's a crowd, even at turkey hunting, so when we parked in a little gap, Phil took off down a dim logging road that skirted a narrow valley. I'd have sent Kayte in the other direction, but she gets lost even in our backyard, and I knew we'd then have to spend the rest of the season looking for her. So she stayed with me, which meant confining my hunting to the more gentle terrain around the car.

As the first dawn light turned the woods from black to gray, a ruffed grouse flashed across the road. Farther down the valley we flushed two more of these colorful birds out of a branch bottom. The dawn was bright and cold as we climbed the point of a low ridge overlooking the valley. From this spot I knew we were high enough to hear turkeys on any of the half dozen ridges sloping away from that massive range around Big Frog Mountain. Kayte and I got settled and waited until the noise we'd made in the frozen leaves was forgotten by the forest creatures around us and they began to move about once more.

On my box I gave the low, plaintive notes of a hen. After a few minutes without an answer, I called much louder. A quarter of an hour later, I rattled the box with the throaty call of a gobbler. All this activity produced exactly no results, except for the raucous notes of a crow across the valley and the loud drumming of a woodpecker on a hollow stub nearby.

Kayte and I climbed over the crest of the ridge into the next valley to repeat our performance. The sun spotlighted the tops of the highest hills and the line of light gradually crept down the mountains until it touched and warmed our half-numb hands and cheeks.

We moved from one ridge to another and heard nothing that resembled the notes of a turkey. At 8:30 A.M. we made our way back over the trail to where we met Phil Stone, who'd also gone through an unproductive session.

The three of us discussed the situation and decided that, with the season so retarded, the birds were not yet courting and probably not even speaking to one another. This evaluation gave me a vast sense of relief, along with some assurance that my big gobbler had not yet been disturbed and that I'd see him again somewhere in these mountain woods.

Kayte and Phil were already in the car, impatiently waiting for me while licking their chops in anticipation over the Bloody Marys they would be soon having at breakfast. I don't know whether it was impulse, instinct, or some strange intuition that suddenly impelled me to step away from the car to the edge of the road with the turkey call in my hand.

I clucked a couple of times, gave the low, breathless notes of a hen, and then listened. No response. I'd expected none. Still, merely to complete the routine, I halfheartedly rattled my box to simulate the call of a gobbler.

There was nothing halfhearted in the challenge that bounced back from the next ridge, almost quickly enough to pass for an echo.

I have no idea how my two partners got out of the car and beside me so fast and so noiselessly, but they now appeared to have lost all interest in breakfast or Bloody Marys. I touched my finger to my lips.

"Stand here a few minutes," I whispered, "and let's see which direction he's headed."

When the buck turkey gobbled again, he was a hundred yards farther down the ridge. That was enough for me. My partners agreed that I could travel faster and get ahead of the gobbler if I went alone, and that I also might have a better chance of seeing and definitely identifying him as the one bird I wanted. As for myself, I already knew.

I climbed the slope and circled the side of the hill in a half-run. At the spot where I hoped to intercept the gobbler, I zipped up my camouflage suit and sat down at the base of a big tree with emerald vegetation growing before it.

I wasn't sure yet who it was the tom answered, but he gobbled again shortly after I'd given him the soft, gentle notes of a hen on my slate-type call. Minutes later a second gobbler, this one with a younger voice, set the woods to ringing off to my left.

The smaller tom definitely was coming to me, but the turkey I had planned to intercept walked off his ridge, crossed a rivulet in the hollow, and climbed to a cove that angled away from where I'd taken my stand.

I left the young buck turkey decoying to my squeal and took off across the slope. I didn't even try to convince myself I was acting foolishly in giving up a bird in the hand for a try at that old boy with the rusty pipes. The big tom had already cost me at least five gobblers since I'd first met him. I figured he should be worth at least one more.

By midmorning the leaves had lost their frosty coating. The drying forest floor became much noisier underfoot. I had to pause every few minutes to get another fix on the gobbler, who continued to answer my calls. We were walking at about the same speed. By the time I reached the road that separated Georgia's Cohutta Range from Tennessee's Ocoee, the tom had crossed the road and climbed the side of a massive mountain into the forbidden area.

This appeared to be the end of the trail. The Ocoee area was closed except for five two-day periods in April, and I wouldn't have another chance at him until then. It looked like old long-beard had once again given me the shaft.

By all sane criteria, I knew it was hardly possible to entice that cagey gobbler to backtrack so late in the day over the route he'd just taken. Especially since he had been intent on going the other way from the moment we'd first heard him.

One thing for sure. I had nothing to lose by trying. I whacked my cedar box with a couple of lusty yelps. Almost instantly, he came back with a high-pitched gobble. I settled down in a little clump of pines in legal territory to wait. At least ten minutes went by before his resonant tones again rolled down the mountain—and this time they seemed to come from farther off. I waited. His next call came from near the top of the mountain. There wasn't any doubt in my mind now that he was walking out of the picture. In desperation I gobbled my box as loud as I could make it quaver.

For a full twenty minutes, complete silence. Then he sounded off again from approximately the same spot where I'd last heard him. My heart gave an extra thump or two. At least I'd stopped his flight . . . momentarily.

I waited. And waited. And waited. I have no idea how long I sat in that one spot, trying to convince myself he'd already gone on and over the mountain. I suppose the only thing that kept the seat of my pants pressed against the unfriendly rocks and roots was the knowledge that many times when a tom stops gobbling, but hasn't been spooked, he's coming to investigate. If so, there wasn't any harm in giving him my exact location. Stealthily I reached for the slate and cedar stick, touched them softly together for a few dainty clucks, then dropped them beside me on the ground. Most novice hunters are likely to call much too much.

To wait—and keep on waiting—requires an enormous amount of patience. Even more so, when there's no hint of any kind whether you are on the verge of success.

At last I gave up. The rocks and roots now seemed to be actively attacking my hindquarters. My legs felt numb from sitting in one position. Phil and Kayte—and beyond them the Bloody Marys, country sausage, eggs, and biscuits—were waiting. I hadn't heard a peep out of my gobbler for three-quarters of an hour. By now he could be in the next county. With disappointment welling through me, I shifted my position to reach for the slate and cedar stick I had dropped to the ground.

Suddenly somewhere a limb or twig cracked; the sound a deer makes as it tiptoes through the woods. I came to full attention again, straining my eyes for a glimpse of feet or head or brown deerhide. For a dozen minutes I sat motionless. At last I decided that the animal or whatever that had cracked that stick must have drifted on by.

Once more I relaxed and prepared to gather up my gear and call it a day. I was on the verge of standing up to give my numb muscles some relief when I heard footsteps in the leaves. The cadence was exactly that of a man who slips stealthily along, stalking unseen quarry.

Again I froze. I couldn't see a man or make out movement of any kind, but at the moment there wasn't anything I needed less than a load of high brass No. 4 or 6 pellets smack in my face.

I had been straining so hard to see some deer or human form that my first glimpse of the gobbler now came as a distinct shock. He was beyond and walking parallel to a contour that dropped off like a terrace about twenty yards in front of my blind. The contour hid all but the meaty, wrinkled top of his head above the wattles. I couldn't see enough yet to definitely identify him as the old patriarch who had led me on a merry three-year chase, but that one glimpse still had me all shook up inside.

He took two more steps, bringing his head higher up above the contour, but I still couldn't see his beard or judge his size. He put his head down to peck at something on the forest floor, and while his eye was out of sight I quickly raised my gun. On its way up, the gun dislodged a dead *Y*-shaped stem. It straddled and lodged on the gun barrel in such a way that I couldn't see the sights. The bird continued to walk, growing taller and taller as it came up the shoulder of the hill, and I moved the barrel slowly to keep it in line with his head.

It was purely a matter of luck that at the same moment my gobbler walked behind a large tree trunk, a protruding twig suddenly flipped the *Y*-stem from my barrel. When the tom stepped past the tree, my sights were directly on his head.

My 12-gauge Winchester pump gun was loaded with shells holding No. 6 shot. Some hunters like large shot—No. 4 or No. 2—but I know I have a better chance of hitting the vital parts of a bird's head and neck with a denser pattern. Most shots in this type of hunting are at a bird's head and neck while he's still on the ground. I often back up my first round of No. 6 with a No. 4 and then a No. 2 load, which gives me a reserve of progressively larger pellets to break down a turkey that flies or runs after the first shot.

There he stood for all of five seconds with his head up in a patch of sunlight, as tall and majestic as I remembered him from two springs before. He was so close it seemed I could reach out and touch him with my gun. The sunlight on his feathers made them ripple in a display of copper, green, and gold so resplendent that I caught my breath. What a beauty. Then I saw his heavy beard and knew beyond any doubt that he was indeed the old patriarch I'd dreamed about for so long.

It was almost sacrilegious to shatter that magnificent moment with a shot—but the powerful impulses developed in a lifetime of hunting triggered the gun. It was a clean, one-shot kill.

That's when all the excitement of the past two hours finally hit me. My hands shook as I tried to unstrap the camera from my shoulder. When I hefted the bird for weight and saw how far I had to lift his feet so that his head would clear the ground, I got the shakes all over again.

He pulled the hand on the corroded old camp scales up to twenty-five and a half pounds—the largest mountain gobbler I've seen, and one of the biggest turkeys I had ever killed, including the heavier breeds from some of the Southern plantations.

Phil peered wonderingly over his glasses at the scales.

"There just ain't no telling," he said, "what this critter might have weighed, if these scales weren't so rusty." (We checked them later on and found that the scales did, in fact, read almost one and a half pounds too low.)

At that moment, though, the gobbler's weight didn't make too much difference. He had given me my finest hunt in turkey woods, and he still remains my most highly prized big game trophy.

This story is actually a letter written from Alaska by Dall DeWeese to a group of hunting friends in Canon City, Colorado. Mr. DeWeese describes his Alaskan hunt and how he killed the largest moose ever recorded—at least it was the largest ever recorded back in 1897, when this hunt took place. The story is best told in a hunter's simple language to his friends. Here's how Dall DeWeese wrote it back in that year. The story, interestingly enough, appeared in the very first issue of Outdoor Life: *January 1898, Volume I, Number 1.*

A Moose Hunt in Alaska—1897

by DALL DEWEESE

CONSISTENT as I am with human nature, boys, I wanted one more moose, and I don't believe you will say "game hog", for you must remember that I am a long way from home and where these animals seem plenty, and I am saving the skins and antlers to be mounted for my museum. Up to this time I could have killed two other moose with small heads (about forty-five to fifty inches) and two cows and one calf moose, but I did not want them. After I secured my first bull, it was then a good one or none. If you give this letter to our home paper and it should fall into the hands of some of the "would-be sportsmen," I will hear them yell "hog," but I should dread to see them have the opportunities for slaughter that I have been surrounded with on this trip.

The next day or two we looked up a better route through the timber to the lake and succeeded by following a well-worn bear trail which led in that direction. Mr. Berg still continued to pack my trophies to the lower camp and did not return that night, so I was alone in these faraway wilds some eighty miles from all but one living man, and he twelve miles away.

As night came on I had a good fire going in front of the lean-to and sat down on some fir boughs. Had you been with me I know how you would have enjoyed your pipe and tobacco, but as I don't use it I sat there long into the night gazing into the fire; yes, all alone, high up on the rolling timbered tablelands at the head of Kusiloff River, and my friend alone down at the lake. With lightning rapidity I recalled all your faces and reminiscences of our grand old times in former years, when I lived in Troy, and we made our campfires on the Au Sable, Manistee, and Fife Lake, Michigan; camps on the Au Plain, Menominee, and Spread Eagle Lake, Wisconsin; Swan River and headwaters of the Mississippi in Minnesota; Devil's Lake, Dakota; camps on Black and White River, Arkansas (where we had those turkey roasts and duck bakes in our "clay ditch oven"); then, dear Jim, the camps on the Savogle and Miramichi in New Brunswick; camps in Wyoming, Utah, Montana, Mexico, and all the streams that head in the big game country of our Colorado from North Park south to head of the Bear, Williams, both forks of the White, the Grand, Eagle, Piney, Gunnison, and southward to the San Juan.

In the burning embers of my campfire, I could in my fancy see all your faces, and how gratifying to know that those of you who were with me were true sportsmen and never a thing occurred to mar the pleasure of our outing, for the good and bad side of man or woman will be revealed in camp. How I wished you all with me that night and tonight, for I am having too much sport on this trip to enjoy it alone.

As my fire burned low I rolled up in my blankets and crawled under the lean-to on a caribou skin thrown on some spruce feathers and then with a thought of the dear ones at home, what tomorrow's luck would be, and with weary body, I was soon in dreamland.

Daylight next morning found me preparing a hurried breakfast of moose steak, boiled rice, tor-te-os (fry pan bread), and tea. I ate heartily, for I intended to make in a new direction that day. I had a birch horn with me and had tried the "call" one evening for three hours, without success and thought I would take it with me this morning.

About seven I tried the "call" more out of curiosity than otherwise; first, the "short call," then the "long call," and repeated several times. An hour passed and finally my patience was rewarded by a light crackling behind me. I listened—then a thud behind the alders. I then made a "low call," and soon his mooseship waded through the patch of alders and stood in open ground (other than the tall grass) not more than sixty yards from me. Oh, for a camera. He would swing his big head to and fro, sniffing the air; then lowering it with muzzle extended stood silently working his ears forward, then back.

I had detected a slight puff of air and noticed it to be in his favor. Suddenly he raised his head high and sniffed loudly and slowly swung around and made for the low timber; not rapidly, but simply as if he had made a mistake. He was a big brute, but his antlers were much inferior to those I had. My curiosity being satisfied, I again moved cautiously along much amused; how plainly I can recall his every move, and I want to tell you I don't like that kind of moose hunting. I was dressed for "still hunting," and as I moved silently along how little I dreamed that I would be rewarded in not killing this last animal by having in my path a much better specimen of moose than I had yet seen.

About ten, while still hunting through rolling ground with patches of spruce and tall grass, I sighted a cow lying down within eighty yards. I looked carefully, knowing the velvet was now off and a bull might be near, and after crawling a rod or so I saw the wide white blade of a bull between the trees close to the edge of the timber. I put my glasses on him to look at his horns, but it seems he had sniffed me, and a startled glance showed his big horns.

The cow ran to my left and the bull to my right, quartering and a little down hill. My first ball caught him in the short ribs on the right side and stopped at the skin in front of the left shoulder; he stopped and swung around broadside. I sent another clean through him. He headed off again and I pitched another one into him. He again stopped broadside and coughed hard, and when his great sides would heave, I saw the blood spout from the wounds. I knew he was done for, and while he stood there with lowered head I ran around and below him as I had heard a terrible rolling through the tall grass (four feet high) below him, and thought it must be a bear making off. I could see nothing and returned to the moose expecting to find him down and dead, but imagine my surprise when on coming up a little raise I found myself within thirty yards of that great brute on his feet and coming toward me with his head lowered, shaking those massive antlers.

I can't tell how I did it, but as I afterward found, I sent a ball at his head which caught him in the brisket. Still he came, and my next ball was better aimed and struck between the eyes. That stopped him, and he sank down upon his limbs but did not roll over. I am frank to acknowledge that I was startled. I am cold, yet never have I had even a grizzly give me such a feeling. As he came through that tall grass breathing the blood and tossing those wicked antlers, truly he looked like an old McCormick self-binder.

I was carrying my new Mannlicher that day and right there saw an advantage in smokeless powder, as well as once more before the day closed. However, I have used the Winchester for twenty-four years; in fact, my first hunt for deer in Henry County, Ohio, when but sixteen years old, was with the old rimfire Henry rifle. When the King's model of 73 Winchester came out, I got that and have used all models since and had them made specially to fit me. I have now in camp my special made 40-70-339 metal patch soft nose, black powder 86 model Winchester, which I have used for the past four years. I brought both my guns on this hunt for fear something might go wrong with one or the other.

Boys, you wanted me to report on this Mannlicher and I must say that it is the most deadly gun I ever carried. Its great velocity of 2000 feet per second and its extreme flat trajectory make it very desirable for long range shooting. At three to four hundred yards, if held on the game, the ball is into it almost the instant you touch the trigger.

I was using the metal patch soft nose which will mushroom on flesh, and the patch seems to be slightly cut with the lands of the barrel when fired and expands by the pressure of the soft nose when it strikes and then goes through the animal like a buzz saw.

The sheep when struck drop as limp as a rag, and the moose, no matter in what part of the body he was struck, seemed paralyzed from the first shot. Again, the gun is very light, which is a great advantage when you pack your loads on your back. You know I am not an agent for the Mannlicher works, but let honor fall where it is due. There is, however, an object to the close range between sights, for you must hold very carefully or you miss. This can be remedied by a peep on the rear of the hammer. I don't think they have any of these small calibers quite perfected; a few years more experiment will doubtless make a great improvement in them.

Well, there I stood by the side of my giant moose, without a camera or a friend with me to admire my prize. Oh, what a carcass. I had my steel tape with me and commenced his measurements and now give them to you as I put them down in my diary. Of course the first measurement was the spread of his antlers, which is sixty-nine inches; length of beam, forty-eight inches; palmations, fifteen inches; circumference of beam burr at head, fourteen and one half inches; circumference of beams at smallest place, ten inches; antlers have thirty-two points.

His great body measured sixteen feet four inches from lip to point of rear hoof; seven feet eight inches from front hoof to top of nithers; girted eight feet nine inches, and six feet seven inches around the neck at shoulders; thirty-three and one-half inches from tip to tip of ears; ears seven inches wide and forty-four inches around the lips of the open mouth.

What a match he will be when mounted for my big elk. Boys, I know that I hew close enough to the line of "true sportsmanship" not to be overcome by selfishness and will say that all points considered, size, massiveness, etc., I believe I have a world beater; but be this as it may, I will be satisfied when I get it packed out and home.

Some hunters saw the heads through the skull and then when being mounted by some they are given more spread; I know of a moose head whose spread was eight inches more when mounted than it was before it was sawed apart and an elk head that is seventeen inches more than it was naturally. I haven't a sawed head in my collection and would not take one as a gift for mounting. This method doesn't belong to true sportsmanship, and it makes the animal look very unnatural. They say it was necessary to saw them apart to get them out of the terrible country. I say that a big game animal doesn't exist in such a country that makes it impossible to get the antlers out whole.

I don't believe there has been game killed in a worse country of access than this. For many miles there is a mass of down timber, crisscrossed and covered with slippery moss, and intergrown with tall grass and bushes; then canyons and ice-cold streams to cross, but I intend to take those antlers down and out without sawing them if it takes all winter.

But back to the moose. It took me till 1 P.M. to dress him, and I then started toward camp in the rain with the neck skin, which was all I could carry, and content in mind that Alaska is the home of the largest moose in the world, and why not when this country affords such wonderful growth for food, and he lives to get age, which he must have to grow large horns; then his healthy condition does the rest.

About 3 P.M., drenched, tired, and hungry, I was at the edge of the heavy spruce and thick willows six to ten feet in height and heard a cracking near me—thought 'twas a moose—then saw the willows shake near me, and stepping upon a rotten log and looking about, there, within twenty-five feet, on his hind legs, looking at me over the willows, stood one of those fighting Alaskan grizzlies.

I had this neck skin of moose, shot-pouch fashion, over my neck with left arm free; but in an instant I cocked my Mannlicher while bringing it in position and plugged him through the neck just under the head. He dropped, and I stepped from the log that I could see better under the willows and sent another ball through his shoulders while he was roaring and fighting the willows and ground. I used lead and gave him another through the neck which settled him. I still kept the neck skin on, thinking to use it for a shield if he charged me. He had evidently scented the skin and was coming right after it.

This was some sport. He is a monster, has claws four inches long, head twenty-two inches from nose to ears, measures ten feet seven inches stretch, foot eight by twelve inches, and has a good coat of hair. It took me till dark to skin him, and after it was off I could not lift it. I dragged it over the willows and left it and got in camp after dark thinking Alaska had bears of uncomfortable size and numbers for night traveling while alone.

As I approached camp I gave my usual shrill whistle and was answered by Mr. Berg through his gun barrel. How glad I was to hear it, and he came out to meet me, gave me a hearty handshake, and then relieved me of my heavy load. As I neared the fire how appetizing was the smell of his good supper already prepared, and I might add that my day's work without food had something to do with my appetite. I was drenched to the skin and after a partial change of footgear we were soon drying, eating, and talking of my "red-letter day," which pleased my big hardy companion seemingly as much as myself; yet we knew that we had both taken great risks in being alone in these wilds.

This ended my hunt in Alaska. I have killed two specimens hard to duplicate, and of the class of animals of which I have had such a desire to add to my collection. I am more than pleased and wish all my hunting friends were here now to take a look and a shake. Mr. Berg says they are more massive and heavier than the record head he killed two years ago, which was mentioned in *Forest and Stream* of March 6, 1897.

It has been raining and snowing all day. We will now pack everything down to the lake, and I will care for my heads and skins and work homeward as fast as possible, for truly I feel that I am well paid for my long and tiresome journey of eight thousand miles, round trip, on land and sea.

I am compelled to travel 185 miles from here on foot and log canoe to reach the steamboat landing. It is now too dark to write and will finish at lower camp. We will make supper of moose steak, boiled rice, wild red currant sauce, and tea.

OUTDOOR LIFE
JANUARY 1898

If you're attacked by a grizzly, play dead. That's the advice you hear often from old hunters and guides in bear country, and this story proves it. But it's tough to play dead when an Alaska grizzly decides to work you over a couple of times . . . even after you're rescued. Here's how Forest Young, an Alaska construction worker, handled the grizzly that was determined to make a meal of him.

Between Life and Death

by BEN EAST

FOREST Young and his hunting partner, Marty Cordes, spent the last half of September 1955 hunting moose north of Haines in Alaska's Chilkat Valley, where they lived and worked as construction men. The first ten days they had no real luck. Young wounded a bull the second day out and followed the blood trail, but the heavy rain that was falling eventually washed out the trail. For a straight week after that they did not lay eyes on a moose with horns, so finally they loaded their gear in the canoe and outboarded ten miles farther up the Chilkat River to moose country that had never failed them in the past. There was a vacant cabin near the river they had used before. They would have gone there sooner, but figured the area might be too crowded with hunters.

There was no cause, however, for complaint on that score. They had things to themselves, and the first day they saw enough moose sign to convince them they had come to the right place. It was only an hour after they started out the second morning, in a patch of willow-grown muskeg about two miles from camp, that they came on two bulls and several cows feeding together. The bulls were good ones. The men dumped both of them.

They spent the balance of that day dressing their two moose and packing part of the meat to camp. The rest of the meat and the two hides were cached in trees, out of reach of bears. Browns and grizzlies were plentiful in the area; the men knew that any meat left where bears could get at it would be almost sure to disappear during the night.

The following morning, which was the last day of September, they packed in enough additional meat to make a canoe load, and Marty cranked up the outboard and took off for Haines. Forest made several more trips to bring in meat during that afternoon and the next forenoon. By the time Marty got back from town late Saturday afternoon, Forest had everything in camp except the hide of Marty's moose. That was still stretched about a dozen feet off the ground in the branches of a birch at the spot where they had made the kill.

Sunday morning Marty said that he wanted to pick up a mess of grouse for a stew. Forest agreed to bring in the moose hide. Both men planned to be back in the cabin about an hour before noon, ready to break camp and head for home with the hides and the balance of the meat.

When Forest arrived at the site of the kill, he found that bears had taken over. The ground looked as if someone had gone over it with a garden rake. There were two neat mounds of grass and moss nearby. Forest knew that the bears had covered up the uneaten portions of the moose entrails. That cache of the bears should have been a warning to him that they would be coming back.

Marty's moose hide was still up in the birch, unmolested. Forest walked over to the tree and threw his packboard down. As he glanced up, he saw movement in the brush about three hundred feet away. Taking a closer look, he was able to make out the backs and heads of two bears over the top of the brush. They were about thirty feet apart.

They didn't scare him. Although he was sure from their color and shape that they were grizzlies, any bear he had ever met had lit out as soon as it discovered him. These would, too. As he watched them, however, they suddenly disappeared from sight. The next thing Forest knew one was coming headlong at him through the thicket. Although he couldn't see the bear, he could see the brush moving. The bear was smashing through the brush, making such a commotion that it was easy for Forest to trace its course.

He still wasn't scared. He jumped up and down and waved his arms, yelling to frighten the grizzly off. Then he suddenly realized that this was one bear that wasn't going to be bluffed. It was still coming hell-bent.

Forest wasn't carrying a gun, or even a hunting knife. He had gone lightly equipped for the job of packing the eighty-pound green moose hide into camp. Quickly sizing up the situation, he jumped for a branch of the birch and started up the tree, hand over hand. But before he had climbed his own height, the grizzly broke out of the brush and came swarming at him.

The bear didn't fool around. It sank its teeth into the back of Forest's right leg just above the knee and pulled him down with one savage yank. He landed on his back, and they tussled for a few seconds. Young wound up sitting up, with the bear's left front leg across both of his, pinning him to the ground. Then the bear grabbed him by the inside of the thigh, just below the crotch, and took a deep, deliberate bite, tearing away a strip of flesh. Forest saw his blood spurt out. He braced himself with his left arm and pummeled the grizzly in the face with his other fist, but the bear paid no more attention to this than it would have to a fly buzzing around its head.

The first moments of the ordeal were pure terror. The bear's face was less than a foot away from Forest's. The grizzly had a big burly head, with long, stiff, gray guard hairs standing out all over its face. Its eyes were red with hate, and its muzzle was screwed up in a sullen mask. It slobbered as it chewed. The bear went on shredding his clothing, skin, and flesh. Every second Forest expected the bear to grab him by the throat and finish him off with one shake. His woolen trousers and heavy underwear were no protection against the grizzly's claws and teeth. He felt the bear grind cloth into flesh with each bite. With horror he realized the bear could tear his legs off and he wouldn't be able to do a thing about it. He punched the grizzly in the face until he broke his hand. The silvertip wasn't fazed a bit.

"I read once that a merciful numbness comes over a man being mauled by a big carnivore," he said to Marty later. "Maybe that happens in some cases, but it certainly didn't in mine. I was anything but numb. I could feel every bite he took, and it hurt like hell!"

He never knew how long he was pinned down by the bear. Maybe a minute, maybe only a few seconds, but it seemed half an eternity. Suddenly it flashed through Forest's mind that his only clear hope for survival was to play dead. He flopped over on his back and side, making himself go limp.

The bear instantly stopped chewing. Instead, it merely stood over its victim, continuing to pin him down with one leg. Forest tried not to breathe. In spite of all his will power, however, and the knowledge that his life hung in the balance, the pain was too intense. He involuntarily emitted a low groan. At that the grizzly grabbed him again, as a cat grabs a mouse. Forest felt another stab of excruciating pain as the long yellow teeth sank deeper into his flesh than before. They slashed through the right side of his scrotum and ripped loose a flap of skin and muscle that exposed his bladder. The pain was awful.

Forest lay inert and let the grizzly continue to tear at him. It took another bite or two and dropped him for the second time.

Then Forest must have inadvertently moved again, or else the bear just decided to make sure of finishing him. It nailed him once more, this time by the back below the right shoulder, and with a lunging bite ripped three ribs loose from the spine and tore a hole that reached all the way into the chest cavity. If the bite had been placed a little lower, in the kidney area, it would have been fatal.

This time Forest didn't fight back, move, or groan. He knew now it was a case of play dead or be dead. The grizzly dropped the limp body; Forest heard the bear walk away. He couldn't see it without turning his head, which he didn't dare risk, so he just lay motionless and hoped it wouldn't come back.

Suddenly, however, he felt the muskeg shake under him and heard heavy feet pounding in. The silvertip was making a queer sort of panting noise, not a bawl and not a growl. Forest braced himself for another mauling, but the bear didn't touch him. He could see its feet and lower legs were only a yard from his face. The bear just stood there looking him over for a minute or so. Then, apparently satisfied, it turned and walked slowly away.

About five minutes later the bear repeated the performance, approaching the man at a panting run, standing over him without molesting him, and then walking off. Forest decided his possum act was working.

For what seemed an interminable length of time, Forest continued to play dead. He couldn't see or hear the bear. All this time it was becoming increasingly difficult to breathe because of the open hole in his back. Forest realized that he was going to strangle unless he turned over on his face and let his nose and mouth drain. He kept still as long as he could, then counting on the bear's having gone for keeps, he slowly and painfully managed to roll over. The movement and the sound provoked no reaction; he began to hope that the worst of his troubles were past.

Quite a while later he thought he heard faint sounds coming from the moose leavings, a hundred feet away, but when he held his breath to listen the noise seemed to stop. That happened three or four times. Forest didn't know what to think. Then he felt the muskeg quake under him once more and heard that familiar, terrifying panting. No noise out of the pit of hell itself could have sounded worse to the tortured man.

The bear must have sensed from Forest's position that he had moved. It let out a murderous roar and tore into him again, grabbing him by the buttocks. The grizzly spanned Forest's entire rear with its jaws, and bit through to the bone. Then it took a deeper bite as if attempting to sever his body in two. Picking him up off the ground, it shook him until he thought his back would break or his head snap off his body. Forest had seen bears kill salmon that way, shattering the spine with one flirt of their jaws. It seemed inevitable that the same thing was going to happen to him. But then the grizzly dropped him as abruptly as it had seized him, turned away and lumbered off. He heard the heavy footfalls fade. It was quiet again.

The bear had dropped him face down, so he was in no danger of choking, but he was in pain beyond all description. The bear had torn the flesh away from the inside of his legs, ripped both buttocks, mangled his right hand, torn one rib entirely out and left two others protruding through the skin, punched a big hole into his lung cavity, and chewed at him from head to knees.

"There is no way to tell you what the agony was like," he said later.

In addition to the pain, Forest was also plagued by the cold water from the muskeg seeping through his clothing.

Forest couldn't stand the pain. He wasn't even granted the mercy of passing out. He decided to prod fate—to kill himself.

He was convinced he was going to die anyway. He couldn't see a chance of getting out alive by himself, hurt as he was. Forest realized it would be hours before Marty would find him lying in the muskeg. Other men badly mauled by bears had killed themselves; now in his mind, clouded by pain, he understood the logic of their action.

It must have taken him half an hour to work his good hand down into the pocket where his small jackknife was lodged. With great difficulty, he managed to extract the weapon. Then he moved his arms up in front of his head, opened the knife and made a deep slash in his left wrist, trying for the big artery. No blood appeared. Hardly feeling the pain from the knife cut over the red flashes of agony that were stabbing all through his body, he slashed again. The third slash exposed the wrist tendons, but still no blood appeared.

It didn't occur to Forest that he might have missed the artery. He took it for granted that he had already lost so much blood that there was none left to flow. That meant he couldn't bleed himself to death through the wrist. If he cut the tendons and then by some miracle survived, he knew he would have a crippled hand the rest of his life. He was willing to kill himself, but not to chance a crippled hand, so he gave up that scheme. Insane from torture? Maybe.

The next idea that came to him, born of pain and desperation, was even more horrible: to find and cut his jugular vein with the knife. He knew that would afford a mercifully quick death. He instinctively knew that he musn't fumble, lest he run the risk of severing his windpipe and thus suffer the added torture of being strangled. He laid the fingers of his good hand against his throat, feeling for the pulse that would mark the location of the big vein, but he couldn't find it. This exertion was almost too much for him. He slumped back and rested. As he was starting to probe again for the vein, he heard Marty off in the brush calling him.

Marty shuddered as he examined the torn body of his partner. His first thought was to try packing him the two miles back to camp. When he started to lift Forest, however, the injured man screamed in agony. Marty had to discard that scheme. The pain was more than Forest could endure. They agreed there was only one alternative. Marty would have to go all the way to Haines for help. While he was gone, Forest would have to take his chances. It wasn't a pleasant prospect.

Before leaving for Haines, Marty made a fast trip to camp and brought back a sleeping bag and an air mattress, a shotgun and shells, cigarettes, a water bottle, food, matches, and a gas lantern. He eased Forest into the bag, and then hung most of his outer clothing on bushes overhead to keep off the rain that was now falling in a cold drizzle. He laid the shotgun beside Forest, lighted the gas lantern and set it down within reach.

"I'll make the fastest trip any man ever made to Haines." Marty promised.

"I'll be here when you get back," Forest told him, but he was far from sure.

It was now midafternoon. The bear had jumped Forest about a quarter past ten in the morning. He was sure of the time, since he had looked at his watch just before he came in sight of the moose hide in the tree. He couldn't expect Marty back before midnight; it was two miles to camp, and a round trip of thirty miles by outboard and sixty by truck to Haines and back. It would also take Marty a little while to round up a rescue party. A glacial river running through very steep country, the Chilkat is quick to flood but also quick to drop. At the time it was at low stage. Forest knew that Marty, without a fast current, would have a slow run. The upstream trip back would take longer than usual, since Marty would be navigating in the dark and probably be bringing at least two extra passengers. Forest knew he would have to wait at least eight hours for help to arrive, perhaps longer. He wasn't sure he could hang on that long. Even if he could, there was still the grizzly to worry about. Forest didn't think it had left the neighborhood.

An hour or so after Marty left, Forest's spirits began to rise. The pain lessened, and he was warming up. He began to think that maybe he was going to make it after all. Soon after that the afternoon light began to fade. Dusk was coming. Everything had been quiet and peaceable for hours. He had almost stopped worrying about the bear, but he fought off the impulse to doze. Then suddenly the muskeg began to shake under him, and once more he heard the snuffling, panting noise that marked the grizzly's approach.

His arms were inside the sleeping bag and his face was covered with the top of it. He didn't move or even breathe. He heard the bear stop a few feet away, let out a blood-chilling roar, and then turn and run off. Forest shuddered with relief. He concluded that Marty's clothes draped over the brush, the glowing gas lantern and the appearance of the bag had caused the bear to bolt.

After about half an hour of dread and fear Forest was beginning to relax when he heard a new noise on his right, something rustling in the brush. His arms were out of the sleeping bag now, and his face uncovered. His hand was on the shotgun. Twisting his head toward the right, he saw, about fifteen feet away, a small bear cub standing in the gathering twilight. The idea flashed through his mind that this cub might belong to the bear that had attacked him. But then Forest knew that couldn't be. He had been mauled by a grizzly; this cub looked like a young black.

Whatever bear it belonged to, Forest was sure the old lady wasn't far off, and he didn't want the cub to bring her down on him. It took a few steps toward the man, watching him with lively curiosity; he didn't know quite what to do. If he scared it and it squalled, he would surely be in for more trouble. He tried a loud, sharp hiss. That did it. The cub swapped ends and ran without squalling. Five minutes later, however, Forest heard another rustling at the edge of the brush. It was back . . . with a twin. He hissed again, and the two of them scrammed. But they were too curious to stay away. With impish persistence, the two little black cubs came back, and for half an hour they kept Forest on pins and needles. Circling around him, they took turns footing in for a look, but neither ever came closer than about fifteen feet. Forest lay quiet, frantically trying to think of a scheme that would drive them off for keeps. He expected the she-bear to come ambling along any minute to investigate what her cubs had found. Eventually, however, they lost interest in Forest and retreated into the brush. All was quiet again.

It was close to full dark when the flame of the gas lantern grew dimmer and then went out. Under normal circumstances that would have been a minor annoyance; however, it was a terrifying experience for Forest. Now he had no protection at all against the night. He couldn't control his fear; it grew to the borders of panic as he thought of the grizzly possibly returning. Then, just as he feared, he heard the frightening, panting noise off in the brush.

The bear wasn't rushing him this time. It was approaching slowly, stalking toward his head from an angle that would make it impossible for Forest to see it. He figured that the grizzly was cautious after the earlier encounter with the lantern. Once it discovered the light was no longer there, he figured the bear would jump him.

In desperation, he raised the shotgun, pointed it in the direction of the noise, elevated the barrel so the shot would pass over the bear. When he pulled the trigger, a red stab of flame flashed from the muzzle. The kick jolted him from head to foot. The blast of the shot ripped the quiet of the night apart. The noise and flash must have scared the bear witless. Forest heard a strangled roar, then the crackling of brush and the pounding of a heavy animal running off. The man was left again with the stillness of the night.

It wasn't long, however, before he heard noise from bears back at the moose remains, a combination of growling and gnawing. That horrible noise went on for three or four hours. During that time, his fear gradually subsided. Forest began to feel that, with any kind of luck, Marty and the rescue party were going to find him alive after all. Sometime later the bears left off feeding and quiet returned.

But that was short-lived. The savage grizzly hadn't forgotten Forest. About an hour before midnight he heard once more the panting that signaled its approach, which this time was from his left. The bear was walking in cautiously; Forest brought the shotgun into position with the barrel laid across his body, and got set to shoot. He knew the risk involved if the shot should only wound, rather than kill the grizzly; however, it was better than lying there and letting it get at him again. He couldn't take another going over. He decided to let the bear come within ten feet. If it approached that close, he would know it meant business. At that range, even in the dark, he would be able to make out its outline; he would give it both barrels together, square in the face. That might drive the bear off, even if it failed to kill.

When the grizzly sounded as though it was about twenty five feet away, it stopped. Forest could hear it panting and snuffling, and then it circled him and started to prowl in from the other side. He trained the gun and waited, but the grizzly didn't come any closer. Apparently something about the setup bothered the grizzly. Maybe it remembered the shotgun blast. After ten minutes or so of nosing around, it moved off. Forest didn't know it, but his bear troubles were over.

Around midnight still awake and alert, Forest caught the far-off thrum of Marty's outboard. He had never heard a more welcome sound. It grew louder and nearer. When it died away abruptly, he knew the rescue party would soon be heading for him on foot.

By this time the rainy night was pitch black. Forest was afraid they might have trouble finding him in the brush, so he took half a dozen matches out of his pocket and held them in his hand, ready for striking as soon as he heard the men approaching. He lay there in the sleeping bag, hanging onto the matches and waiting for what seemed hours. It was actually only about thirty minutes. While he was waiting, he heard again the sound of a distant outboard. His hopes sank pretty low. Forest thought the rescuers had turned back; he was too far gone to figure out that a second boat, still a long way off, was feeling its way up the Chilkat.

A little later he couldn't believe his ears when he heard voices in the brush close by. He struck all the matches at once.

"There he is! There's a light!" somebody said.

Flashlights winked toward him through the darkness. Half a minute later Forest was looking up into the faces of Marty and two companions. He took the first easy breath he had drawn since the bear had first grabbed him. They laid a stretcher on the ground beside the sleeping bag. He asked the time. It was nearly one in the morning. The ordeal had lasted fourteen and a half hours. That's a long time to lie helpless, waiting for a grizzly to finish you off.

The two men Marty had brought back with him were Carl Heinmiller and Walt Dueman. Heinmiller was a retired Army major, who had lost three fingers and an eye in the South Pacific during World War II. Despite his handicaps, he was the top first-aid man around Haines. Heinmiller immediately set to work giving Forest a shot of penicillin and then one of morphine. After that the three of them eased him onto the stretcher. While carrying him back to the cabin, they lost the trail in the darkness. It took them three and a half hours to get through the brush and timber. The pain from his injuries, plus the jolting from the stretcher ride, were pretty bad; however, the morphine, which was dulling Forest's consciousness, helped. Actually the trip was about as tough for the rescuers as it was for him.

The grizzly didn't seem to want to give up. The men heard it bawl in the distance twice on their way back to camp. They thought it was trailing them; each time the bear bawled the sound seemed just as close to them. They imagined that it was sullen and quarrelsome but not willing to jump so large a party.

When the rescuers reached the cabin, they found a second rescue party of three men waiting. Their boat was the one Forest had heard away off down the Chilkat. They had reached the camp just before the stretcher bearers arrived with their burden. They decided to get some sleep, knowing that nothing further could be done for Forest until the next day.

Shortly after eight in the morning, Dr. Robert Schuler reached the cabin. Although a resident of Juneau, he had been in Haines the evening before when Marty brought in the word about Forest. The doctor started for the cabin at daylight by airboat with John Fox. They hadn't dared to tackle the river in the dark, but once it was light the fast airboat got them to the cabin in forty-five minutes. It had taken Marty four hours, and the other boat party almost eight. The Chilkat is tough to run at night.

By the time the doctor was attending to Forest, machinery of a full-scale rescue, utilizing Alaskan and Canadian volunteers and equipment, was in motion. At midmorning a big helicopter from the RCAF base at Whitehorse, one hundred miles away, settled down in the little clearing in front of the cabin. The 'copter had been torn down for overhaul the day before; however, when word of the mishap reached the base late in the evening, the repair crew worked all night to get it back together and in shape to undertake the rescue.

The whirlybird was big enough to carry a five-man rescue crew, including a doctor and nurse, plus a complete supply of drugs and plasma. The medics, however, didn't waste time treating Forest at the camp; he was a critical hospital case by that time. They bundled him aboard, and he was airlifted to Haines. During the short hop, he received transfusions. A Coast Guard PBY flew him from Haines to Juneau, where he was taken by ambulance to St. Anne's Hospital. Just twenty-seven hours after the bear nabbed him, Forest was on the operating table being patched up by a Juneau surgeon, Dr. Cass Carter.

Surgical attention was long overdue. Forest had more than a hundred tooth marks on the front of his body, from his shoulders to his knees, plus countless other cuts and gashes in his back and side. Several ribs were broken and one had been torn out. Dr. Carter had to remove part of two; the end of one had pressed in against a lung, which fortunately had not been punctured. The surgeon cut and sewed and patched for three hours. During surgery, it was necessary to give Forest additional blood transfusions. After operating, the doctor said he wouldn't have believed that any man who had been injured as seriously as Forest could have stayed alive more than six hours without medical help.

Forest's life hung by a thread for days. With time, however, his name was removed from the critical list. He was in the hospital from October 3 to December 10. When released, he was thirty pounds underweight, but he soon gained it back. The mauling left him short three ribs and marked by some ugly scars. His right hand was permanently banged up and the third finger was half an inch shorter than it had been, but Forest still had the use of the hand. Within a year he had recovered almost completely and was back on the job.

Following his return to work, Forest and Dr. Carter, who was an enthusiastic big game hunter, and Marty built a hunting cabin in the same area in which Forest had been attacked. That fall the three of them hunted there. Doc Carter and Forest both accounted for a moose. Forest killed his only about four hundred yards from the place where the bear had mauled him.

The hunters were to discover that grizzlies were still in the area. When Carter shot his moose, he only had time to dress it out and cover it with a tarp before nightfall. The men had been told that if they built a low fence of sticks around a kill it would keep bears off, so they tried it. When they went back the next morning, however, the fence had been knocked down, the tarp pulled away, and the moose head dragged off to one side. In a patch of sand, they found a round depression, which had been made by the fat rump of a big bear as it sat beside the kill and sized things up. From the size of the tracks and the shape of the claw marks, they knew the outlaw was a silvertip. Apparently the noise of their airboat or their approach had spooked the grizzly. It had left without feeding on the moose at all. Forest wondered if it was the same grizzly he had tangled with. He guessed he would never know. They packed the meat to the cabin without further delay. Although they saw no more of the bear, they kept a close grip on their rifles while moving the meat.

In fact, Forest never went into the woods a minute during this trip without his rifle, and he'll probably never be in the woods again without one, at least not as long as he lives in that part of the country. While he was hunting moose he was also watching for that big grizzly with stiff gray whiskers all over its face, always waiting for the chance to even the score. Although Forest never got that chance, it's a safe bet that no bear will ever catch him with his guard down again.

OUTDOOR LIFE
JUNE 1957

It's safe to say that every hunter who strays from a familiar logging road will someday get lost—it's just a matter of degree. Most of us will lose our bearings for an hour or so, then breathe a sigh of relief when we stumble onto the logging road. Most of the time we won't even tell our buddies back in camp about our short encounter with anxiety and fear. Try to imagine, then, getting lost for ten days. To make matters worse, this hunter and his guide were caught in a snowstorm and lost their clothing, tent, matches, and compass. There's a lesson here—if you're a hunter, learn it well.

Ten Terrible Days

by ELWYN (BUD) MYERS

I want to say something right at the beginning that has been said a thousand times before, but I want to say it louder: don't ever leave camp or walk off a trail in wild country without a map, compass, and matches in a waterproof container.

My ordeal started out as a moose hunt that promised to be about as dangerous as a game of Ping-Pong. It turned into a life-and-death affair, and death almost won.

I got out of high school at Pentwater, Michigan, in 1953, out of the Marines in 1957, and out of Central Michigan University in June of 1961. I had a job waiting in the fall with the Fish and Wildlife Service, and I also had plans to get married in about a year.

I had hunted since I was a kid—foxes, deer, partridges, and ducks—I loved it. All along, however, I wanted to go to Canada for a moose. With the job and the girl in the offing, I concluded the fall of 1961 might be my last chance for quite a spell.

I picked the area northeast of Lake of the Woods, in western Ontario, left Pentwater on Wednesday, October 25, drove twenty-eight hours, and reached the town of Vermilion Bay, fifty miles east of Kenora, before noon the next day.

I had reservations at a hunting camp, but I learned that an early

231

freeze had forced it to close three days before. So here I was, a thousand miles from home, all set for my first moose hunt, with no place to go. On the advice of a restaurant counterman, I got in touch with Archie Webb, who operates a bush-flying service, does some outfitting, and maintains tent camps on a few remote lakes. We made arrangements in a hurry. Webb would fly me to Portal Lake, thirty-five or forty miles to the north, for a four-day hunt. He'd supply a guide, tent, boat, sleeping bags, and the rest of the gear. We wrapped it all up and in two hours were airborne.

Archie landed at McIntosh, on the Canadian National Railroad, to pick up guide Tom Strong, a local Indian, thirty-one years old, who had lived all his life in the area and knew it well. Quiet, he looked and acted capable, and I liked him from the start.

From McIntosh we flew to a small lake where Webb had a tent camp, and he left us there for the night. Next day he moved us and the camp to Portal Lake, setting us down shortly after noon. We got the gear ashore and Archie gunned his plane off the water, leaving the guide and me with a good outfit, plenty of provisions, and a big chunk of roadless bush. Webb would fly over every day or so, check to make sure things were okay, and fly my moose out if I was lucky.

The sun was up when Tom nudged me awake next morning, Saturday. "Look out the flap," he said. A big cow moose was standing at the edge of the lake about forty yards away. I could have killed her without leaving my sack, but I hadn't come to Canada to get a moose that way; besides, I wanted a good head for mounting.

I had a hard case of moose fever by the time she wandered back into the woods, and we didn't wait for breakfast. We paddled the twelve-foot aluminum boat down the lake, spotting two more cows but no moose with horns. Finally we went back to camp for breakfast.

The morning was so still that Tom was sure if there were bull moose knocking their antlers against trees we'd hear them. "All cows here," he said.

When we finished eating he proposed a hike to a small bog lake he knew about. It was only two miles away, and we'd be back in time for lunch. "Lots of bulls back in there," he said.

We paddled across the lake, pulled the boat up on shore, and left it there. That probably saved our lives.

The idea of making any special preparations never entered my mind. We'd be gone only a few hours, the guide had been to the place before, and it was a fine, warm October day. There was no reason to think about survival gear.

We were both lucky in our clothing. I was wearing light underwear, a sweatshirt, cotton shirt, wool vest, insulated hunting pants, an army field jacket, fur cap, two pairs of sweat socks, and thermal rubber boots. Strong had on long underwear, two shirts, two pairs of pants, a wool jacket and cap, and low rubber pacs over two pairs of wool socks. By sheer accident I had a pair of wool mittens in my pocket. Tom was less fortunate on that score. Paddling, he used only one glove, and that was all he had with him.

I carried my .30/06 converted Springfield and eight shells. I also had a hunting knife and binoculars. Strong had a few kitchen matches and I was carrying some paper matches. We had maybe a dozen between us, enough for a cigarette now and then.

We reached the bog lake in less than an hour and found fresh tracks. The place looked good, so we waited. The clear, warm day was changing now. The sky turned overcast and a raw wind came up. When we started to get cold the guide suggested we head for camp. We'd go back another way, he said, to keep out of muskeg and swamp. We crossed a ridge and struck into the bush. The sky was getting darker, the wind was blowing harder, and soon it began to snow, a blinding squall of big wet flakes that whitened the ground fast. We walked an hour, and I expected to see Portal Lake any minute. Then we came over the top of a ridge and looked down on the bog lake we had just left.

I had heard about men walking in circles, but I found it hard to believe we had done it. There was no doubt about it, however, so we turned back and trudged away once more. We walked two hours that time, broke out of a dense swamp, and stared in disbelief at the bog lake.

"I walk circles," Tom grunted. "You try."

So I took the lead, lining up one tree with another. In about an hour we came out on a smaller lake we had not seen before.

"I here last fall," the guide assured me. "Camp that way," and he drew a crude map in the snow with a stick. But after two more hours of hard hiking we came back to the same spot and found our own tracks. When we tried again, the same thing happened.

Once more I took the lead, and we did not see that lake again. By late afternoon we were mixed up in a chain of lakes and ponds connected with channels winding through bogs.

An hour before dark we came to a large lake that Strong was sure he recognized. "Camp over there," he said, "beyond big swamp." We found the swamps and fought our way through, but by then it was getting dusk and we decided to camp for the night.

The snow had turned to rain and sleet, and everything was dripping. We had six matches left, some of them wet. We stripped bark off a birch tree, gathered half-dry wood from windfall, and Tom tried to get a fire going. He did—with our last match.

We built up a roaring blaze, dried our wet clothing, and gathered wood and green boughs for a bed. We slept fitfully, getting up often to replenish the fire. The storm let up before daybreak, but the morning was gray and cheerless with a cold wind. We had no food but found a few wintergreen berries, which we munched while debating the next move.

We faced a grave decision. With our matches gone, this would be our last fire. Should we stay beside the fire and wait for rescue or try to get back to camp? I hated to leave, but Tom insisted he knew how to get to Portal Lake, and in the end I gave in.

We had been without food for more than twenty-four hours, and when we spotted a grouse in a tree I concluded raw meat would be better than nothing. I tried to blow the bird's head off with the .30/06 but only cut a feather or two from its topknot. Shortly after that I did better on a snowshoe hare. We picked up the headless rabbit and took it along.

We walked the rest of that day without finding anything the guide recognized. An hour before dark we came to a chain of small lakes. "You know these?" I asked.

"Never see before," he admitted.

"Then we're really lost." He nodded gravely.

It was a tough thing to face. I'd heard and read about it but had never thought it would happen to me, and knowing we'd let ourselves in for it by our own mistakes didn't help any. Right then I'd have given a year of my life for a map and compass. We were trapped in country as wild and rough as any in western Ontario, all hills and swamps, lakes and streams, muskeg, beaver ponds, and windfalls. Twenty-odd miles south was the Canadian National Railroad, running east from Winnipeg to Sioux Lookout and through Tom's home town of McIntosh. About the same distance east was Highway 105, leading north from Vermilion Bay to Goldpines. Tom and I both thought the road lay southeast of us rather than east, however—a mistake that came close to finishing us.

We built a crude lean-to by propping logs against a ledge, covering it with green boughs, and gathered more for a bed. Then we tried to start a fire by shooting into a handfull of birchbark shavings and a piece of crumpled paper from my wallet, but we had no way to extract the bullet. The blast charred the paper but blew away the shavings. Nothing ignited, and we realized we could not make fire that way.

Next we tried to eat some of the raw rabbit, but it tasted too strong and wild. Maybe we were not yet hungry enough. We each managed two or three bites of fat but couldn't choke down the unsalted lean and finally threw the whole thing away.

Snow began to fall at dark, and the night was bitterly cold. We slept in snatches, getting up often to walk warmth into ourselves. We were undecided next morning whether to wait for rescue or try to find our way out. I had flown enough to know how slim our chances would be of being spotted from the air without a fire, so in the end we walked away. But before we left we laid four logs together to form a rectangle in an open place on the rocks, with an arrow to point our direction. We were not able, after that, to write signals in the snow because we could find no open areas big enough that were free of brush and grass.

An hour after we left we found a blazed trail. Bark had been chipped off trees and the scar marked with an S in red paint. We figured the S meant south, so we followed the blazes in what we thought was that direction.

That morning Archie Webb flew over our camp and noticed our boat on the shore across the lake from the tent. He had seen it there the day before and went down to investigate. He found the camp unused, our clothing still packed, no sign of recent fire, and only the rifle missing. He taxied across the lake to the boat, discovered old footprints leading into the bush, and realized he had a pair of lost men on his hands. The boat, left there on the shore, had touched off a prompt alarm. Webb flew back to McIntosh, picked up an experienced Indian guide, Tom Payash, and returned to Portal Lake to launch a search that was to grow into one of the biggest and most intensive manhunts ever carried out in that part of Canada.

Strong and I followed the blazes all day. Late in the afternoon we saw that they crossed a river rimmed with new ice. The barrier was formidable, but we could see the blazes on the far side so we hunted along the bank until we found a log to cross on. It was under almost a foot of water and so slippery it seemed doubtful for footing, but we had no choice. We pulled off our boots and socks, for the first time in four days, and when I saw my feet I was scared. They were white and puckered and Tom's weren't much better. Unless we could get our feet out of the boots at night we were in for trouble.

We got poles for balancing, and I tied my boots around my neck, slung my rifle on one shoulder, and inched out on the log. It was like grease, but I kept going. When I was safe on the other side Tom followed. A mile farther on, the blazed trail petered out at the edge of a big marsh. That was as bad a letdown as I'd ever had.

We built a lean-to against an upturned stump and cut marsh grass for our bed. It was dry and warm, and our camp that night was one of the best we had. But now I had another reason to worry. Cutting boughs in the dusk, I'd sliced a finger to the bone. I tore off a strip of shirt for bandage, but it worked loose in the night and the cut was dirty and swollen next morning. It looked as if I might have an infected finger added to my other troubles.

We decided to follow the blaze line back. Maybe hunters had blazed it out from a fly-in cabin on a lake. That would mean shelter and fire. Starting at first light, we recrossed the river on the sunken log, and went on.

We had seen deer frequently, and I decided to kill the next one. We needed meat if we were to keep going, and more important maybe we could wrap our feet in the skin at night and get our socks partially dry. Late in the afternoon we saw a doe sixty yards away and shot her.

We stopped for the night and tried to eat some of the warm venison. Tom couldn't get the lean down but ate a few bites of the fat. I didn't like the unsalted stuff but ate a slice half as big as my hand and felt better.

That night we took our boots off for the first time and put our socks inside our shirts to dry, wrapping our bare feet in the deerskin, hairy side in. It was even warmer than we'd expected.

Our pants had been ripped from brush and windfalls, and wads of insulation were hanging out of mine. Next morning we sewed them up with strips of deer hide, but they soon tore again. When we left the lean-to, in a hard snowstorm, I carried a hindquarter of the doe and Tom was wearing the green skin around his shoulders.

In the early afternoon the blazed trail ended on the shore of a lake. The last blaze was a crude picture of a cabin, and for a little while we were sure we'd find the cabin nearby, but we searched in vain. I'd still like to know who blazed that apparently meaningless trail, and why they did it.

About an hour after we left the lake, a rifle shot rapped out in the distance. We listened, hardly daring to believe our ears. In the next few minutes two or three more shots followed. They seemed to come from all around us. Then, sounding from less than a mile away, two were fired in quick succession. Certain they were a signal, I touched off two quick ones in answer, and almost instantly we heard a single shot reply.

This was the first proof we'd had that a search was under way. We had heard distant aircraft a few times but never close enough to raise our hopes. Now, however, we felt sure that rescue was near.

Of the eight shells with which I had left camp, I had but two left and dared not risk them except as a last resort. We waited for another signal, but none came. We decided to go and meet the searchers.

I was sure of the location of the last shots, but when Strong jerked a thumb and said, "Come from over there," he pointed in the opposite direction. For a second I lost my temper. "What's the matter with you? They came from that way."

Tom shook his head. "Over there," he said.

It was the only argument we had, and I knew better than to let it grow into a quarrel. If we separated I was certain at least one of us would wander until he died. "Okay," I said at last, "we'll try it your way." We'll never know which was right.

That morning Webb had enlisted the help of two more pilots, Ron Booi of North Star Camp on Clay Lake and Emile Mayling of Vermilion Bay. He had also flown a party of twelve ground searchers to Portal Lake, established a camp there, and put Walter Booi, owner of the North Star Camp, Ron's father and a veteran bush man, in charge. Then Webb, Ron, and Mayling began an air search that would eventually cover more than one thousand square miles.

Ground searchers had fired the shots. At that moment we were hardly more than a mile from help, but we missed contact completely, and those were the last shots we heard. The next day the searchers gave up their firearms. Those in charge knew that shooting in an area where men are lost is likely to confuse them or even excite them to panic.

Strong and I walked three hours, stopping now and then to yell and wait hopefully for an answer, before we gave up. I'd never been more discouraged than I was right then, but there was greater disappointment to come.

We found a place to camp at the edge of a muskeg and were gathering dry grass when we heard the drone of a plane. The sound grew louder, and the plane came into sight just over the trees bordering the marsh, flying low and less than five hundred yards away.

We ran for the open muskeg, stripping off our coats, waving and screaming like madmen, but the aircraft kept its course. It was a small bush plane and we could see the pilot, but he did not see us. We watched until he went out of sight above the timber. I guess that was the worst disappointment I ever faced.

Before dark, a second aircraft came over, flying a little higher. Again we raced for the marsh, but again the plane flew on, passing directly over our heads. I said grimly to Tom, "That settles it. If we're going to get out at all we'll have to walk out on our own." I didn't admit even to myself that I wasn't sure we'd make it.

That night our feet were in better shape. Our socks, tucked inside our shirts, never really dried but were drier in the morning than when we lay down, and the deerskin was warm on our bare feet. I debated shooting a second deer so we'd each have a skin, but with only two shells left decided to wait.

The final days of our ordeal blurred into a nightmare of torment, wandering while daylight lasted and huddling under open shelters at night, shaking with cold. I kept my watch wound and tried to keep track of time, but I must have lost count because we were lost two days longer than I thought.

We were turning into gaunt scarecrows. When we broke ice for a drink, I studied my reflection in the black water and hardly knew myself. We grew weaker each day. I was eating a little raw venison. It was almost like cold cuts out of a refrigerator. I realized I was risking dysentery by eating raw meat, but that possibility was better than eating nothing. Tom had given up on it, however, and was in worse shape than I. Once, when we were crossing a big muskeg, he dropped so far behind he was barely in shouting distance. After that I was careful to watch and wait for him.

The quarter of doe meat froze so hard at last that we threw it away. Neither of us seemed hungry, and we told ourselves that if we needed more we could kill another deer. We didn't suffer much actual discomfort from lack of food, but I dreamed constantly of hot chicken dinners.

The cold and wet were far harder to bear. There were about five inches of snow on the ground, and the bogs and sluggish creeks, often flooded by beaver dams, were frozen over but not hard enough to hold us. In many places we broke through, occasionally sinking above our knees. Our boot laces were broken and knotted, our tattered and ice-caked pants flapped around our legs, and at night our wet clothing froze stiff. At first I had slept with my mittens on, but when they became soaked I drew my arms out of my sleeves and folded them inside. I had lost my fur cap the first day (I also lost my binoculars, but I don't know when) and at night I tied a red handkerchief around my head, pulled the jacket up over it, and buttoned it tight. Tom and I crowded close for warmth, each pressing his bare feet against the other inside the deerskin. But in spite of all we did the cold kept us awake, and the nights were long. As we grew weaker we slept more soundly, however, and toward the end the cold no longer bothered us much.

We didn't know it then, of course, but I have learned since from official Canadian weather records that the daytime temperature in the Kenora area never climbed much above 40 degrees the ten days we were lost, that it was below freezing most of the time, and that the nights got down as low as 15 above.

My cut finger was swollen to bursting, but I had too much on my mind to worry about it. I wondered a lot about my family and my girl. I knew they'd be praying, waiting hopefully for the phone to ring, lying awake at night.

The tantalizing thought of our well-supplied tent was seldom out of my mind. I'm sure we were never more than ten miles from it, most of the time much less. It was hard to realize we might die of cold and starvation so close to it. In fact, I never really admitted that possibility; I told myself over and over we'd get out somehow. I don't know what Tom thought, for he said little. His wife had been ready to go to the hospital to have a baby the day we left McIntosh, however, and he worried openly about her.

There were days when we walked in circles, coming back repeatedly to our own tracks. Each night we built our lean-to at the edge of an open marsh where we'd have a chance of being seen by aircraft. We saw or heard planes every day, but after the first sighting when the two flew overhead none came close.

The plight of lost men begets a peculiar kind of universal pity. Certainly that was true in our case. We were headline news in cities a thousand miles away, and the Canadians pressed the search for us in every way they knew.

More bush planes volunteered, and the Search and Rescue Wing of the RCAF at Winnipeg came in until there were eleven aircraft flying and two helicopters standing by. The country for twenty miles around Portal Lake was laid out in a grid pattern and all of it covered. All the lakes big enough to land on were combed by small planes that taxied around the shore as their pilots looked for tracks, a dead fire, any sign of us.

High winds and snow hampered the searchers, and there were days when the planes could go up for only an hour or so. Archie Webb and Ron Booi flew under almost impossible conditions, when trim tabs and pontoon rudders froze and they had to land to break the ice off, even cracking shell ice with their pontoons to taxi ashore. My dad flew up from Pentwater to the search camp and went out on flights or waited helplessly for word of us.

On Saturday, November 4—a week from the day we had wandered into the bush—the Kenora Bush Search and Rescue Unit, a volunteer outfit made up of experienced bush men and timber cruisers, was called in. Constable George Orosy of the Ontario Provincial Police, area commander of the unit, flew to the camp and took charge. By that time he had twenty men.

The searchers began to feel they were looking for dead men. From what had been found in our tent they knew we were without food, and because no smoke had been sighted, they were sure we had no fire. There was a limit to the time we could survive, and many believed we had reached it. Hope was almost gone, but there was no thought yet of abandoning the search.

Orosy was more optimistic. We were both young and in good condition. Strong was used to roughing it, and he thought I would last as long as the guide. "It will take more than a week to finish them," he told Dad confidently.

The ground search was widened to cover more territory. Four members of the Kenora group walked twenty miles east to Highway 105 in three days but found no sign of us. Next, Orosy had three-man teams flown to lakes from five to ten miles north, south, east, and west of Portal with instructions to walk a compass course back to the search camp. If they found us they'd light two fires as a signal, and bush planes were assigned to support these teams.

Everything that seasoned rescue workers could think of was being done. Every man in the quest knew that unless we were found soon there would be no further use to look for us.

The morning the widened ground search got under way, Tom and I awoke to see the sky clearing and the sun breaking through for the first time since we had walked away from the bog lake on October 28. Now at last we could get our bearings. That first sight of the sun seemed to put new life in us. We'd walk out now. Just a few more days and we'd be back safe and sound.

Which way to go? It was no use to look for Portal Lake since we had no idea of its location or ours. We agreed our best chance was to try for Highway 105, which we believed lay to the southeast. We struck out in that direction, walking as fast as we could.

Actually, we were headed toward the railroad and Quibell, thirty-odd miles away, and I know now we could never have made it. The Wabigoon River and a chain of big lakes was in our way, and we would not have been able to get across. Our strength was about gone, and our wanderings would have ended somewhere along the Wabigoon. Orosy told me later that we walked in a more southerly direction than southeast, I suppose partly because our way was barred time after time by streams and flooded bogs.

We tried to hurry all that day, setting our course by the sun. When we stopped for the night we thought we'd covered twelve to fifteen miles. It was more likely five or less.

Now, at last, the search was closing in. While we stumbled weakly on that Sunday afternoon, one of Orosy's search teams—Louis Ashopenace, Tom Payash, and Charlie Fobister—cut our tracks going south two miles west of Portal Lake. They were old, but the three Indians followed them until shortly before dark and camped on a lake. Just after they got their fire built, an RCAF plane flew over, misread their signals, and reported we had been found.

Tom and I spent that night, our ninth in the bush, as we had spent the others, shivering under a lean-to. But we were only a few miles ahead of the search party. The sun was still out the next morning, and we started off to the southeast once more.

Orosy doubted that we had been found, and at daylight he and Archie Webb flew out to investigate. They went back to the base camp and airlifted three more Indians out to help the search team. About noon they came on the camp where we had spent the night and found blood on the snow from Tom's frostbitten legs. They made four miles through a dense swamp in the next hour.

My recollections of that day are hazy. Once when we stopped to rest in the thickets of a big swamp, Tom looked at me dully and said, "I don't think I make it."

That was the first admission of defeat from either of us, and I knew I couldn't be of much help. We even talked of throwing the deerskin away but decided against it. Tom was still carrying it around his shoulders with his bare hands wrapped in it, and I staggered along with the rifle.

About three o'clock we came to a low ridge, the first dry land we'd seen for hours. There was a big windfall with plenty of dead poles, so we stopped for the night. Before the lean-to was finished, Tom crawled into it and wrapped the deerskin around his feet without taking his boots off. He had not done that before, and I realized he was at the end of his rope.

I was helping him tuck the half-frozen hide around his legs when I saw a man walk out of the swamp, following our tracks. He saw us in the same instant, whistled sharply, and broke into a run, and then five more came in sight in single file behind him. We were found!

It took the idea a few minutes to soak in, then we shook hands all around. One of the Indians told us, "You're tough guys. We think you both dead." Then they went to work.

They had axes, food, coffee, tea, and dry socks. In minutes a big fire was crackling. They pulled a log up in front of it, and Tom and I soaked up the most wonderful heat I had ever felt, while our clothes started to steam dry. We drank tea and half a cup of hot soup apiece, and when that stayed down we tried a few bites of bread and cheese. About that time Ron Booi flew over.

He counted eight men and knew the long search was ended. He came down low enough to shout for us to wait where we were, then flew off to make his report. Our rescuers started to clear a place for a helicopter to land, but Booi was back in a little while, circling low again, pointing south and shouting, "Lake. Go that way."

We walked less than a mile before we came to the lake and found Archie Webb's plane waiting at the shore. We learned later that two 'copters standing by at Winnipeg and Kenora were grounded by fifty five-mile winds. Waves were hammering against the pontoons of Webb's plane, the sun was gone, and it was a dark, dreary November day. Tom and I climbed weakly up into the cabin. "You're late," Archie greeted us with a dry grin.

"About a week," I acknowledged.

Minutes later we were looking down into the snowy bush where we had spent those ten terrible days. Suddenly the whole thing seemed like a hideous dream.

Webb landed us at McIntosh, and my dad and Orosy met us there. Orosy said later that he did not think Strong could have survived another night in the open. "And I'd have given you just one more day after he went," he added. I hadn't realized either of us was that far along, but maybe he was right. We were both in pretty rough shape.

Webb's wife, who had kept the search camp supplied with hot soup and food, drove us to the General Hospital at Dryden, forty miles southeast of McIntosh. We were there shortly after dark, but by that time it was snowing hard.

My weight had dropped twenty-two pounds, and Tom, thin to begin with, had lost about as much, but neither of us suffered any lasting damage. My finger healed quickly, Tom's frostbite was not severe, and by some miracle—and thanks to the deerskin—we escaped frozen feet. I spent three days in the hospital, eating about every two hours, and Tom was there a little longer. His wife had a baby boy before he got home and they named it Bud, for me. I couldn't have had a nicer compliment.

I still want a moose, and one of these days I'll go back and get one. But when I do you can be sure that every minute I'm in the bush I'll know exactly where I am.

OUTDOOR LIFE
JULY 1962

Modern bowhunters kill bears with a fair amount of regularity. Black bears, and even Alaska brown bears and grizzlies, fall to the bow. It is an admirable accomplishment, but it is no longer a near impossible feat. But try to picture how the first bowhunter whoever faced a grizzly must have felt. That hunter was Saxton Pope, the man who gave birth to the Pope and Young Club. Pope did not have a modern magnesium compound bow with stabilizers and sights. He carried a wood longbow with wood arrows and crude broadheads. And Pope didn't know if he could kill a grizzly with his equipment. After all, he would be the first to try it.

First Grizzlies
With a Bow

by SAXTON POPE

THE very idea of shooting grizzly bears with the bow and arrow strikes most people as so absurd that they laugh at the mention of it. The mental picture of the puny little archery implements of their childhood opposed to that of the largest and most fearsome beast of the Western world produces merriment and incredulity.

Because it seemed so impossible, I presume, this added to our desire to accomplish it.

Ever since we began hunting with the bow, we had talked of shooting grizzlies. We thought of an Alaskan trip as a remotely attainable adventure, and planned murderous arrows of various ingenious spring devices to increase their cutting qualities. We estimated the power of formidable bows necessary to pierce the hides of these monsters. In fact, it was the acme of our hunting desires.

We read the biography of John Capen Adams and his adventures with the California grizzlies, and Roosevelt's admirable descriptions of these animals. They filled out our dreams with detail. And after killing black bears we needed only the opportunity to make our wish become an exploit.

The opportunity to do this arrived unexpectedly, as many opportunities seem to, when the want and the preparedness coincide.

The California Academy of Sciences has in its museum in Golden Gate Park, San Francisco, a collection of very fine animal habitat groups, among which are deer, antelope, mountain sheep, cougars, and brown bear. While an elk group was being installed, it happened that the taxidermist, Mr. Paul Fair, said to me that the next and final setting would be one of grizzly bears. In surprise, I asked him if it were not a fact that the California grizzly was extinct. He said this was true, but the silvertip bear of Wyoming was a grizzly and its range extended westward to the Sierra Nevada Mountains; so it could properly be classified as a Pacific Coast variety. He cited Professor Merriam's monograph on the classification of grizzlies to prove his statements. He also informed me that permit might be obtained from Washington to secure these specimens in Yellowstone National Park.

Immediately I perceived an opportunity and interviewed Dr. Barton Everman, curator of the museum, concerning the feasibility of offering our services in taking these bears at no expense to the academy. Incidentally, we proposed to shoot them with the bow and arrow, and thereby answer a moot question in anthropology. The proposition appealed to him, and he wrote to Washington for a permit to secure specimens in this National Park, stating that the bow and arrow would be used. I insisted upon this latter stipulation, so that there should be no misunderstanding if, in the future, any objection was raised to this method of hunting.

In a very short time permit was given to the academy, and we started our preparations for the expedition. This was late in the fall of 1919, and bear were at their best in the spring, just after hibernation; so we had ample time.

It was planned that Mr. Compton, Mr. Young, and I should be the hunters, and such other assistance would be obtained as seemed necessary. We began reviewing our experience and formulating the principles of the campaign.

Our weapons we now considered adequate in the light of our contact with black bears. We had found that our bows were as strong as we could handle, and ample to drive a good arrow through a horse, a fact which we had demonstrated upon the carcasses of recently dead animals.

But we decided to add to the length of our arrowheads, and use tempered instead of soft steel as heretofore. We took particular pains to have them perfect in every detail.

Then we undertook the study of the anatomy of bears and the location and size of their vital organs. In the work of William Wright on the grizzly, we found valuable data concerning the habits and nature of these animals.

In spite of the reputation of this bear for ferocity and tenacity of life, we felt that, after all, he was only made of flesh and blood, and our arrows were capable of solving the problem.

We also began preparing ourselves for the contest. Although habitually in good physical condition, we undertook special training for the big event. By running, the use of dumbbells and other gymnastic practices, we strengthened our muscles and increased our endurance. Our field shooting was also directed toward rapid delivery and the quick judgment of distances on level, uphill, and falling ground. In fact, we planned to leave no factor for success untried.

My brother, G. D. Pope, of Detroit, being a hunter of big game with the gun, was invited to join the party, and his advice was asked concerning a reliable guide. He gladly consented to come with us and share the expenses. At the same time he suggested Ned Frost, of Cody, Wyoming, as the most experienced hunter of grizzly bears in America.

About this time one of my professional friends visited the Smithsonian Institution at Washington, where he met a member of the staff, who inquired if he knew Doctor Pope, of San Francisco, a man that was contemplating shooting grizzlies with the bow and arrow. The doctor replied that he did, whereat the sage laughed and said that the feat was impossible, most dangerous and foolhardy; it could not be done. We fully appreciated the danger involved—therein lay some of the zest. But we also knew that even should we succeed in killing them in Yellowstone Park, the glory would be sullied by the popular belief that all park bears are hotel pets, live upon garbage, and that it was a cruel shame to torment them with arrows.

So in my early correspondence with Frost, I assured him that we did not want to shoot any tame bears and that we would not consider the trip at all if this were necessary. He assured us that this was not necessary, and reminded us that Yellowstone Park was fifty miles wide by sixty miles long, and that some of the highest portions of the Rocky Mountains lay in it. The animals in this preserve, he said, were far from tame and the bears were divided into two distinct groups, one mostly composed of black and brown with a few inferior specimens of grizzlies that frequent the dumps back of the camps and hotels, and another group of bears that never came near civilization, but lived entirely up in the rugged mountains and were as dangerous and wary as those in Alaska or any other wild country. These bears wander outside the park and furnish hunting material throughout the neighboring state. He promised to put us in communication with grizzlies that were as unspoiled and unafraid as those first seen by Lewis and Clarke in their early explorations.

After explaining the purposes of our trip and the use of the bow,

Ned Frost agreed that it was a real sporting proposition and took up the plan with enthusiasm. I sent him a sample arrow we used in hunting, and his letter in reply I take the liberty of printing. It is typical of the frontier spirit and comes, not only from the foremost grizzly hunter of all times, but discloses the man's bigness of heart:

My dear Doctor:

Your letter of the 18th was received a day or so ago, and last night I received "Good Medicine" [a hunting arrow] on the evening train, and I feel better away down deep about this hunt after a good examination of this little Grizzy Tickler than I have at any time before. I have, by mistake, let it simmer out in a quiet way that I was going to see what a grizzly would really do if he had a few sticks stuck in his innerds, and my friends have been giving the Mrs. and me a regular line of farewell parties. Really, I think it has been a splendid paying thing to do; pork chops are high, you know, and I really feel I am off to the good about nine dollars and six bits worth of bacon and flour right now on this deal. Maybe I'll be in debt to you before green-grass if I don't look out.

Well, anyway, here is hoping we will all live through it and have a dandy time. Don't worry about coming to blows with the bear; I have noticed from long experience that it is not the times that you think a bear is going to give you trouble that it happens, but always when least expected. I have trailed wounded grizzlies time and time again, and was more or less worried all the while, but never had one turn on me yet. Then, too, I have had about three experiences with them that made my hair stand straight up, and when it finally settled, it had more *frost* in it than ever before; and let me add right here, that one of the worst places I ever got into was when I had sixteen of the best bear dogs that were ever gotten together, I believe, after an old she-grizzly, and I was like you, thought they would hold the bear's attention. *But,* don't let any notion like this get you into trouble. Now, I am not running down dogs as a means of getting bear; I love them and would now have a good pack if it was possible to run them in the game fields of this state, but you don't want to think that they can handle a grizzly like they do a black bear. In fact, I would place no value on them whatsoever as a safeguard in case a grizzly got on the pack, and I am speaking from experience, mind you. No, a good little shepherd would do more than a dozen regular bear dogs, but there is only about one little shepherd like I speak of in a lifetime.

If you can use the bow from horseback, here is a safe proposition, and I believe a practical one, too. But I don't feel that there is really so much danger in the game after all, as it is only once in a great while that any bear will go up against the human animal, and then is most likely to be when you are not expecting it at all. Don't worry about it. What I am thinking about most is to get the opportunity to get the first arrow into some good big worthy old boy that will be a credit to the expedition.

There are lots of grizzlies in the park all right, and some of them are not very wild, but if you get out away from the hotels a few miles, they are not going to come up and present their broadsides to you at thirty yards. So, as I say, I am thinking mostly about the chances of getting the opportunities. I don't know, of course, just how close you can place your arrows at thirty yards, and it is getting the first hole into them that I am most interested in now. I feel that we ought to get some good chances, as I have seen so many bear in the park; but, of course, have never hunted them and don't know just how keen they will be when it comes right down to getting their hides. There are some scattered all over the park that will rob a camp at night, and some of them will even put up a fight for it, but most of them will beat it as soon as one gets after them.

It would be impossible, I believe, to keep dogs still while watching a bait, as they would get the scent of any approaching bear, and then you would not be able to keep them quiet, and they would most likely scare the bear out of the country. I can rustle a few dogs to take along if you want them, and pretty good dogs, too; but I am not strong for them myself, only in this way, to put them on the trail of a bear and take a good horse apiece, so that we could get up to the chase and have a chance to land on him. This might be a good thing to try if all others failed.

I know how you feel about killing clean with the bow and not having any shooting, and I can assure you that I would let 'em get just as close as you want them, and not feel any concern about their getting the best of anybody, and you would have a chance to use the bow well in this case; but I am more prone to think they will beat it off with a lot of your perfectly good arrows than anything else.

Yours truly,
Ned Frost

It was apparent from the first that dogs were of little use in taking grizzly. It would be necessary to shoot from blinds set conveniently near bait. Frost assured us that bears of this variety, when just out of hibernation and lean, would run out of the country if chased by a pack of dogs, and incidentally kill all that they could catch. In the fall of the year, when the bears are fat, they refuse to run, but wade through the pack, which is unable to keep him from attacking the hunter.

As an example of this, he related an instance where he started a grizzly with eight or ten Russian bear hounds, and chased the beast about thirty miles. As he followed on horseback, he found one after the other of his dogs torn to pieces, disembowled, and dismembered. At last, he came upon the bear at bay in deep snow, against a high cliff. Only two of his hounds were left, and one of these had a broken leg. Mad with vengeance, Frost shot the grizzly. It charged him at forty yards. In quick succession he fired five bullets in the oncoming bear, seemingly with no effect. Up to his waist in the snow, he was unable to avoid its rush. It came on and fell dead on his chest, with the faithful hound hanging to it in a desperate effort to save his master.

This is one of the three or four maulings that Ned has received in his hunting experiences, which, he says, "have added frost to my golden locks." The dog became a cherished pet in the family for many years.

Frost killed his first bear when fourteen years of age, and has added nearly five hundred to this number since that time.

It is characteristic of the grizzly that he will charge upon the slightest provocation, and that nothing will turn him aside from his purpose. Later we found this particularly true where the female with cubs is concerned.

Instances of this are too well known to recount, but one coming under our own experience was related to me by Tom Murphy, the bear hunter of California.

In early days in Humboldt County, there lived an old settler named Pete Bluford, who was a squaw man. He shot a female grizzly with cubs within a quarter of a mile of what are now the town limits of Blocksburg. The beast charged and struck him to the ground. At the same time she ripped open the man's abdomen. Bluford dropped under a fallen tree, where the bear repeatedly assaulted him, tearing at his body. By rolling back and forth as the grizzly leaped over the log to reach him from the other side, he escaped further injury. Worried by the hunter's dog, she finally ceased her efforts and wandered off. The man was able to reach home in spite of a large open wound in his abdomen, with protruding intestines. This was roughly sewed together by his friend, Beany Powell. He recovered from the experience and lived many years with the Indians of that locality. As an example of Western humor, it is related that Beany Powell, when sewing up the wound with twine and a sack needle, found a large lump of fat protruding from the incision, of which he was unable to dispose; so he cut it off, tried out the grease in the frying-pan and used it to grease his boots.

Old Bluford became a character in the country. He was, in fact, what is colloquially known as "an old poison oaker." This is an individual who sinks so low in the scale of civilization that he lives out in the backwoods or poison oak brush and becomes animal in type. His hair grew to his shoulders, his beard was unkempt, his fingernails were as long as claws and filthy with dirt. Rags of unknown antiquity partially covered his limbs, vermin infested his body, and he stayed with the most degraded remnants of the Indians.

One cold winter they found him dead in his dilapidated cabin. He lay on the dirt floor, his ragged coat over his face, his hands beneath his head, and two house cats lay frozen, one beneath each arm. These old pioneers were strange people and died strange deaths.

In our plans to capture grizzlies we took into consideration the proclivity of this beast to attack. We knew his speed was tremendous. He is able to catch a horse or a dog on the run. Therefore, it is useless for a man to try to run away from him. There is no such thing as being able to climb a tree if the animal is at close quarters. Adams has shown that it is a mistake to attempt it. One only stretches himself out inviting evisceration in the effort.

We decided if cornered either to dodge or to lie flat and feign death. So we practiced dodging, our running being more for the purpose of gaining endurance and to follow the bear if necessary.

Ishi, the Yana Indian, said that grizzlies were to be overcome with arrows and if they charged, they were to be met with the spear and fire. So we constructed spears having well-tempered blades more than a foot in length set upon heavy iron tubing and riveted to strong ash handles six feet in length. Back of the blade we fashioned quick lighting torches of cotton waste saturated with turpentine. These could be ignited by jerking a lanyard fastened to a spring faced with sandpaper. The spring rested on the ends of several matches. It was an ingenious and reliable device.

The Esquimaux used a long spear in hunting the polar bear. It was ten or twelve feet in length. After being shot with an arrow, if the bear charged, they rested the butt of the spear on the ground, lowered the point and let the bear impale himself on it.

When the time came to use our weapons, Ned Frost dissuaded us from the attempt. He said that he once owned a pet grizzly and kept it fast with a long chain in the back yard. This bear was so quick that it could lie in its kennel, apparently asleep, and if a chicken passed within proper distance, with incredible quickness she reached out a paw and seized the chicken without the slightest semblance of effort. And when at play, the boys tried to stick the bear with a pitchfork, she would parry the thrusts and protect herself like a boxer. It was impossible to touch her.

The fire, Frost thought, might serve at night, but in the daylight it would lose its effect. So he insisted that he would carry a gun to be used in case of attack. On our part, we stipulated that he was to resort to it only to prevent disaster and protested that such an exigency must be looked upon by us as a complete failure of our plans. We knew we could not stop the mad rush of a bear with our arrows, but we hoped to kill at least one by this means and compromise on the rest if necessary.

Indians, besides employing the spear, poisoned arrows, and fire, also used protected positions, or shot from horseback. We scorned to shoot from a tree and were told that few horses could be ridden close enough, or fast enough, to get within bowshot of a grizzly.

Inquiry among those qualified to know led to the estimate of the number of all bears in the Park to be between five hundred and one thousand. Considering that there are some three thousand square miles of land, that there were nearly sixty thousand elk, besides hundreds of bison, antelope, mountain sheep, and similar animals, this does not seem improbable. I am aware that recent statements are to the effect that there were only forty grizzlies there. This is palpably an underestimate, and probably takes into account only those that frequent the dumps. Frost believes that there are several hundred grizzlies in the Park, many of which range out in the adjacent country. So we felt no fear of decimating their ranks, and had every hope of seeing many. In fact, their number has so increased in recent years that they have become a menace and require killing off.

During the past five years four persons have either been mauled or killed by grizzlies in Yellowstone. One of these was a teamster by the name of Jack Walsh. He was sleeping under his wagon at Cold Springs when a large bear seized him by the arm, dragged him forth and ripped open his abdomen. Walsh died of blood poison and peritonitis a few days later.

Frost himself was attacked. He was conducting a party of tourists through the preserve and had just been explaining to them around the campfire that there was no danger of bears. He slept in the tent with a horse wrangler by the name of Phonograph Jones. In the middle of the night a huge grizzly entered his tent and stepped on the head of Jones, peeling the skin off his face by the rough pressure of his paw. The man waked with a yell, whereupon the bear clawed out his lower ribs. The cry roused Frost, who having no firearms, hurled his pillow at the bear.

With a roar, the grizzly leaped upon Ned, who dived into his sleeping bag. The animal grasped him by the thighs, and dragged him from the tent out into the forest, sleeping bag and all. As he carried off his victim, he shook him from side to side as a dog shakes a rat. Frost felt the great teeth settle down on his thigh bones and expected momentarily to have them crushed in the powerful jaws. In a thicket of jack pines over a hundred yards from camp, the bear shook him so violently that the muscles of the man's thighs tore out and he was hurled free from the bag. He landed half-naked in the undergrowth several yards away.

While the frenzied bear still worried the bedding, Frost dragged himself to a nearby pine and pulled himself up in its branches by the strength of his arms.

The camp was in an uproar; a huge fire was kindled; tin pans were beaten; one of the helpers mounted a horse and by circling around the bear, succeeded in driving him away.

After first aid measures were administered, Frost was successfully nursed back to health and usefulness by his wife. But since that time he has an inveterate hatred of grizzlies, hunting them with grim persistency.

It is said that nearly forty obnoxious grizzlies were shot by the Park rangers after this episode and Frost was given a permit to carry a weapon. We found later that he always went to sleep with a Colt automatic pistol strapped to his wrist.

We planned to enter the Park in two parties. One, comprised of Frost, the cook, horse wrangler, my brother, and his friend, Judge Henry Hulbert, of Detroit, was to proceed from Cody and come with a pack train across Sylvan Pass. Our party consisted of Arthur Young and myself; Mr. Compton was unexpectedly prevented from joining us by sickness in his family. We were to journey by rail to Ashton. This was the nearest point to Yellowstone Station on the boundary of the reservation that could be reached by railroad in winter.

We arrived at this point near the last of May, 1920. The roads beyond were blocked with snow, but by good fortune, we were taken in by one of the first work trains entering the region through the personal interest and courtesy of the superintendent of the Pocatello division.

We had shipped ahead of us a quantity of provisions and came outfitted only with sleeping bags, extra clothing, and our archery equipment. This latter consisted of two bows apiece and a carrying case containing 144 broadheads, the finest assembly of bows and arrows since the battle of Crecy.

Young had one newly made bow weighing eighty-five pounds and his well-tried companion of many hunts, "Old Grizzly," weighing seventy-five pounds. He later found the heavier weapon too strong for him in the cold weather of the mountains, where a man's muscles stiffen and lose their power, while his bow grows stronger.

My own bows were seventy-five pounds apiece—"Old Horrible," my favorite, a hard hitter and sweet to shoot, and "Bear Slayer," the fine-grained, crooked-limbed stave with which I helped to kill our first bear. Our arrows were the usual three-eighths birch shafts, carefully selected, straight and true. Their heads were tempered steel, as sharp as daggers. We had, of course, a few blunts and eagle arrows in the lot.

In the Park we found snow deep on the ground and the roads but recently cleared with snowplows and caterpillar tractors. We traveled by auto to Mammoth Hot Springs and paid our respects to Superintendent Albright, and ultimately settled in a vacant ranger's cabin near the Canyon. Here we awaited the coming of the second party.

Our entrance into the Park was well known to the rangers, who were instructed to give us all the assistance possible. This cabin soon became a rendezvous for them and our evenings were spent very pleasantly with stories and fireside music.

After several days, word was sent by telephone that Frost and his caravan were unable to cross Sylvan Pass because of fifty feet of snow in the defile, and that he had returned to Cody where he would take an auto truck and come around to the northern entrance to the Park, through Gardiner, Montana.

At the expiration of three days he drove up to our cabin in a flurry of snow. This was about the last day in May.

Frost himself is one of the finest of Western types; born and raised in the sagebrush country, a hunter of big game ever since he was large enough to hold a gun. He was in the prime of life, a man of infinite resource, courage, and fortitude. We admired him immensely.

With him he had a full camp outfit, selected after years of experience, and suited to any kind of weather.

The party consisted of Art Cunningham, the cook; G. D. Pope, and Judge Henry Hulbert. Art came equipped with a vast amount of camp craft and cookery wisdom. My brother came to see the fun, the Judge to take pictures and add dignity to the occasion. All were seasoned woodsmen and hunters.

We moved to more commodious quarters, a log cabin in the vicinity, made ourselves comfortable, and let the wind-driven snow pile deep drifts about our warm shelter while we planned a campaign against the grizzlies.

So far, we had met few bears, and these were of the tourist variety. They had stolen bacon from the elevated meat safe, and one we found in the woods sitting on his haunches calmly eating the contents of a box of soda crackers. These were the hotel pets and were of nothing more than passing interest to us.

Contrary to the usual condition, no grizzlies were to be seen. The only animals in evidence were a few half-starved elk that had wintered in the Park, marmots, and the Canadian jay birds.

We began our hunts on foot, exploring Hayden Valley, the Sour Creek region, Mt. Washburn, and the headwaters of Cascade Creek.

The ground was very wet in places and heavy with snow in the woods. It was necessary, therefore, to wear rubber pacs, a type of shoe well suited to this sort of travel.

Our party divided into two groups, usually my brother and the Judge exploring in one direction while Young and I kept close at the heels of Frost. We climbed all the high ridges and swept the country with our binocular glasses. From eight to fourteen hours a day we walked and combed the country for bear signs.

Our original plan was to bring in several decrepit old horses with the pack train and sacrifice them for bait. But because of the failure of this part of our program, we were forced to find dead elk for this purpose. We came across a number of old carcasses, but no signs that bear had visited them recently. Our first encounter with grizzly came on the fourth day. We were scouting over the country near Sulphur Mountain, when Frost saw a grizzly a mile off, feeding in a little valley. The snow had melted here and he was calmly digging roots in the soft ground. We signaled to our party and all drew together as we advanced on our first bear, keeping out of sight as we did so.

We planned to go rapidly down a little cut in the hills and intercept him as he came around the turn. Progressing at a rapid pace, Indian file, we five hunters went down the draw, when suddenly our bear, who had taken an unexpected cutoff, came walking up the ravine. At a sign from Ned, we dropped to our knees and awaited developments. The bear had not seen us and the faint breeze blew from him to us. He was about two hundred yards off. We were all in a direct line, Frost ahead, I next, Young behind me, and the others in the rear. Our bows were braced and arrows nocked.

Slowly the bear came feeding toward us. He dug the roots of white violets, he sniffed, he meandered back and forth, wholly unconscious of our presence. We hardly breathed. He was not a good specimen, rather a scrawny, long-nosed, male adolescent, but a real grizzly and would do as a starter.

At last he came within fifty yards, stopped, pawed a patch of snow, and still we did not shoot. We could not without changing our position because we were all in one line. So we waited for his next move, hoping that he would advance laterally and possibly give us a broadside exposure.

But he came onward, directly for us, and at thirty yards stopped to root in the ground again. I thought, "Now we must shoot or he will walk over us!" Just then he lifted his head and seemed to take an eyeful of Young's blue shirt. For one second he half reared and stared. I drew my bow and as the arrow left the string, he bounded up the hill. The flying shaft just grazed his shoulder, parting the fur in its course. Quick as a bouncing rubber ball, he leaped over the ground and as Young's belated arrow whizzed past him, he disappeared over the hill crest.

We rose with a deep breath and shouted with laughter. Ned said that if it had not been for that blue shirt, the bear would have bumped into us. Well, we were glad we missed him, because after all, he was not the one we were looking for. It is a hard thing to pick grizzlies to order. You can't go up and inspect them ahead of time.

This fiasco was just an encouragement to us, and we continued to rise by candlelight and hunt till dark. The weather turned warmer, and the snow began to melt.

At the end of the first week we saw five grizzlies way off in the distance at the head of Hayden Valley. They were three or four miles from us and evening was approaching, so we postponed an attack on them. Next morning, bright and early, we were on the ground again, hoping to see them. Sure enough, there they were! Ned, Art, and I were together; my brother and the Judge were off scouting on the other side of the ridge. It was about half past eight in the morning. The bears, four in number this time, were feeding in the grassy marshland, about three miles up the valley. Ned's motto has always been: "When you see 'em, go and get 'em."

We decided to attack immediately. Down the river bank, through the draws, up into the timber we circled at a trot. It was hard going, but we were pressed for time. At last we came out on a wooded point a quarter of a mile above the bears, and rested. We knew they were about to finish their morning feeding and go up into the forest to lay up for the day. So we watched them in seclusion.

We waxed our bowstrings and put the finishing touches on our arrowheads with a file.

Slowly the bears mounted the foothills, heading for a large patch of snow, where Frost thought they would lie down to cool before entering the woods. It seems that their winter coat makes them very susceptible to heat, and though the sun had come out pleasantly for us, it was too hot for them. There was an old female and three half-grown cubs in their third year, all looking big enough for any museum group.

At last they settled down and began to nuzzle the snow. The time had come for action. We proposed to slip down the little ravine at the edge of the timber, cross the stream, ascend the hill on the opposite side, and come up on our quarry over the crest. We should thus be within shooting distance. The wind was right for this maneuver, so we started at once.

Now as I write my muscles quiver, my heart thumps, and I flush with a strange feeling, thinking of that moment. Like a soldier before a battle, we waded into an uncharted experience. What does a man think of as he is about to enter his first grizzly encounter? I remember well what passed through my head: "Can we get there without alarming the brutes?" "How close will they be?" "Can we hit them?" "What will happen then?"

Ned Frost, Young, and I were to sneak up on four healthy grizzlies in the open, and pit our nerve against their savage reaction. Ned had his rifle, but this was to be used only as a last resort, and that might easily fail at such short range.

As we walked rapidly, stepping with utmost caution, I answered all the questions of my subconscious fears. "Hit them? Why, we will soak them in the gizzard; wreck them!" "Charge? Let them come on and may the best man win!" "Die? There never was a fairer, brighter, better day to die on." In fact, "Lead on!" I felt absolutely gay. A little profanity or a little intellectual detachment at these times is of material help in the process of autosuggestion. As for Young, he was silent, and possibly was thinking of camp flapjacks.

Halfway up the hill, on the opposite side of which lay our grizzlies, we stopped, braced our bows, took three arrows apiece from our quivers, and proceeded in a more stealthy approach.

Young and I arranged ourselves on each side of Frost, abreast with him. Near the top Ned took out a green silk handkerchief and floated it in the gentle breeze to see if the wind had changed. If it had, we might find the bears coming over the top to meet us. Everything was perfect, so far! Now, stooping low, we crept to the very ridge itself, to a spot directly above which we believed the bears to be. Laying our hats on the grass and sticking our extra arrows in the ground before us, we rose up, bows half-drawn, ready to shoot.

There on the snow, not over twenty-five yards off, lay four grizzly bears, just like so many hearth rugs.

Instantly, I selected the farthest bear for my mark and at a signal of the eye we drew our great bows to their uttermost and loosed two deadly arrows.

We struck! There was a roar, they rose, but instead of charging us, they rushed together and began such a fight as few men have seen. My bear, pinioned with an arrow in the shoulder, threw himself on his mother, biting her with savage fury. She in turn bit him in the bloody shoulder and snapped my arrow off short. Then all the cubs attacked her. The growls and bellowing were terrific.

Quickly I nocked another arrow. The beasts were milling around together, pawing, biting, mad with rage. I shot at my bear and missed him. I nocked again. The old she-bear reared on her haunches, stood high above the circling bunch, cuffing and roaring, the blood running from her mouth and nostrils in frothy streams. Young's arrow was deep in her chest. I drove a feathered shaft below her foreleg.

The confusion and bellowing increased, and, as I drew a fourth arrow from my quiver, I glanced up just in time to see the old female's hair rise on the back of her neck. She steadied herself in her wild hurtling and looked directly at us with red glaring eyes. She saw us for the first time! Instinctively I knew she would charge, and she did.

Quick as thought, she bounded toward us. Two great leaps and she was on us. A gun went off at my ear. The bear was literally knocked head over heels, and fell in backward somersaults down the steep snowbank. At some fifty yards she checked her course, gathered herself, and attempted to charge again, but her right foreleg failed her. She rose on her haunches in an effort to advance, when, like a flash, two arrows flew at her and disappeared through her heaving sides. She faltered, wilted, and as we drew to shoot again, she sprawled out on the ground, a convulsed, quivering mass of fur and muscle—she was dead.

The half-grown cubs had disappeared at the boom of the gun. We saw one making off at a gallop, three hundred yards away. The glittering snowbank before us was vacant.

The air seemed strangely still; the silence was oppressive. Our nervous tension exploded in a wave of laughter and exclamations of wonderment. Frost declared he had never seen such a spectacle in all his life; four grizzly bears in deadly combat; the din of battle; the wild bellowing; and two bowmen shooting arrow after arrow into this jumble of struggling beasts.

The snow was trampled and soaked with blood as though there had been an Indian massacre. We paced off the distance at which the charging female had been stopped. It was exactly eight yards. A mighty handy shot!

We went down to view the remains. Young had three arrows in the old bear, one deep in her neck, its point emerging back of the shoulder. He shot that as she came at us. His first arrow struck anterior to her shoulder, entered her chest, and cut her left lung from top to bottom. His third arrow pierced her thorax, through and through, and lay on the ground beside her with only its feathers in the wound.

My first arrow cut below the diaphragm, penetrated the stomach and liver, severed the gall ducts and portal vein. My second arrow passed completely through her abdomen and lay on the ground several yards beyond her. It had cut the intestines in a dozen places and opened large branches of the mesenteric artery.

The bullet from Frost's gun had entered at the right shoulder, fractured the humerus, blown a hole an inch in diameter in the chest wall, opened up a jagged hole in the trachea, and dissipated its energy in the left lung. No wound of exit was found, the soft nose copper-jacketed bullet apparently having gone to pieces after striking the bone.

Anatomically speaking, it was an effective shot, knocked the bear down and crippled her, but was not an immediately fatal wound. We had her killed with arrows, but she did not know it. She undoubtedly would have been right on us in another second. The outcome of this hypothetical encounter I leave to those with vivid imaginations.

We hereby express our gratitude to Ned Frost.

Now one of us had to rush off and get the rest of the party. Judge Hulbert and my brother were in another valley in quest of bear. So Ned set off at a rapid tramp across the bogs, streams, and hills to find them. Within an hour they returned together to view the wreckage. Photographs were taken, the skinning and autopsy were performed. Then we looked around for the wounded cub. Frost trailed him by almost invisible blood stains and tracks, and found him less than a quarter of a mile away, huddled up as if asleep on the hillside, my arrow nestled to his breast. The broken shaft with its blade deep in the thorax had completely severed the head of his humerus, cut two ribs, and killed him by hemorrhage from the pulmonary arteries. Half-grown as he was, he would have made an ugly antagonist for any man.

His mother, a fine mature lady of the old school, showed by her teeth and other lineaments her age and respectability. In autumn she would have weighed four or five hundred pounds. We weighed her in installments with our spring scales; she registered three hundred and five pounds. She was in poor condition and her pelt was not suitable for museum purposes. But these features could not be determined readily beforehand. The juvenile Ursus weighed one hundred and thirty-five pounds. We measured them, gathered their bones for the museum, shouldered their hides, and turned back to camp.

That night Ned Frost said, "Boys, when you proposed shooting grizzly bears with the bow and arrow, I thought it a fine sporting proposition, but I had my doubts about its success. Now I know that you can shoot through and kill the biggest grizzly in Wyoming!"

Our instructions on leaving California were to secure a large male *Ursus Horribilis Imperator,* a good representative female, and two or three cubs. The female we had shot filled the requirements fairly well, but the two-year-old cub was at the high school age and hardly cute enough to be admired. Moreover, no sooner had we sent the news of our first success to the Museum than we were informed that this size cub was not wanted and that we must secure little ones.

So we set out to get some of this year's vintage in small bears. Ordinarily, there is no difficulty in coming in contact with bears in Yellowstone; in fact, it is more common to try to keep some of the hotel variety from eating at the same table with you. But not a single bear, black, brown, or silvertipped, now called upon us. We traveled all over that beautiful Park, from Mammoth Hot Springs to the Lake. We hunted over every well-known bear district. Tower Falls, Specimen Ridge, Buffalo Corrals, Mt. Washburn, Dunraven Pass (under twenty-five feet of snow), Antelope Creek, Pelican Meadows, Cub Creek, Steamboat Point, and kept the rangers busy on the lookout for bear. From eight to fifteen hours a day we hunted. We walked over endless miles of mountains, climbed over countless logs, plowed through snow and slush, and raked the valleys with our field glasses.

But bears were as scarce as hen's teeth. We saw a few tracks but nothing compared to those seen in other years.

We began to have a sneaking idea that the bear had all been killed off. We knew they had been a pest to campers and were becoming a menace to human life. We suspected the Park authorities of quiet extermination. Several of the rangers admitted that a selective killing was carried out yearly to rid the preserve of the more dangerous individuals.

Then the elk began to pour back into the Park; singly, in couples, and in droves they returned, lean and scraggly. A few began to drop their calves. Then we began to see bear signs. The grizzly follow the elk, and after they come out of hibernation and get their fill of green grass, they naturally take to elk calves. Occasionally they include the mother in the menu.

We also began to follow the elk. We watched at bait. We sat up nights and days at a time, seeing only a few unfavorable specimens and these were as wild and as wary as deer. We found the mosquitoes more deadly than the bear. We tracked big worthy old boys around in circles and had various frustrated encounters with she-bears and cubs.

Upon one occasion we were tracking a prospective specimen through the woods, proceeding with great caution, when evidently the beast heard us. Suddenly, he turned on his tracks and came on a dead run for us. I was in advance and instantly drew my bow, holding it for the right moment to shoot. The bear came directly in our front, not more than twenty yards away and being startled by the sight of us, threw his locomotive mechanism into reverse and skidded toward us in a cloud of snow and forest leaves. In the fraction of a second, I perceived that he was afraid and not a proper specimen for our use. I held my arrow and the bear, with an indignant and disgusted look, made a precipitous retreat. It was an unexpected surprise on both sides.

They say that the Indians avoided the Yellowstone region, thinking it a land of evil spirits. In our wanderings, however, we picked up on Steamboat Point a beautiful red chert arrowhead, undoubtedly shot by an Indian at elk years before Columbus burst in upon these good people. In Hayden Valley we found an obsidian spearhead, another sign that the Indian knew good hunting grounds.

But no Indian was ever so anxious to meet grizzly as we were. We hunted continually, but found none that suited us; we had to have the best. Frost assured us that we had made a mistake in ever trying to get grizzlies in the Park—and that in the time we spent there we could have secured all our required specimens in the game fields of Wyoming or Montana.

A month passed; the bears were beginning to lose their winter coats; our party began to disintegrate. My brother and the Judge were compelled to return to Detroit. A week or so later Ned Frost and the cook were scheduled to take out another party of hunters from Cody and prepared to leave us. Young and I were determined to stick it out until the last chance was exhausted. We just had to get those specimens.

Before Frost left us, however, he packed us up to the head of Cascade Creek with our bows and arrows, bedrolls, a tarpaulin, and a couple of boxes of provisions.

We had received word from a ranger that a big old grizzly had been seen at Soda Butte and we prepared to go after him. At the last moment before departure, a second word came that probably this same bear had moved down to Tower Falls and was ranging between this point and the Canyon, killing elk around Dunraven Pass.

Young and I scouted over this area and found diggings and his tracks.

A good-sized bear will have a nine-inch track. This monster's was eleven inches long. We saw where he made his kills and used certain fixed trails going up and down the canyons.

Frost gave us some parting advice and his blessing, consigned us to our fate, and went home.

Left to ourselves, we two archers inspected our tackle and put everything in prime condition. Our bows had stood the many wettings well, but we oiled them again. New strings were put on and thoroughly waxed. Our arrows were straightened, their feathers dried and preened in the sun. The broadheads were set on straight and sharpened to the last degree, and so prepared we determined to do our utmost. We were ready for the big fellow.

In our reconnaissance we found that he was a real killer. His trail was marked by many bloody episodes. It seemed quite probable that he was the bear that two years before burst in upon a party of surveyors in the mountains and kept them treed all night. It is not unlikely that he was the same bear that caused the death of Jack Walsh. He seemed too expert in planning murder. We saw by his tracks how he lay in ambush watching a herd of elk, how he sneaked up on a mother elk and her recently born calf on the outskirts of the band, and with a great leap threw himself upon the two and killed them.

In several places we saw the skins of these little wapiti licked clean and empty of bodily structure. No other male grizzly was permitted to enter his domain. He was, in fact, the monarch of the mountain, the great bear of Dunraven Pass.

We pitched our little tent in a secluded wood some three miles from the lake at the head of Cascade Creek, and began to lay our plan of attack. We were by this time inured to fatigue and disappointment. Weariness and loss of sleep had produced a dogged determination that knew no relaxation. And yet we were cheerful. Young has that fine quality so essential to a hunting companion, imperturbable good nature, never complaining, no matter how heavy the load, how long the trail, how late or how early the hour, how cold, how hot, how little, or how poor the food.

We were there to win and nothing else mattered. If it rained and we must wait, we took out our musical instruments, built up the fire and soothed our troubled souls with harmony. This is better than tobacco or whiskey for the purpose. In fact, Young is so abstemious that even tea or coffee seem a bit intemperate to him, and are only to be used under great physical strain; and as for profanity, why, I had to do all l the swearing for the two of us.

We were trained down to rawhide and sinew, keyed to alertness and ready for any emergency.

Often in our wanderings at night we ran unexpectedly upon wild beasts in the dark. Some of these were bears. Our pocket flashlights were used as defensive weapons. A snort, a crashing retreat through the brush told us that our visitant had departed in haste, unable to stand the glaring light of modern science.

We soon found that our big fellow was a night rover also, and visited his various kills under the cloak of darkness. In one particularly steep and rugged canyon, he crossed a little creek at a set place. Up on the side of this canyon he mounted to the plateau above by one of three possible trails. At the top within forty yards of one of these was a small promontory of rock upon which we decided to form a blind and await his coming. We fashioned a shelter of young jack pines, constructed like a miniature corral, less than three by six feet in area, but very natural in appearance. Between us and the trail was a quantity of down timber which we hoped would act as an impediment to an on-rushing bear. And the perpendicular face of our outcropping elevated us some twelve or thirteen feet above the steep hillside. A small tree stood near our position and offered a possibility in case of attack. But we had long ago decided that no man can clamber up a tree in time to escape a grizzly charging at a distance less than fifty yards. We could be approached from the rear, but altogether it was an ideal ambush.

The wind blew steadily up the canyon all night long and carried our scent away from the trail. Above us on the plateau was a recently killed elk which acted as a perpetual invitation to bears and other prowlers of the night.

So we started watching in this blind, coming soon after dusk and remaining until sunrise. The nights were cold, the ground pitiless, and the moon, nearly at its full, crept low through a maze of mist.

Dressed in our warmest clothing and permitting ourselves one blanket and a small piece of canvas, we huddled together in a cramped posture and kept vigil through the long hours. Neither of us smoked anyway, and of course, this was absolutely taboo; we hardly whispered, and even shifted our positions with utmost caution. Before us lay our bows ready strung, and arrows, both in the quiver belted upright to the screen and standing free close at hand.

The first evening we saw an old she-bear and her two-year-old cubs come up the path. They passed us with that soft shuffling gait so uncanny to hear in the dark. We were delighted that they showed no sign of having detected us. But they were not suited to our purpose and we let them go. The female was homely, fretful, and nervous. The cubs were yellow and ungainly. We looked for better things.

Bears have personality, as obvious as humans. Some are lazy, some alert, surly, or timid. Nearly all the females we saw showed that irritability and irascible disposition that go with the cares of maternity. This family was decidedly commonplace.

They disappeared in the gloom, and we waited and waited for the big fellow that some time must appear.

But morning came first; we stole from our blind, chilled and stiffened, and wandered back to camp to breakfast and sleep. The former was a fairly successful event, but the latter was made almost impossible by the swarms of mosquitoes that beset us. A smudge fire and canvas head-coverings gave us only a partial immunity. By sundown we were on our way again to the blind, but another cold dreary night passed without adventure.

On our way to camp in the dim light of early dawn, a land fog hung low in the valley. As we came up a rough path there suddenly appeared out of the obscurity three little bear cubs, not thirty-five yards away. They winded us, squeaked, and stood on their hind legs, peering in our direction. We dropped like stones in our tracks, scarcely breathing, figuratively frozen to the ground, for instantly the fiercest-looking grizzly we ever saw bounded over the cubs and straddled them between her forelegs. Nothing could stop her if she came on. A little brush intervened and she could not locate us plainly for we could see her eyes wander in search of us; but her trembling muscles, the vicious champing of her jaws, and the guttural growls, all spoke of immediate attack. We were petrified. She wavered in her intent, turned, cuffed her cubs down the hill, snorted, and finally departed with her family.

We heaved a deep sigh of relief. But she was wonderful, she was the most beautiful bear we had ever seen; large, well proportioned, with dark brown hair having just a touch of silver. She was a patrician, the aristocrat of the species. We marked her well.

Next day, just at sunset, we got our first view of the great bear of Dunraven Pass. He was coming down a distant canyon trail. He looked like a giant in the twilight. With long swinging strides he threw himself impetuously down the mountainside. Great power was in every movement. He was magnificent! He seemed as large as a horse, and had that grand supple strength given to no other predatory animal. Though we were used to bears, a strange misgiving came over me. We proposed to slay this monster with the bow and arrow. It seemed preposterous!

In the blind another long cold night passed. The moon drifted slowly across the heavens and sank in a haze of clouds at daybreak. Just at the hush of dawn, the homely female and her tow-headed progeny came shuffling by. We were desperate for specimens, and one of these would match that which we already had. I drew up my bow and let fly a broadhead at one of the cubs. It struck him in the ribs. Precipitately, the whole band took flight. My quarry fell against an obstructing log and died. His mother stopped, came back several times, gazed at him pensively, then disappeared. We got out, carried him to a distant spot and skinned him. He weighed one hundred and twenty pounds. My arrow had shaved a piece off his heart. Death was instantaneous.

We packed home the hind quarters and made a fine grizzly stew. Before this we had found that the old bears were tough and rancid, but the little ones were as sweet and tender as suckling pigs. This stew was particularly good, well seasoned with canned tomatoes and the last of our potatoes and onions. Sad to relate the better part of this savory pot next day was eaten by a wandering vagabond of the *Ursus* family. Not content with our stew, he devoured all our sugar, bacon, and other foodstuffs not in cans, and wound up his debauch by wiping his feet on our beds and generally messing up the camp. Probably he was a regular camp thief.

That night, early in the watch, we heard the worthy old boy come down the canyon, hot in pursuit of a large brown bear. As he ran, the great animal made quite a noise. His claws clattered on the rocks, and the ground seemed to shake beneath us. We shifted our bows ready for action, and felt the keen edge of our arrows. Way off in the forest we heard him tree the cowardly intruder with such growls and ripping of bark that one would imagine he was about to tear the tree down.

After a long time he desisted and, grunting and wheezing, came slowly up the canyon. With the night glasses we could see him. He seemed to be considerably heated with his exercise and scratched himself against a young fir tree. As he stood on his hind legs with his back to the trunk and rubbed himself to and fro, the tree swayed like a reed; and as he lifted his nose I observed that it just touched one of the lower branches. In the morning, after he had gone and we were on our way to camp, we passed this very fir and stretching up on my tiptoes, I could just touch the limb with my fingers. Having been a pole vaulter in my youth, I knew by experience that this measurement was over seven feet six inches. He was a real he-bear! We wanted him more than ever.

The following day it rained—in fact, it rained nearly every day near the end of our stay; but this was a drenching that stopped at sunset, leaving all the world sweet and fragrant. The moon came out full and beautiful, everything seemed propitious.

We went to the blind about an hour before midnight, feeling that surely this evening the big fellow would come. After two hours of frigidity and immobility, we heard the velvet footfalls of bear coming up the canyon. There came our patrician and her royal family. The little fellows pattered up the trail before their mother. They came within range. I signaled Young and we shot together at the cubs. We struck. There was a squeak, a roar, a jumble of shadowy figures and the entire flock of bears came tumbling in our direction.

At that very moment the big grizzly appeared on the scene. There were five bears in sight. Turning her head from side to side, trying to find her enemy, the she-bear came toward us. I whispered to Young, "Shoot the big fellow." At the same time, I drew an arrow to the head, and drove it at the oncoming female. It struck her full in the chest. She reared; threw herself sidewise, bellowed with rage, staggered and fell to the ground. She rose again, weakened, stumbled forward, and with great gasps she died. In less than half a minute it was all over. The little ones ran up the hill past us, one later returned and sat up at its mother's head, then disappeared in the dark forever.

While all this transpired, the monster grizzly was romping back and forth in the shaded forest not more than sixty-five yards away. With deep booming growls like distant thunder, he voiced his anger and intent to kill. As he flitted between the shadows of the trees, the moonlight glinted on his massive body; he was enormous.

Young discharged three arrows at him. I shot two. We should have landed, he was so large. But he galloped off and I saw my last arrow, at the point blank range of seventy-five yards, fall between his legs.

He was gone. We thought we had missed the beast and grief descended heavy upon us. The thought of all the weary days and nights of hunting and waiting, and now to have lost him, was very painful.

After our palpitating hearts were quiet and the world seemed peaceful, we got out of our blind and skinned the female by flashlight. She was a magnificent specimen, just right in color and size for the Museum, not fat, but weighing a trifle over five hundred pounds. My arrow had severed a rib and buried its head in her heart. We measured her and saved her skull and long bones for the taxidermist.

At daybreak we searched for the cubs and found one dead under a log with an arrow through his brain. The others had disappeared.

We had no idea that we hit the great bear, but just to gather up our shafts, we went over the ground where he had been.

One of Young's arrows was missing!

That gave us a thrill; perhaps we had hit him after all! We went further in the direction he had gone; there was a trace of blood.

We trailed him. We knew it was dangerous business. Through clumps of jack pines we cautiously followed, peering under every pile of brush and fallen tree. Deep into the forest we tracked him, where his bloody smear was left upon fallen logs. Soon we found where he had rested. Then we discovered the fore part of Young's arrow. It had gone through him. There was a pool of blood. Then we found the feathered butt which he had drawn out with his teeth.

Four times he wallowed down in the mud or soft earth to rest and cool his wound. Then beneath a great fir he had made a bed in the soft loam and left it. Past this we could not track him. We hunted high and low, but no trace of him could we find. Apparently he had ceased bleeding and his footprints were not recorded on the stony ground about. We made wide circles, hoping to pick up his trail. We searched up and down the creek. We cross-cut every forest path and runway, but no vestige remained.

He was gone. We even looked up in the tree and down in the ground where he had wallowed. For five hours we searched in vain, and at last, worn with disappointment and fatigue, we lay down and slept on the very spot where he last stopped.

Near sundown we awoke, ate a little food, and started all over again to find the great bear. We retraced our steps and followed the fading evidence till it brought us again to the pit beneath the fir tree. He must be near. It was absolutely impossible for any animal to have lost so much blood and travel more than a few hundred yards past this spot. We had explored the creek bottom and the cliffs above from below, and we now determined to transverse every foot of the rim of the canyon from above. As we climbed over the face of the rock we saw a clot of dried blood. We let ourselves down the sheer descent, came upon a narrow little ledge, and there below us lay the huge monster on his back, against a boulder, cold and stiff, as dead as Caesar. Our hearts nearly burst with happiness.

There lay the largest grizzly bear in Wyoming, dead at our feet. His rugged coat was matted with blood. Well back in his chest the arrow wound showed clear. I measured him; twenty-six inches of bear had been pierced through and through. One arrow killed him. He was tremendous. His great wide head; his worn, glistening teeth; his massive arms; his vast, ponderous feet and long curved claws; all were there. He was a wonderful beast. It seemed incredible. I thumped Young on the shoulder: "My, that was a marvelous shot!"

We started to skin our quarry. It was a stupendous job, as he weighed nearly one thousand pounds, and lay on the steep canyon side ready to roll on and crush us. But with ropes we lashed him by the neck to a tree and split him up the back, later box-skinning the legs according to the method required by the museum.

By flashlight, acetylene lamp, candlelight, firelight, and moonlight, we labored. We used up all our knives, and having neglected to bring our whetstones, sharpened our blades on the volcanic boulders, about us. By assiduous industry for nine straight hours, we finished him after a fashion. His skin was thick and like scar tissue. His meat was all tendons and gristle. The hide was as tight as if glued on.

In the middle of the night we stopped long enough to broil some grizzly cub steaks and brew a pot of tea; then we went at it again.

As we dismembered him we weighed the parts. The veins were absolutely dry of blood, and without this substance, which represents a loss of neary ten per cent of his weight, he was 916 pounds. There was hardly an inch of fat on his back. At the end of the autumn this adipose layer would be nearly six inches thick. He would then have weighed over fourteen hundred pounds. He stood nearly four feet high at the shoulders, while his skull measured eighteen and a half inches long; his entire body length was seven feet four inches.

As we cleaned his bones we hurled great slabs of muscle down the canyon, knowing from experience that this would be a sign for all other bears to leave the vicinity. Only the wolves and jays will eat grizzly meat.

At last we finished him, as the sun rose over the mountain ridges and gilded all the canyon with glory.

We cleaned and salted the pelts, packed them on our backs, and, dripping with salt brine and bear grease, staggered to the nearest wagon trail. The hide of the big bear, with unskinned paws and skull, weighed nearly 150 pounds.

We cached our trophies, tramped the weary miles back to camp, cleaned up, packed and wandered to the nearest station, from which we ordered a machine. When this arrived we gathered our belongings, turned our various specimens over to a park ranger, to be given the final treatments, and started on our homeward trip.

We were so exhausted from loss of sleep, exertion, and excitement, that we sank into a stupor that lasted almost the entire way home.

The California Academy of Sciences now has a handsome representative group of *Ursus horribilis imperator*. We have the extremely satisfactory feeling that we killed five of the finest grizzly bear in Wyoming. The sport was fair and clean, and we did it all with the bow and arrow.

HUNTING WITH THE BOW AND ARROW
G.P. PUTNAM'S SONS, 1947

Okay, so you'll have to read slowly to grasp the dialect here, but it's worth it. There's no question that Nash Buckingham played a major role in the birth of outdoor literature. He was a Southern gentleman, and hunting was a way of life back in the mid-1930s. Buckingham knew how to capture it in words. He wrote so much that it's difficult to pick the very best. Here's my choice. It takes place in the deep South, so it had to be a quail story.

Bobs of the Bayou Bank

by NASH BUCKINGHAM

A raw January morning! She-Who-Presides peers past Ollie's bulky shoulder into the ice chest. Deep concern mantles her countenance. She keeps repeating, "Are you certain, Ollie? Are you positive?"

And old Ollie moans, "Naw'm, Miss Irma, I ain' pos'tive, but I sho' is sho' dey ain' but fo' quails in hyar, sho' as de worl'—dey ain't but fo' lef', honey." And, at the same dramatic instant, out in the dog's run, Joe and Black Boy try out several canine barbershop chords.

Ollie straightens and faces me accusingly: "An' you, Mistah Boss, you done et three o' dem quails yo'se'f! You knows you done it, too. Now what you gwi' say 'bout dat?"

"Well," I defend myself, "what did you cook 'em for, to admire?"

At such attempted wisecracking, She-Who-Presides promptly gets her dander up and turns on the heat.

"In that case, Rip," she fires at me, "you can just hustle your lazy self and your dog Snyder out of my house and bring home a dozen birds or not come back for another twenty years. The girls at the Duplicate Bridge Club's meeting are expecting quail because—Well, because I promised. And besides, any man who deliberately wolfs down three of his hardworking wife's birds—" Stage business of dabbing at the eyes with a silly little wad of cambric.

My own eyes have been taking stock, out of doors. Two days' down-pour have the region soggy. A pretty greeting, to be literally foraged out of the house like this! Ostentatiously I turn backstairward in time to overhear Ollie snicker, "He mek out lak he don't wanna go, but he do, honey, he do."

Since she happens to know so much, I hand her some instructions. "Give Joe and Black Boy their feed right away, then, and leave the kennel gate open." And, as a parting shot to Madame, "For my break-fast, my good woman, I demand grits fried in red ham gravy and poached eggs on anchovy toast. Exactly that, or I'll call off the deal, defy you, and ring the police."

A brisk fifteen minutes! Boots heavily vaselined in anticipation of gummy going. Breakfast satisfactory. "It is now," concludes Madame, "exactly seven forty-five. I am to drive you over to Arkansas, deposit you on Decker Bayou near the duck club, and return to the same spot by five o'clock. Remember," she bargains, "I 'suspect' company for dinner at seven this evening!"

"If it's birds you want," I come back at her, "less talk and more action!"

Seeing me thrust two cans of their iron rations and my own paper sack of cold victuals into my suspender pouch, is a signal to Black Boy and Joe. Ensues no end of high bouncing, rumpus in general, and back-of-the-neck licking as the car, with Madame at the wheel, heads westward. An exchange of looks between the two dogs says, more plainly than words, "What a break!"

A shade past nine o'clock, Madame rolls the car into a plantation road and about-faces for the unloading. Scarce needing invitation to "scram," Joe and his brace mate stand not upon the order of their going. In two wags of a sheep's tail they jump the roadside gully and highball Decker Bayou's bank. I wave good-bye to homeward bound Madame. I'll get those birds for her or bust a hamstring.

Two minutes later I am in hot pursuit of the dogs, now quartering furiously a corn patch to my right. I slow down to watch maneuvers! A proper morning to make haste slowly. I hang to the cattle-stamped bank path for firmer footing.

Two hundred yards farther along, I catch unmistakable glimpses of a well-bunched bevy of quail, out over midstream of the bayou, and flashing toward me. I can scarce believe my eyes. Something has undoubtedly flushed them below, a straying cur or strolling share-cropper. To my chagrin, instead of pitching our way, they hold past and suddenly whip into the west bank's tall tangle. Black Boy, Joe, and I meet in a pocket where the heavy woods take in. Companions at heel through the brushy path, I finally emerge amid rolling wastes of corn and stripped cotton stalks. Now I realize what is really in store as to footing. Dump two days' rain into alluvial East Arkansas and jump in after it, if you don't believe me. I noticed—few and far between, however—scattered cotton pickers braving even this direful weather to glean a few pounds "extry" of fleecy staple. They are sticking to the ridges, at that. It is, I tell myself, a silly business at my age, this pulling one's lungs and spare parts out of place trying for a quail limit in behalf of a lot of bridge-frolicking damsels. I should have stalled for time this morning, until the clubhouse road dried. I thought fondly of easier and drier hunting ahorseback.

BIRDS, I opine, will have taken to deep ditches and thicket. Needle and haystack hunting! The dogs can take just so much of this sledding and no more. A pretty kettle of fish! Altogether, as the old Indian used to grunt, "too damn much howdy-do!" I strive mentally to clothe myself in Crusader's garb—Field of the Cloth of Gold, chain mail, two-handed sword and mace—Sir Lancelot out to do himself high honor for Cause and Fair Lady. But I lurch through ten inches of green water and almost topple! Sir Lancelot needing skid chains in a welter of gumbo instead of gore.

Fair Lady, my eye! I decide to regain the footpath and stick to it as much as possible. Reluctantly, but relentlessly, it comes to me that I am not definitely slowing up, but unquestionably slipping. Why, five years ago this would have been like shooting fish in a barrel! And just then, ahead and directly in the path himself, Black Boy suddenly sticks his nasal indicator skyward, caves in his spine a trifle, and pussyfoots into a classic point. Joe sights the deal and stiffens by the rule book.

Just before I take that inevitable one step too many which is parent to the shot, I compose myself to make hay while the sun shines. "These fellows," I reason, "will hop directly against this head wind and whip sharply back the way I've come. Well, let 'em—but a couple will stay behind."

How now, hounds, and have at ye! Fully fifteen winter-plumaged streaks buzz from the slope 'twixt Joe and the water. Easy pickings! Halfway through the webbed grasstops I select a cock bird and pin ahead of his spotted cheeks. Now!

Oh! you, too, gentle reader, must sometime have yanked, and grown livid, at a gun that wouldn't shoot. I even try all over again, in a frenzy. And at a fat laggard, too, coming out of the ditch slowly.

Black Boy and Joe almost turn a back flip and stand aghast! I bawl out the cypresstops! Summon High Heaven and Fate to witness that there is no justice! Oh! for a long, gray beard to pluck out, hair by hair!

Now, rage pretty well spent, I investigate, fully prepared to kick myself for falling like a sap for the ancient, uncocked-gun gag. At that, I've fallen for such things before. And worse still, even forgotten to load! I open and close the gun. I work the safety slide. No "pushee," no "pullee," no "shootee!" I begin methodical examination. I finger-print the selective single-trigger shift—possibly a clue and indictment there. I shift and reshift the mechanism and actually box the weapon's jaws. Now try to cock it! Eureka! The slide catches! Now try to snap it. Saints be praised, she clicks. But only the left tube. The starboard chamber and safety are definitely out of commission. I slip a shell into the left barrel, turn its muzzle into a cotton row and let go. "W-h-a-a-a-m!" Well, better half a loaf than none. But, cheerio, dogs! The hunt will go forward on one cylinder. If, as Adage has it, the stern chase is a long one, here's a fine chance to check up on the Old Man. Forward—dogs!

Mazes of cornfield. Mud enough to supply the muckrakers and-slingers of the world. Joe and Black Boy, wet as rats and plastered to their ears, stand nobly to the going. We pass the Caldwell home and pause for a breather on the wagon bridge spanning Decker. It might be better, I conjecture, to push more deeply north—across the "Mud Line" railroad to what proved extra fruitful covey ground last winter. But keeping my appointment at five with Madame might be another story in case I strayed too far. So—let's be on our way, dogs!

Now, I bargain with myself, for some sure-enough soupy plowing. Lake bank, new ground, and "first bottom" corn. I "sojer" along the ridges awhile, Blacky and Joe prowling denser cover.

Unexpectedly, at the extreme tip of a coffee bean belt, Joe lams into a point labeled "birds!" Up behind him and the backing Black Boy I pant, fingering the safety catch to be sure my one and only load is available. The covey rise is accommodatingly scattered. One plump masculine member of a nine- or ten-bird outfit turns head over heels. Feathers at last! Black Fellow makes the retrieve while I mark down singles. Two drop ahead into some thick, open pasture grass. The rest split and apparently dive into the lake's backwater. Pretty nearly "home free," those chaps. My canine companions, bidden sharply to "hunt close," soon pin those two nearest hiders-out. How I now long for that missing second shot!

"Fellow," I whisper to myself, "there's a long, long trail acomin' to you this day." But one shot must suffice, and does, for the first bob off the ground. Better so, as giving more time to watch his running mate's landing place. If I find him, I'll need a duck boat, however. A hundred yard's mushing, and out of a brush pile whirs a surprise. A fine cock bird of a fellow who makes a final mistake by not getting a great oak tree between us.

A half mile more of fruitless gouging. Distant plantation bells sound the "Ring In." Coming high noon. Over the lake bank's slope and across the fields toward Decker, a darky's wide log cabin with hospitable "dog trot" attracts my attention. If I can make it that far, we'll sound mess call and maybe do a bit of bunk fatigue. Black Boy and Joe, spotting my change of course, instantly lope toward inevitable skirmish with a yapping outpour of five and hound-puppy keynoters.

A neat old colored woman answers my hail and smilingly accepts what amounts to my own invitation to enter and eat my snack by her fireside. My dogs, having by now toothed the "egg-busters" into cover beneath the cabin, first remove mud from their own hides by rolling in the woodpile chips, and then open negotiations for "chow." Three or four gulps each, and that show is over.

Meanwhile, the good old soul whose spotless kitchen I have invaded welcomes me as only her fast-fading race can when caring for their "white folks." She and her "old man" are identified as "Williamson darkies." "Yaas, suh, Cap'n, us bin wid Mistah Frank er long, long time—nev' wuz no finah man den him." To which finest of living epitaphs I add a mental "Amen, Aunty!"

She has been bustling about over something. Almost like fog wisps, coffee fragrance spreads from a purring stove. About now, "Uncle," her man, clumps in for his own noontime bait of greens, fat meat, and corn dodger. That's what I've been pot-and-pan sniffing. I wonder whether my appetite might stand a nominal amount of such addition to my own provender. "Uncle" and "Aunty," I learn, upon inquiry, are members of the same Fraternal Order and Sewing Circle Burial Society as our colored folks down at the clubhouse. Such identification via the "grapevine" firmly establishes my position in the household. Urged to tableside, I now admit that greens, tender hog jowl, and strong coffee go hand-to-mouth with a chicken salad sandwich and slice of coconut cake.

My black goodman graciously accepts a two-bit donation to the Fraternal Order and departs for an afternoon round with his wood wagon and jugheads. I readjust the rocker for foot space and bid Aunty awaken me upon the tick of two. Stillness. Peace. Comfort. Through drowsy mist I note the wary house puss reoccupying her abandoned stove corner. Across the dog trot I see wood ashes whirling up the chimney's throat. The mud isn't deep here—anymore.

"Boss," laughs Aunty, "de clock done jes' struck two—das de orders, ain't it?"

We repair to the dog trot and sound "Inspection." Joe and Black Boy come running. The best route, I surmise, is to circle what was once a two-covey stretch down toward Sherman's field. Failing a find, then to recross Decker on the highway bridge and take a chance on starting all over again where we took off this morning. Nine birds behind schedule and three hours to go. Another two bits for Aunty's sewing circle, and the shoot is definitely afoot again. But Sherman's is utterly barren. That route's two bunches must be hanging back in the lake-bank woods.

The bayou path again! My own hobnailed boot tracks, half-dried out by the wind! Joe has decided on another whack at the corn. Why not. It has peas for a flooring. But Black Boy, with maybe some sort of hunch tickling his long, square nose, begins a crafty workout of Decker's fringed slope. And, all at once, putting on the brakes to avoid even a side slip through the greasy silt, he halts barely outside a brambled morass. I give the underfooting a rustle. Into the clear darts a single! But only to crumple just as he almost gained a bend in the trail. Bird in mouth on the return trip, Black Boy freezes into an aside! 'Attaboy, Black Fellow! Up again, down again. Thence, along a hundred and fifty yards, Black Boy potters into pantherish points. Doing himself proud this trip! Three additional quail for the bridge addicts.

Joe, attracted by the firing, has cut short his cast and dashed in to offer his services. But Black Boy's blood is up. It is his own private deal, Black Boy is telling the world! Practically waved aside, Joe takes a chance and drops in behind, to rework the ground. Something tells me to look backward, and, sure enough, the setter has trailed a bob to the very water's edge. It flushes a straight away course across the bayou. And foolishly through an open space on the bank top, I cut him down too soon. Never mind if it is nine straight, there he floats a good twenty feet offshore in extremely deep, cold water.

At the shot, and just as I open the gun and start downhill through dense cover to investigate, another bird catapults toward freedom. Caught helpless, I watch him depart and, by chance, look down to resume reloading. No! I'm not dreaming! Just off my booted left foot, the coiled mass of it undulating into attack, ugly head switching to the roll of a darting, forked tongue, is a thick, six-foot snake. The fingered shell drops tubeward; the bore closes gently; muzzles twist cautiously past my left knee. W-h-a-m! Loam and snake innards spout into the bushes. The serpent head vanishes. Caught him just right.

Looking ahead, I discover that fate and a keen nose have thrown another single right down Black Boy's alley. Good fellow, you held to that snake shot, too. About now, Joe comes rolling into the picture and spots the curved Black Boy. He checks instantly and seems to say: "Well, he's probably landed the gentleman okay, or he wouldn't take the trouble to twist his spine out of shape like that." Boy's victim is sacked. Ten straight! Then I remember number nine, the cock bird floating offshore back yonder in Decker. He must be salvaged at all

cost. That snake business all but drove him out of my mind. I retrace
the path and reconnoiter fruitlessly for a makeshift bateau or raft.
Wood chopping comes to ear from the heavy copse. Three colored
brothers at leisurely fuel gathering. Negotiations for loan of an ax,
with the inevitable two bits in dual role of retainer and collateral, are
successful.

I locate two thirty-foot second growth luckily almost overhanging
Decker. I fell their trunks out over the stream toward the quail. The
mass, caught from above by clinging withes of rattan, descends reluctantly, but I finally manage to pull the two main stems down until
a sort of crude suspension bridge dangles across the soil-stained water.
Ticklish business. I cut a long, light reaching pole and mount the tree
bases for this semi-tightrope act. Now for the symphony orchestra to
render "Deep River."

With a vine in one fist, for balance and life line in case of a give-
away and ducking, and my "fetcher" in the other, I ease off shore.
Fifteen feet from the bank I wish I hadn't come. My weight sags both
treetops beneath the surface. I am ankle deep myself. Viny cables are
taut as bowstrings. If even a tiny strand pops somewhere, I'll topple
off anyhow, in sheer fright. Snakes and tightrope walking! My wispy
ruler extends, gropes for Bob, and twitches him back, inch by inch.
Guiding as I retreat, my nerve finally gives way four feet from shore.
One despairing leap. Hooray! Bob is quickly raked ashore! Over more
quickly than I figured!

My colored ax owner, apparently vastly relieved at having caught
up with his implement, appears. Does he, by any chance, know the
whereabouts of a covey of birds around here any which way?

My query meets intense deliberation, then, "Yaas, suh, Boss. Does
you-all see dat 'ar leanin' tree wid mistletoe in de top, p'intin' to'ds
dat shotgun house on de leveee banquette away across't de fiel' yonder?" The various objectives are finally oriented. "Well, Boss man,
whin you-all 'rives nyarbouts to de leanin' tree, dar bees 'bout er fo'
acre patch o' sorghum an' ol' tall clumpy grass. Well, suh, I bin noticin'
er pertickler big hover o' pott'idges whut mos' inginally visits right in
dar."

With my first move, off scud Joe and Black Boy toward yon leanin'
tree. For the first time I realize that our journeying has awakened
dormant tendons in even my pretty well hike-hardened underpinning.
Two hundred yards of mucky slogging. A small voice whispers, "You
have ten birds. With what she has at home, that'll be enough for the
party. Why not quit?"

Another fifty yards of punishment! If I stop I'll fall down sure as
shooting. "What," shouts Old Man High Resolve, "fixing to fold up

with the goal in sight, eh? You'd disappoint the Madame, would you? After all her trouble driving you over here? And your eating three of her birds?"

Hopping a lateral ditch, I roll heavily over its low levee. Reclining among the weeds, trying halfheartedly to see if there is mud in my gun tubes, I wonder if I'd best yield to common sense and sleep right here tonight. "This morning," I sneer at myself cynically, "you gabbed to yourself about Sir Lancelot. A great break for you the fair dames can't clap eyes on you now! Sir Lancelot! Sir Stick-in-the-Mud!"

Groggily I stumble through a belt of towering weed stalks and out into what must be the sorghum patch and clumpy grass. Joe and Black Boy, ignorant of my downfall of a moment ago, are combing the opening's outer rim. Twenty yards out into the clearing a dozen or more bobs, scattered feeding, set the stalks about me abuzz. Desperately I shove at the safety! Pin onto an almost overhead darter! Realize that, fairly struck, it will be blown to bits; I steady and whip off ahead of a cock skimming the weed tops. Down he hurtles! I almost fall over backward trying to keep an eye on three singles splitting off toward the highway.

"Fellows," I tell the dogs, "as the situation stands, we are only one bob shy of Madame's order. Without said bob, her luncheon may degenerate into a washout. Somewhere in yon gumbo stew are three adult quail! Are you with me, boys?" Tail wagging and knee rubbing. Black Boy maintains a head of steam sufficient to attempt face licking! So, together, we mush a quarter mile of breast-high cotton stuck in glue.

Not one chance in a hundred, I tell myself. Those three bobs, I figure, darted over the hedge and whirled for the big woods, common-sense thing for today's smart birds. I begin a desperate struggle down the home stretch. Somewhere ahead my game dogs are at work. The cotton lowers and thins. There they are, Joe and Black Boy. They galvanize! Well ahead, off to their right, three birds, whose trail they have just struck, flush wild and wing across my line of fire. Old "One Shot" aims a wavering wallop. The captain slithers below the stalk tops! My dogs wheel!

I might as well admit it, we all break shot! What a race for the spot where that cock fellow disappeared! Too tired to aid my trailers, I give out the "Wanted—Dead or Alive" yell. I hastily bend down some cover, sink atop it, and lend loud vocal aid to the chase. Five minutes pass. Oh, joy! Oh, rapture! Bird in mouth, and with Black Boy trailing unenviously, up trots Joe!

We reel to the highway. In a "borrow pit," I slosh the mud from my boots and person. At the cabin I make application for fireside chair space. Joe and Black Boy are rubbed down with a tow sack and check in a the very andirons. Nobody minds. Colored folks after my own heart. Before long, She-Who-Presides will be sounding her recall. Well, I have her dozen birds, and here I am. Pretty soft—this armchair by the open fireplace. Her dozen bobs all safely sacked, too. Good old Joe and Black Boy!

My colored hostess shakes my shoulder gently. "Boss," she apologizes, "dar's a 'mobile bin settin' down dar by de bridge fer ten minutes, blowin' de hawn—an'—an'—de white lady whut's in it sont dis hyar boy t'ask wuz de a white gemman bin seed roun' hyar wid a gun an' two ol' big huntin' dawgs."

"Aunty," I reply, easing stiffly into my pack while clucking up the dogs and feeling for the customary two bits, "I've been asleep, haven't I?"

And she, honest black countenance agrin, answers my query with one of her own: "Boss, whin you sleeps, you show-Gawd does so some snorin', don't you?"

MARK RIGHT!
1936